D1460121

Reporting the
Second World War

'In wartime, truth is so precious that she should always be attended by a bodyguard of lies.'

Winston Churchill

Reporting the Second World War

The Battle for Truth

Brian Best

Pen & Sword
MILITARY

First published in Great Britain in 2015 by
PEN AND SWORD MILITARY
an imprint of
Pen and Sword Books Ltd
47 Church Street
Barnsley
South Yorkshire S70 2AS

Copyright © Brian Best, 2015

ISBN 978 1 47383 420 0

Printed and bound in England by
CPI Group (UK) Ltd, Croydon, CR0 4YY

Typeset in Times by CHIC GRAPHICS

Pen & Sword Books Ltd incorporates the imprints of
Pen & Sword Books Ltd incorporates the imprints of Pen & Sword Archaeology,
Atlas, Aviation, Battleground, Discovery, Family History, History, Maritime,
Military, Naval, Politics, Railways, Select, Social History, Transport, True Crime,
Claymore Press, Frontline Books, Leo Cooper, Praetorian Press,
Remember When, Seaforth Publishing and Wharncliffe

For a complete list of Pen and Sword titles please contact
Pen and Sword Books Limited
47 Church Street, Barnsley, South Yorkshire, S70 2AS, England
E-mail: enquiries@pen-and-sword.co.uk
Website: www.pen-and-sword.co.uk

Contents

Prologue vi

Chapter 1   The Spanish Rebellion – Prelude To War 1

Chapter 2   The Early Days 15

Chapter 3   1940 – The Collapse of Europe 24

Chapter 4   1940–41 – Britain Alone 34

Chapter 5   Propaganda and the Media.......................................43

Chapter 6   Africa and the Eastern Mediterranean 52

Chapter 7   The First Assaults on Mainland Europe........................75

Chapter 8   The Russian and Pacific Fronts 1941-42 85

Chapter 9   Italy 99

Chapter 10 Fight Back in the East 114

Chapter 11 Bombing Correspondents.......................................132

Chapter 12 D-Day...145

Chapter 13 Paris and the Race for the German Border.......................164

Chapter 14 Arnhem...174

Chapter 15 The Rhineland Campaign 185

Chapter 16 Final Days 196

Bibliography 211

Notes 213

Index 221

Prologue

With the end of the First World War came recriminations and downright fury over the way the war had been reported in the newspapers. In just ten years, the brilliantly shining stars of journalism, the war correspondents, had seen their popularity destroyed in the war years by the combination of heavy censorship, a readiness to embrace the military hierarchy's version of the truth and a blatant misrepresentation of life at the sharp end. In particular, they faced the scorn of the millions of soldiers who had suffered the horrors of the front line and had not been truthfully portrayed.

Belatedly, decent correspondents like Philip Gibbs wrote books revealing what conditions were like for the troops and criticising the deadly folly of the High Command's wasteful strategies. For the public, the pursuit of truth had arrived years too late. Practically all the accredited correspondents were middle-aged or physically unfit for service and soon retired to write their memoirs. Any future war would be covered by a fresh younger batch of journalists, with the addition of female war correspondents – something never thought possible at the end of the Great War.

Britain staggered through the 1920s, a period of depression and steady decline in her former economic pre-eminence. Poverty and stagnant growth were epitomised by the General Strike of 1926, which sowed the seeds of mistrust and militancy for decades. In contrast, America was enjoying a period of prosperity and achievement, dubbing the 1920s as the 'Roaring Twenties', but there was little evidence of such vibrancy in Britain.

As the world moved into the 1930s, there were signs that its citizens were trying to lay its past to rest with new innovations and a promise of a brighter future with the development of cars, airplanes, entertainment in the shape of 'talkies', radio and television. For the newspapers, there was much debate about the resurgence of Germany under Adolf Hitler's Nazi Party from the desperate days of hyperinflation and riots, to apparent affluence and national pride. One of Germany's admirers was Viscount Rothermere, owner of the *Daily Mail*, who was fulsome in his praise for the new German Chancellor. Other papers were less sure. Alarm bells rang when the British home-grown version of the Nazis, Oswald Mosley's Blackshirts, began to show their true side in their provocative and violent rallies.

Then in 1936 came the 'Reign of Three Kings'. On 28 January, King

George V died and was succeeded by his eldest son, Edward VIII. In December, Edward signed his abdication to marry the American divorcée, Wallis Simpson. The throne then passed to the next in line, Edward's reluctant younger brother, George VI.

Also vying for attention in the newspapers was the outbreak of the Spanish Civil War on 17 July 1936. This afforded the first chance since the Great War for journalists to go and report a European war. Most national newspapers were poorly prepared to cover this rebellion but it enabled new correspondents to gain experience for the greater conflict that was about to engulf the world. It also brought into prominence the American correspondents, who, with their country's involvement in the Second World War, became increasingly dominant in all the war fronts around the world.

Unlike their Great War predecessors, the Second World War correspondents were free to visit the sharp end of the fighting, even taking part in bombing missions, parachute drops and amphibious landings. They were able to write about the conditions in which servicemen fought, something never before articulated. It also brought increased dangers.

The toll on war correspondents was considerable. Many suffered death and wounds alongside the servicemen: sniper, machine gun, mortar and artillery fire. Others strayed on to mine fields, were bombed or drowned at sea. Some were captured along with the men about whom they were reporting and one American correspondent was executed by the SS. One of the most common causes of death amongst the correspondents was travelling by air. Aviation was still in its unreliable stage and this, coupled with overworked and poorly maintained aircraft, was the cause of so many air accidents in which war correspondents died.

The unexpected decision by the Royal Air Force to allow the BBC's Richard Dimbleby to record his impressions of a bombing raid on Berlin paved the way for many correspondents to follow suit. As the average life of a bomber crew was tragically short, this was a stunt that should only be pulled off once or twice. Instead, many correspondents risked their necks to take part in this perilous exercise despite one bombing mission being much the same as any other. In fact Dimbleby flew a further nineteen times, despite hating flying and suffering air sickness. Ed Murrow was another who did not have to fly but, like Dimbleby and others, wanted to feel he was supporting the efforts of Allied aircrew.

Increasingly, war correspondents identified themselves with the fighting man and the fighting man generally reciprocated. A good example of this was the American reporter, Ernie Pyle, who established a strong bond with the ordinary GI infantryman and gained great fame in America for his heartfelt reports on the soldier's life on campaign. A depressive, he suffered a breakdown, but still kept coming back and reporting under fire until he was killed within weeks of the war's end.

Women correspondents had to overcome the reluctance of their newspapers and the military to allow them anywhere close to the front line. In spite of this imposition, reporters like Martha Gellhorn, Margaret Bourke-White and Clare Hollingworth managed to outflank the authorities and scoop their male colleagues.

The war introduced thousands of correspondents to warfare and made an impact on most of them. After the war, some became household names like Richard Dimbleby, Ed Murrow and Walter Cronkite, all three of whom made the transition from radio to television. Many went on to write bestselling books like Alan Moorehead and Cornelius Ryan. Others went on reporting the many colonial wars for independence that quickly followed 1945, and some continued to be killed in the process.

Thanks to the pioneering efforts of their Second World War models, female war correspondents have become an increasingly familiar sight on today's battlefields. It is to the Second World War we must look for the enormous impact on the way today's wars are reported.

Chapter 1

The Spanish Rebellion –
Prelude To War

The outbreak of the Spanish Civil War divided world opinion. The Right and the Catholics supported the rebellious military-led Nationalists as a bulwark against the expansion of Bolshevism. The Left, including the unions, student groups and intellectuals saw the democratically elected Republicans as an anti-Fascist shield. There were also clearer heads that saw the civil war escalating into another world war.

Britain maintained a position of strong neutrality and placed an embargo on the supply of arms to the point of sending warships to intercept shipments. In a move that has been mirrored in the recent civil war in Syria, the British Government made it a crime to volunteer to fight in Spain, but about 4,000 went anyway.

The Republicans were fragmented by several factions, including centrists who supported the weak liberal government, but who were bitterly opposed by socialists, anarchists and communists. They were reliant on volunteers who were heroic but untrained against professional soldiers.

The Nationalists were far more united and embraced the Fascist *Falange Española*, the religious conservative Carlists and the Monarchists. They also had the Army of Africa made up of the Spanish Legion and Moroccan *Regulares*, feared for their professionalism and brutality. With their experience of desert warfare suited to the open Spanish countryside, they were able to move swiftly from Seville to Madrid between August and November 1936.

Foreign press coverage was extensive and it was estimated a thousand correspondents and photographers were sent to cover the war. This was probably an exaggeration and a figure of one to two hundred was nearer the mark with journalists departing and being replaced. Many worked for more than one newspaper or bureau with most tending to gravitate to the Republican side of the fight. Initially this was because the censorship was less strict and the correspondents were largely free to go where they dared. Once armed with a pass to visit the front and supplied with a car and driver by the Ministry of War, the journalist was able to wander where he liked. This freedom brought its own danger with a front that was liable to change without warning. Several correspondents inadvertently found themselves in the Nationalists' zone and were held captive.

This happened to Denis Weaver of *News Chronicle* and James Minifie of the *New York Herald Tribune*, who suffered the horror of watching their driver and escort executed in front of them, before being subjected to days of rough treatment and then expelled.

Another reason the correspondents tended to side with the Republicans was the deliberate bombing of civilians in the cities by the German and Italian air units sent to support General Franco's Nationalists. There was also an initial feeling that the Republicans were fighting a just cause. Despite the efforts of the Soviet Union to create a Bolshevik satellite in Western Europe, the journalists continued in their support of the legitimate government. As the war dragged on, the continuing highjack by these ruthless elements caused disharmony, confusion and vulnerability.

Most of the foreign newspapers tended to favour the rebel Nationalists. Prominent amongst them were Lord Beaverbrook's *Daily Express* and Lord Rothermere's *Daily Mail* and *Evening News*. None was more supportive than Rothermere, the champion of Adolf Hitler and Oswald Mosley, who saw Fascism as the only antidote to Bolshevism.

Fewer correspondents covered the Nationalist side and they tended to be the more seasoned journalists like Noel Monks, Webb Miller, Francis McCullagh and *The Daily Telegraph*'s Percival Phillips. Phillips had an intimate knowledge of the situation, far more than he could possibly get past by the censors. He believed that most of the American and British correspondents who went to Spain were pro-Franco, but that Franco's press bureau, run by the insufferable Luís Bolín, alienated most of them to the point where they became pro-government. Surprisingly, Bolín was particularly harsh towards the blatantly supportive *Daily Mail*'s Harold Cardozo, because Bolín's articles had been turned down by the paper. Bolín had a positive genius for preventing news getting out and, in so doing, he actually hurt Franco's cause. So much information was quashed that most of the correspondents would later publish their observations in books. Phillips had to rely on *The Daily Telegraph* sending a daily bulletin to keep him informed of the situation in Spain.

Phillips spoke about fellow correspondents:

> *'I have met dozens of fellows who are in Barcelona and Madrid, and they told me that though there was hopeless confusion, they were always treated like brothers. Bolin's opposite number isn't dressed up like an officer... as a general rule he is a real journalist wearing civilian clothes and working hard in his office, and glad to see colleagues from London and New York. No need to wait three hours for an audience, and then be told that you must come back tomorrow: you just blow in through the open door of the office, and help yourself to a drink or a cigar if the censor is busy.'*

Percival Phillips had been one of the Great War's accredited war correspondents who covered events on the Western Front, for which he was knighted. He was a vastly experienced journalist covering all the major stories around the world. He accompanied the Prince of Wales on many royal trips and they became good friends.

Steadily he became disillusioned and frustrated by the constrictions to which he and his fellow correspondents were subjected. He was particularly alarmed to the extent that Germany and Italy had become involved, almost as a training ground for a greater conflict. He observed:

> *'Spain had to import foreign mercenaries to fight for it, even in a civil war. Foreign artillery is blowing Spain to bits. Officials won't let us mention Italians and Germans in our despatches, but they are here all the same.'*

Ill health and depression forced him to request a letter of safe conduct from Bolin, which he refused to issue. Fearing that he was now not safe in Spain, Phillips managed to cross the border into Portugal and make his way to Gibraltar. Here he sent a despatch to the *Telegraph* dated 3 December 1936 reporting that he had observed a build up of German troops in nearby Algeciras. He also wrote that the Nazis were gaining control of the commercial exports from captured parts of Spain and seizing stocks of olive oil, oranges, wood, cork and iron as payment for the assistance they had offered Franco. Soon after, he collapsed with nephritis (disease of the kidneys) and was returned to London where he died.

Reporting on the Republican side for *The Daily Telegraph* was Henry Buckley, the resident correspondent. He had been assigned to Spain in 1929 and knew the politics and personalities of the main players in the war. He admired and disliked men from both camps and was not intoxicated by the romance of the anti-Fascist cause, unlike many fellow correspondents. Widely regarded as a truthful and humane reporter, he was befriended by most of the prominent war correspondents, including Ernest Hemingway. Small and self-effacing, Buckley was not an obvious candidate for friendship with the boisterous and alcoholically-boorish Hemingway. Yet he was described by the celebrated writer as 'a lion of courage, though a very slight, even frail, creature with jittery nerves'.

Before the arrival of Ernest Hemingway and Martha Gellhorn to Spain, the glamour couple associated with the war were Robert Capa and Gerda Taro. Their real names respectively were the Jewish couple, André Friedman and Gerta Pohorylle. Lovers and photographic partners since 1934, they reinvented themselves by changing their names to overcome the increasing political intolerance towards Jews. They planned to sell their photographs through the fictious American photographer, 'Robert Capa', as a way of breaking into the lucrative American market. André Friedman, a native of Budapest, used his street nickname 'Capa', which means 'shark' in Hungarian. Pohorylle adopted the professional name of Gerda Taro after the Japanese artist, Tarõ Okamoto and the Hollywood actress, Greta Garbo.

Initially, they covered the war together until Taro gained some independence when her pictures were taken up by several important European publications. She refused Capa's marriage proposal and began to commercialise her photos under a separate label. Popular publications like *Life* and the *Illustrated London News* used her photographs and she was in great demand.

On 25 July 1937, she was covering the retreat from the Battle of Brunete with her new lover, a Canadian journalist named Ted Allen, when she met her death. Hopping onto the running-board of a car carrying wounded from the battle, it was hit by a Republican tank that had lost control. Gerda Taro died the next day. In the climate of suspicion and political killings, it was suggested that she had been a victim of Stalin's purge of communists and socialists in Spain not aligned to Moscow.

Robert Capa went on to become the outstanding photographer of the

Second World War, but he is probably best known for the image of the 'Falling Soldier', taken early in the civil war. It is of a communist militiaman caught in the moment he was shot dead and was considered the iconic image of the war. In recent years, a debate about its authenticity has divided opinion, some saying that it was staged, while a recent Japanese documentary even suggests that it was taken by Gerda Taro.

The Nationalists quickly occupied about a half of the country, leaving the north coast, almost all the east coast and the central area around Madrid in Republican control. Franco's forces were advancing on Madrid, which was not heavily defended, and if the capital had fallen, then it would have probably shortened the war considerably. Instead, they concentrated their efforts in lifting the Siege of the Alcázar in Toledo, south of Madrid. The military governor of the province refused the Republican government the munitions stored at the Alcázar, About 8,000 militia men were sent to seize the fortress but were met by about 800 Guardia Civil, 300 male civilians and 650 women and children who had barricaded themselves within the stone-built fortification. Armed with rifles, the defenders faced machine-guns, artillery and air attacks from 21 July until the siege was lifted on 27 September.

The 23-year-old South African correspondent, O'Dowd Gallagher, sent a report of the relief to the *Daily Express* dated 29 September. He was in a hotel in Talavera when a military officer walked into the dining room and was recognised as one of the Alcázar defenders. Dinner was forgotten as the man related his experiences:

'For nearly two and a half months he had lived underground, on water, black bread as hard as the stones of the Alcázar itself, and twice a week on the flesh of mules or horses. Talking quickly, he told his story and answered the questions shot at him by the officers, among whom were some who led the relief columns.

There were 1,100 people capable of using arms in the Alcázar, he said, and all had signified their willingness to accept the leadership of Colonel Moscardó. It was soon obvious that the fight was going to be a long one. Provisions were rationed. Each had about a pint of water a day. Washing was strictly forbidden.

There were several attempts to undermine the Alcázar. A young officer kept watch on a high point to calculate the effect of each explosion. One day after a heavy mine had been blown he did not

5

return. He was listed among those who had "disappeared", meaning those who had been blown completely to pieces.

To the now silent officers in the dining-room the man from the Alcázar – almost a man back from the dead – told how the besiegers built up a battery of four guns only a few hundred yards from the Alcázar itself. They began to batter the ancient masonry and made great breaches. On some days women arrived to watch.

"I think they were from Madrid. They used to sit and drink wine; sometimes actually fire guns at us. They made it a sort of a holiday."

The imprisoned occupants of the Alcázar were soon driven underground in the dungeons. In one comparatively small cellar beneath the eight-feet-thick walls seventy-five women and children spent four weeks without moving out. The man from the Alcázar told us: "constantly moving about were five pale-faced nuns and three doctors. They performed thirty amputations. There was not one case of infection, despite the tainted air in the dungeon hospital."

The walls of this 400-year-old castle, from whose battlements bows and arrows and arquebuses were used, might have been built for modern warfare. They withstood the most violent bombardments and only crumbled after sustained short-range shelling.

One million cartridges were seized by officers of the Alcázar when the revolt began. Of these, 400,000 rounds were fired.

Normal food soon ran out, but the Alcázar was well stocked with grain. Women baked crude bread in the cellars, enough for one or two weeks at a time. When the siege began there were ninety-seven horses and twenty-seven mules within the walls. When it ended only one horse and five mules remained. The rest had been eaten.

Several times insurgent airplanes dropped stores to the defenders. At first the defenders feared the provisions had been dropped by government machines and that they were poisoned. A young chemist in the Alcázar analyzed the food and declared it wholesome.

Though unable to communicate with the outside world the defenders heard radio war bulletins given out by Lisbon. Sometimes a jazz programme was turned on; then the younger people danced and sang among the ruins.

'When the garrison was relieved they had to leave through some second-floor windows and stumble to the ground level over tons of shattered rock.'

Another journalist covering the Nationalist side was *The Times* correspondent, Harold 'Kim' Philby, already recruited as a Soviet agent. He was also reporting to British intelligence who, like their Soviet counterpart, wanted information of the new Messerschmitt Bf109 fighter and the Panzer tank which was deployed by Franco's forces. Philby passed on to MI6 that he had been personally assured by Franco that German troops would never be permitted to cross Spain to attack Gibraltar.

For their part, the Soviet NKVD asked Philby to check for weak points in Franco's security and to initiate an assassination, a suggestion that Philby showed a great reluctance to explore.

In December 1937, during the Battle of Teruel, the car in which Philby was travelling was hit by a Republican shell. Philby emerged with a slight head wound but his companions were not so fortunate; Brandish Johnson of *Newsweek* was killed outright while Edward Neil of Associated Press (AP) and Ernest Sheepshanks of Reuters soon died of their injuries. Ironically the committed communist Kim Philby was decorated with the Red Cross of Military Merit by Franco.

One of the earliest fatalities amongst the journalists was Louis Delaprée of *Paris-Soir*. Although his political inclination was to the right and his newspaper regarded as apolitical, Delaprée was reporting from the Republican side in Madrid. The capital had become about the most vulnerable target as it suffered massive bombing by the Nationalists, who enjoyed the airpower supplied by fellow Fascists, Germany and Italy. With no air-raid shelters to protect them, the citizens took refuge in caves, under brick archways and the metro. It was generally believed that more Spaniards were killed in the cities than at the front. On 25 November 1936, Delaprée reported the dread felt as the enemy aircraft approached the defenceless city:

> *'The darkness shrouding Madrid is so thick that you could cut it with a knife. We cannot see the sky, but from the sky they can see us. Humming, rumbling, pounding, the rebel planes appear in an awesome crescendo.... Defenceless, we hear above us this deep and musical vibration, herald of Death.*
>
> *Blasts, cushioned and then ear-splitting...Window panes rattling inaudibly.. ..Windows thrown open by an invisible force and all the sounds that will soon become so familiar to us. The trampling of people as they escape, the sirens of ambulances transporting the*

wounded, the sobbing women beside you as they bury their heads in their scarves, the to-and-fro of men who click their heels to convince themselves that they are not afraid. And above all – above all else – the sound of your own heart beating ever faster.

A terrible confusion reigns in the night, as it is lit up by deadly flares. We stumble against stretchers, knock into the wounded who watch as their blood flows on the asphalt by the light of the flames.

On the corner of Alcalá and Gran Vía, a hand clutches my leg. I free myself and light a match while I bend over the person who has grabbed this lifesaver. It is a young woman, her nose already pinched by approaching death. I don't know what her wounds are, but her robe is stained with blood. She whispers: "Look what they've done..."

And her hand makes an indeterminate gesture. Another match.

"Look, look", the voice again.

The bloodless hand is still showing me something. At first, I think it's the pool of blood on the sidewalk.

"Look..."

I bend again, and I perceive a small child, lying crushed under broken glass.

The white hand calls on the sky to bear witness and drops again.

Another match. With my companion, Flasck of the Journal, who has joined me, we bend over the wounded woman.

"She's dead," he says.

The whole city is full of similar scenes, of comparable pictures that seem to have been conjured up on the whim of a macabre genius, a necrophilous god. I have painted this scene in some detail because it was the first that showed me the reality of this butchery, and not the abstract and victim-free bombing from which I fled, like everyone else in the tortured city.'

Delaprée wrote so passionately about the terrible sights he saw that his mass-circulation newspaper began to heavily edit his reports and even relegate them to the obscurity of an inner page. When the journalist learned how his reports were being emasculated, he entered into a slanging match with his editor which resulted in them being rejected altogether.

Delaprée filed his last report from Madrid on 4 December 1936, as the British constitution crisis deepened and just a week before Edward VIII announced his abdication, which added to the journalist's bitterness. He wrote in his accompanying note:

'You've only published half my articles. I know that... I'll fly back on Sunday unless I suffer the same fate as Guy de Traversay [a fellow correspondent killed by the Nationalists in Majorca], *and that'd be fine, wouldn't it? Because that way you'd have your own martyr.*

Until then, I won't send you anything else. Not worth it. The killing of a hundred Spanish kids is less interesting than a sigh from Mrs Simpson, the royal whore.'

This message proved to be prescient, for Louis Delaprée died in the plane that was returning him to Madrid on 11 December. As it approached Madrid, it was attacked and shot down by what was assumed to be a Nationalist fighter plane. Survivors believe the plane was downed by a Republican plane flown by a Soviet pilot, either deliberately or in error.

So died a journalist whose brief career as a war correspondent led to something of great significance that came to symbolise the tragedy of the civil war. Pablo Picasso, who lived in France, took inspiration from Delaprée's reports and painted his most famous work, 'Guernica'.

Four correspondents who were the first to arrive within hours of the bombing of Guernica were the *Daily Express* reporter, Noel Monks, Christopher Holmes of Reuters, the Belgian reporter Mathieu Corman of *Ce Soir*, and *The Times* reporter George Steer. In what was one of the most important articles produced during the war, Steer's account alerted the world to that small Basque market town of Guernica which had been subjected to systematic aerial bombing by the airplanes of the German Condor Legion. In a war that had more than its fair share of acts of atrocity, the bombardment of helpless civilians stood out as a symbol of the horror of industrialised warfare.

Steer's account appeared in *The Times* dated 27 April, 1937:

'Guernica, the most important town of the Basques and the centre of their cultural tradition, was completely destroyed yesterday afternoon by insurgent air raiders. The bombardment of this open town far behind the lines occupied precisely three hours and a quarter, during which a powerful fleet of aeroplanes consisting of three German types, Junkers and Heinkel bombers and Heinkel fighters, did not cease unloading on the town bombs weighing from 1,000lb downwards and, it is calculated, more than 3,000 two-pounder aluminium incendiary projectiles. The fighters, meanwhile, plunged low from above the centre of town to machine-gun those of the civilian population who had taken refuge in the fields...

9

At 2am today when I visited the town the whole of it was a horrible sight, flaming from end to end. The reflection of the flames could be seen in the clouds of smoke above the mountains from 10 miles away. Throughout the night houses were falling until the streets became long heaps of red impenetrable debris...

In the form of its execution and the scale of the destruction it wrought, no less than in the selection of its objective, the raid on Guernica is unparalleled in military history. Guernica was not a military objective. A factory producing war material lay outside the town and was untouched. So were two barracks some distance from the town. The town lay far behind the lines. The object of the bombardment was seemingly the demoralisation of the civil population and the destruction of the Basque race...

Monday was the customary market day in Guernica for the country round. At 4.30pm when the market was full and peasants were still coming in, the church bells rang the alarm for approaching aeroplanes, and the population sought refuge in cellars and in dugouts prepared following the bombing of the civilian population in Durango on 31 March...

Five minutes later a single German bomber appeared, circled over the town at a low altitude, and then dropped six heavy bombs, apparently aiming for the station. The bombs, with a shower of grenades, fell on a former institute and on houses and streets surrounding it. The aeroplane then went away. In another five minutes came a second bomber, which threw the same number of bombs into the middle of the town. About a quarter of an hour later three Junker bombers arrived to continue the work of demolition, and thenceforward the bombing grew in intensity and was continuous, ceasing only with the approach of dusk at 7.45. The whole town of 7,000 inhabitants, plus 3,000 refugees, was slowly and systematically pounded to pieces. Over a radius of five miles round a detail of the raiders' technique was to bomb separate caserios or farmhouses. In the night these burned with the same intensity as the town itself, and at Mugica, a little group of houses at the head of the Guernica inlet, the population was machine-gunned for 15 minutes.'

Steer followed this up the following day. *The Times* 28 April 1937:

'In the form of its execution and the scale of destruction it wrought, no less than the selection of its objective, the raid on Guernica is unparalleled in military history. Guernica was not a military objective...The object of the bombardment was seemingly the demoralisation of the civil population and the destruction of the cradle of the Basque race.'

Two years later, Steer covered the brief Winter War between Finland and Russia in 1939. In 1940, Steer ran the Ethiopian Forward Propaganda Unit and later in the war was appointed head of the Indian Field Propaganda Unit. While he was working for this unit, he was killed in a car crash on 25 December 1944.

Picasso's famous interpretation of Guernica appeared at the Spanish Pavilion in the November 1937 Exhibition in Paris. His vision has ensured that this outrage lasted beyond the even greater crimes of the Second World War. It was the precursor to the military struggle of the war, with Guernica symbolising the vulnerability of civilian populations in an age of total war.

Noel Monks, the Melbourne-born correspondent for the *Daily Express*, was a devout Catholic and initially sympathetic to Franco, but was deeply shocked by what he witnessed at Guernica. On arriving at the devastated town he was pressed into helping Basque militia collect the charred bodies:

'Some of the soldiers were sobbing like children. There were flames and smoke and grit, and the smell of burning flesh was nauseating. Houses collapsing into the inferno...A sight that haunted me for weeks were the charred bodies of several women and children huddled together in what had been the cellar of a house. It had been a refugio.'

He later wrote:

'Airplanes, bombs, bullets, fire. Within twenty-four hours Franco was going to brand those shocked homeless people as liars before the whole world. So-called British experts were going to come to Guernica months afterwards, when the smell of burnt human flesh had been replaced by petrol dumped here and there among the ruins, and make pompous judgements: "Guernica was set on fire by the Reds". My answer to them is unprintable. No government official accompanied me to Guernica. I wandered among the ruins and

survivors at will. I drove back to Bilbao and had to wake up the
operator – it was two in the morning – to send my message.
Censorship had been lifted. The man who sent my urgent dispatch
couldn't read English. If the "Reds" had destroyed Guernica, I for
one could have blown the whole story for all they knew. And how I
would have blown it had it been true!'

In March 1939, Monks sued the publishers of a book entitled *The Spanish Arena* which included a chapter called The Fiction Factory, which was an outright attack on the British press, accusing it of misrepresenting facts in a way that was purely anti-Franco. Monks was singled out for distorting the facts and was expelled from Spain. In the event, the publishers withdrew the allegation and paid damages.

On 1 January 1939, Monks married Mary Welsh, a *Time Magazine* correspondent, but lengthy periods apart during the war were not conducive to a stable married life. In 1945 she divorced him in order to marry Ernest Hemingway. She must have wondered what she was letting herself in for exchanging the easy-going, genial Monks for the unpredictable and domineering Hemingway. Shortly after she accepted his proposal of marriage in Paris, Hemingway was given a present of two German pistols in a velvet-lined case. Loading them, Hemingway began stalking around the room taking aim at imaginary enemies.

Spotting a photograph of Mary with her estranged husband, Hemingway grabbed it and dashed into the bathroom. After a pause, there was a burst of gunfire followed by howls of laughter and the sound of running water. Hemingway had set the photo on the toilet bowl and opened fire, obliterating Monk's image. He also managed to destroy the bowl and plumbing. The management of the Ritz just gave a Gallic shrug and sent for the plumber. Mary was furious and seriously considered ending the relationship.

The war acted as a magnet for several celebrated writers who arrived to add their support to the Republican side. George Orwell and John Dos Passos were initially passionate about the Republican cause but became disillusioned by the splintering of the various factions. Probably the most famous writer was the aforementioned Ernest Hemingway, who used his experiences to write one of his best known novels, *For Whom the Bell Tolls*.

Hemingway arrived in Spain in 1937 having agreed to report for the North American Newspaper Alliance (NANA). The writer, at the peak of his art, was obsessed with all things Spanish since he first visited the country and became an aficionado of bull fighting. As an individual with strong leftist sympathies, he was naturally a supporter of the Republican cause and paid four visits to the war-stricken country. At no time did he consider reporting from the Nationalist side to give a semblance of balance. He was joined by his latest object of desire, Martha Gellhorn, an exceptional correspondent, reporting the war for *Collier's Weekly*.

Hemingway was insistent that he had a ringside seat at the front line and this is reflected in his inimitable style. He was present at the Battle of Teruel, probably the bloodiest and most decisive of the war. Fought in the mid-winter of 1937-1938, it cost both sides over 140,000 casualties. Hemingway wrote of the Republican attack in the blizzard-like conditions:

> *'On our left, an attack was starting. The men, bent double, their bayonets fixed, were advancing in the awkward first gallop that steadies into the heavy climb of an uphill assault. Two men were hit and left the line. One had a surprised look of a man first wounded who does not realise the thing can do this damage and not hurt. The other knew he was hit very bad. All I wanted was a spade to make a little mound to get my head under, but there weren't any spades within crawling distance...Suddenly we heard cheering run along the line and across the next ridge we could see the Fascists running from their first line.*
>
> *They ran in the leaping, plunging gait that is not panic but a retreat, and to cover that retreat their farther machine-gun posts slithered our ridge with fire. I wished very strongly for a spade...'*

Having taken Teruel from the Nationalists, the Republican army was counter-attacked and the town fell in February 1938, a turning-point in the war. Attention now centred on Madrid. Hemingway wrote from the capital:

> *'They say you never hear the one that hits you. That's true of bullets, because, if you hear them, they are already past. But your correspondent heard the last shell that hit this hotel. He heard it start from the battery, then come with a whistling incoming roar like a subway train to crash against the cornice and shower the room with broken glass and plaster. And while the glass still tinkled down and you listened for the next one to start, you realised that now finally you were back in Madrid.'*

He was able to include a subject dear to his heart – alcohol:

> *'Beer is scarce and whiskey is almost unobtainable. Store windows are full of Spanish imitations of all cordials, whiskies and vermouths. These are not recommended for internal use, although I am employing something called "Milords Ecosses Whiskey" on my face after shaving. It smarts a little, but I feel very hygienic. I believe it would be possible to cure athlete's foot with it, but one must be careful not to spill it on one's clothes because it eats wool.'*

By 1938, the war was no longer avidly followed in the newspapers and most of the experienced war reporters had left Spain for other assignments. These mostly centred on Germany's muscle-flexing with the annexation of Austria and Sudetenland, which was meekly accepted by the rest of Europe and epitomised by the British Prime Minister, Neville Chamberlain, holding aloft a piece of paper and declaring, 'peace for our time'.

The Spanish Civil War offered correspondents a comparatively free rein that enabled them to give a vivid picture of the war. Regrettably, this freedom would not be available in the war that was about to start.

Chapter 2

The Early Days

On New Year's Day 1939 the newspapers were divided on how Britain should consider itself. The *News of the World* declared that: *'we must be ready to meet a life-and-death challenge'* in the face of the current tense international situation. The *Daily Express*, on the other hand, ever supportive of appeasement, sought to pacify its readers with: *'That is why you can sleep soundly in 1939'*.

Viscount Rothermere, after spending much of the 1930s assuring the people that Hitler was a wonderfully good fellow and very fond of Britain, changed tack with a leader in the *Daily Mail* dated 4 September 1939, the day after Britain declared war on Germany:

'No statesman, no man with any decency could think of sitting at the same table with Adolf Hitler or his henchmen, the trickster von Ribbentrop, or any other of the gang. We fight against the blackest tyranny that has ever held men in bondage. We fight to defend and to restore freedom and justice on earth.'

On 28 March 1939, Madrid had surrendered to General Franco's Nationalists so ending the civil war, the repercussions of which would rumble on for decades. Three days later, Britain and France, finally awakening from self-delusion, opposed Nazi expansion by pledging aid to Poland in the event of a threat to its independence by Germany.

This followed Germany's annexation on 15 March of the Czech territories of Slovakia, Bohemia and Moravia and, on 22 March, the seizure of the Baltic port of Memel from Lithuania. On 7 April, Italy got in on the act by over-running the small Balkan state of Albania. It was now abundantly clear that the forces of fascism were on the move.

It came as a shock to the British and French governments when they learned that Germany and the Soviet Union had signed a non-aggression pact on 23 August. What wasn't revealed until later was the dividing of Poland between them. A week later, Germany invaded Poland.

In order to have a legitimate reason for going to war, the Nazis staged a cynical exercise to show that Poland had instigated an attack on German territory. Taking ethnic-Poles from concentration camps, they dressed them in Polish uniforms and shot them at the border town of Gleiwitz, claiming they had fired the first shots.

On 31 August, Clare Hollingworth, who had been working as a journalist for less than a week for *The Daily Telegraph*, was sent to Poland to report on the worsening situation. She stayed with friends in Katowice and managed to persuade the British Consul-General to loan her his official car to explore the border area. In her book, *The Three Weeks' War in Poland*, published the following year, she wrote of her experiences:

'Since all British correspondents had been expelled from Berlin some days before, I decided to have a look around in German Silesia. Katowicz was too quiet for news. I crossed the frontier at Beuthen without trouble. (Though news of my crossing so upset the Polish Foreign Office that the British Embassy was required to vouch for me.) The German frontier town was nearly deserted. It was open to enfilading fire from Polish batteries, and the Germans evidently thought it prudent to evacuate civilians...

I drove along the fortified frontier road via Hindenburg to Gleiwitz, which had become a military town. On the road were parties of motor-cycle despatch-riders, bunched together and riding hard. As we came over the ridge into the town, sixty-five of them burst past us, each about ten yards behind the other. From the road I could see bodies of troops, and at the roadside hundreds of tanks, armoured cars and field guns stood or moved off toward the frontier. Here and there were screens of canvas or planking, concealing the big guns; they seemed not to be camouflaged against air-attack. I guessed that the German Command was preparing to strike north of Katowicz and its fortified lines, the advance which was to reach Czestochowa in two days of war... .'

The following day, 1 September, she was awoken in the early hours:

'Slam! Slam! ...a noise like doors banging. I woke up. It could not be later than five in the morning. Next, the roar of airplanes and more doors banging. Running to the window I could pick out the planes, riding high, with the guns blowing smoke-rings below them. There was a long flash into the town park, another, another. Incendiary bombs? I wondered... .'

I grabbed the telephone, reached the Telegraph *correspondent in Warsaw and told him my news. I heard later that he rang straight through to the Polish Foreign Office, who had had no word of the attack. The* Telegraph *was not only the first paper to hear that Poland was at war – it had, too, the odd privilege of informing the Polish Government itself.'*

Hollingworth had a momentary fear that she had committed a terrible gaffe when the Secretary of the Consulate was convinced that it was just an air-raid practice; she had visions of her career ending prematurely for reporting a non-existent war.

Another correspondent witnessed the unprovoked invasion on 1 September at the Polish port of Danzig. Associated Press correspondent Lynn Heinzerling witnessed the shelling of the Polish naval base by the pre-Dreadnought veteran battleship, *Schleswig-Holstein*, in what were the first shots of the Second World War. Heinzerling wrote:

'It came rolling up from the harbour like the rumble of doom. Men began to die here as Hitler stepped out on the road to ruin.'

These were about the only on-the-spot pieces of reportage that appeared in the newspapers for the foreseeable future. Arrangements were made for four accredited British journalists to join the French army on the Maginot Line, the fortified complex of forts on the Franco-German border and where the first action was anticipated. Alexander Clifford left London on 19 September to take up his new position as the Ministry of Information's official 'Eyewitness' with the British Expeditionary Force in France.

After a month during which nothing of importance happened, Clifford was hard pressed to find anything to report and when he did, he found it had been heavily censored. In exasperation he resigned, joining the *Daily Mail* and later enhanced his reputation for his reporting of the North African campaign.

The war that Clifford and his colleagues had been sent to cover became dubbed as the Phoney War or the Bore War. The *New Statesman* decided it was: *'Four months of the strangest war in history.'* In fact Hitler proposed to invade France on 25 October, but was talked out of it by the military that needed time to recover from the Polish campaign. Instead, he gave poor weather as the official reason for the postponement.

At the same time, a global game of consequences began to be played out which indirectly led to Hitler's planned invasion of Britain being scrapped. It started in the early months of the war when the German raider, the pocket battleship *Admiral Graf Spee*, sank nine British merchant ships in the Indian Ocean and South Atlantic. Each time, the *Graf Spee* took off a total of 300 crewmen before sinking their ships. Hosting so many extra guests was impractical and her captain passed them onto their supply ship, the *Altmark*, to carry them to a neutral port. On 13 December, *Graf Spee* was intercepted by a Royal Naval cruiser squadron who, despite being outgunned, managed to damage the battleship enough to put her into Montevideo in neutral Uruguay for repairs.

There was an influx of American correspondents to this South American backwater capital to cover this unusual story. NBC sent their correspondent, James Bowen, with a portable microphone and a clear shortwave channel to New York to cover the unfolding drama from the dockside. After three days of waiting, the *Graf Spee* began to move slowly through the channel to Buenos Aires. NBC promised Bowen that when something happened he would be immediately put on the air. Suddenly the unexpected did happen: *'Something's going on, but we can't tell what yet.'* There was a pause, then: *'Give me the air, quick! She's exploded!'*

Thinking he was trapped by a superior force, the *Graf Spee*'s captain, Hans Langsdorff, had scuttled his ship in the River Plate estuary and later committed suicide.

The *Altmark*'s ruthless Captain Dau ignored Langsdorff's order to land his British prisoners in a neutral port and chose them to bring to Germany and captivity. Meanwhile, the *Altmark* had sailed hundreds of miles out of her way to avoid the shipping lanes. Passing between Iceland and the Faroe Islands she reached the neutral waters of Norway. Now she could make the long voyage down the Norwegian coast to Germany. Her progress was spotted by an RAF Coastal Command plane and reported to the Royal Navy. Sending the destroyer, HMS *Cossack*, to intercept her, and despite protests from the Norwegian government, a naval boarding party overwhelmed the *Altmark*'s crew and freed the captive seamen.

While the action brought a much-needed morale boost to the British public, it did spur German into planning an occupation of Norway to protect the supply of Swedish iron ore through the ice-free port of Narvik.[1]

The same thought occurred to Britain, who despatched a destroyer flotilla to sink German ore ships at Narvik. This was successfully done but, as the British warships left the scene of destruction, they ran into a flotilla of German destroyers. In the ensuing Battle of the Fjords, all the newly-built German destroyers were sunk or beached. The consequence of the complete destruction of the German flotilla contributed to Hitler's reluctance to invade Britain until his naval losses could be replaced. By that time, his eyes were focused to the east – and Russia.

All the Norwegian events occurred without a single journalist being on hand to report them. There was, however, one short-lived shooting war that took place at the eastern end of the Baltic Sea: the Winter War fought between Finland and the Soviet Union. This came about as a result of the accord between Germany and Russia, which saw the Soviets absorb eastern Poland and the Baltic states of Estonia, Latvia and Lithuania. Russia wanted bases and territory from Finland but the Finns saw it as a threat to their independence and refused to negotiate. Stalin decided that he would invade and incorporate Finland into the Soviet Union.

On 30 November 1939, half a million Russian troops launched an assault across the Finnish border against 130,000 Finnish soldiers. The Finnish air force was also heavily outnumbered ten to one and a swift victory was expected. Instead, masses of Russian troops came up against the well-sited fortified positions known as the Mannerheim Line and many perished in the thick snow.

The 'Phoney War' in France was not generating any news, so this invasion of a small country by its huge neighbour became the focus of international attention. Hugo Mäkinen, an American of Finnish origin, operated as liaison officer for the foreign correspondents and ensured that a good impression was made on his new charges. He ensured that every effort was made to facilitate the work of the correspondent with accommodation, translator, vehicle and driver to ease their path. Very few restrictions were placed on the journalists, up to and including the front lines. It was all that a correspondent could ever wish. Those that wanted could have a cursory military training which enabled them to accompany the soldiers into battle.

One of them was the American journalist, Virginia Cowles, who reported the Spanish Civil War and Czechoslovakia. Described by one writer as: 'One of the most attractive women I have ever met – and certainly one of the bravest', she had been fashion correspondent with Hearst newspapers, until she got her teeth into war reporting, admitting, 'I had no qualifications as a war correspondent except curiosity.'

Using her charm and good looks, she managed to get some of the more reticent interviewees to relax and reveal some interesting snippet. Having recently returned from the Munich Conference, Prime Minister Neville Chamberlain was honoured with a dinner at the Ritz. Virginia Cowles was sitting on the same table as Chamberlain, who went out of his way to seek her opinion on how the Czechs had received the news of the Munich Agreement.

> *'I was so astonished for a moment I couldn't reply. Then I described some of the things I had seen and heard and he listened with grave attention. From what I saw, the Czechs behaved with extraordinary self-control. All the stories of Czechs persecuting Germans were completely unfounded – manufactured by German propaganda.'*

Cowles then asked Chamberlain of his impressions of the Nazi leaders.

> *'What did you think of Ribbentrop? I asked.'*
> *"A terrible fellow."*
> *And Hitler?*
> *"Not very pleasant either. I thought he had an extraordinary face – almost sinister. And a temper that's quite unmanageable. Several times at Godesburg he got so excited I was able to carry on a conversation only with extreme difficulty. In fact, several times I had to tell Herr Schmidt [the interpreter] to say we would get nowhere by such a demonstration, and ask him to keep to the subject. A most difficult fellow. It's hard to understand the fascination he has for the German people… ."'*

Virginia Cowles recorded another insight of Hitler's personality when Chamberlain recalled: '*Someone reported to me that Hitler was shocked when he was told I enjoyed shooting and remarked that it was a cruel sport. Now, fancy anyone with Hitler's record objecting to shooting birds!*'

Cowles then mentioned that she had waited by the radio until three o'clock on the night of the Munich Conference, waiting for the final report, and asked Chamberlain why it had taken so long. '*German inefficiency,*' he replied with a smile.

'I had always been led to believe that the Germans were a thoroughly efficient people, but when we arrived in Munich we found nothing was prepared. There were no interpreters. No stenographers, no pencils, not even any paper. It took hours to get the thing arranged. But the climax came at two-thirty in the morning when the document was finally ready for signature, and Hitler jumped up from the table, walked over to the desk, and plunged his pen in the inkwell to find there wasn't even any ink! Now even in London we could have had ink!'

Now based in London, she was writing for *The Sunday Times*. After a six weeks trip to Russia to gauge the current conditions there, she was then sent to Finland to join other journalists reporting this David and Goliath war. On her first day in Helsinki, she lunched with the veteran Pulitzer-prize winning journalist, Webb Miller of the United Press (UP). He told her that there were two wars going on:

'The first war was the regular trench warfare, based on the Western Front methods being fought behind the Mannerheim defences on the Karelia Isthmus; the second war was the guerrilla fighting staged through the forests on all the other fronts in Finland. In the trench war, the Russian attack on the Mannerheim Line had been repulsed; and the guerrilla war, not only had the Russian thrusts been halted, but the Finns, by brilliant strategy and ferocious courage, had succeeded in wiping out entire divisions.'

This was to be Webb Miller's last assignment for he became America's first war fatality. This happened not under fire, but in blacked-out London, when he mistakenly stepped out of a stationary train, thinking he was at a station platform, and hit his head on the tunnel wall; a rather inglorious end to a life filled with adventure.[2]
Virginia Cowles, along with fellow-Americans, Edward Beattie of UP and Edwin Hartrich of the *New York Herald Tribune*, made the long three day trip from the capital to the front by Lake Ladoga.
On arrival, Cowles recalled:

'The roads were continuously swept by enemy planes it was impossible to travel by daylight and we didn't set out until late afternoon.... We passed a long line of lorries hauling back captured

field guns, then a column of white-hooded soldiers in small horse-drawn sleds, stacked high with ammunition. For the next five miles the road and woods were alive with Finnish soldiers hauling back their war booty. It was getting dark and we could only half distinguish the objects that passed us.

The scene at the front was even more terrible than that of the "dead man's land" of Suomussalmi.³ The night accentuated the gruesomeness; a full moon shone uncertainly through dark-moving clouds and the rising wind moaned through the pine-trees, blowing sudden gusts of snow across the roadway like a fitful passage of evil spirits.

Before us lay the dreadful wreckage of battle. The road was strewn with the hulks of tanks turned half over like giant beetles, with field-kitchens, battered lorries and heavy guns. And on either side of the road, scattered through the woods lay hundreds of frozen bodies of the dead, shapeless mounds beneath a blanket of snow.

It was only when you saw the carnage of the battles that you realised how deadly and dramatic these forest wars had been. You can visualise the Russian columns moving down the roads, every now and then the heavy tanks and tractors floundering into the snow-banks, blocking the advance for hours; you could picture the Russian soldiers, with their deep superstitious fear of the forests, clinging in bewilderment to the roadside, and the invisible, white-coated Finns creeping up behind the trees to launch their attack. I remember one of the Russian prisoners in the internment camp summing it up naively: "The trouble was, we never could see the Finns!"'

Another American journalist, Edmund Stevens of the *Christian Science Monitor*, an experienced skier, joined Finnish troops as they penetrated into Russian territory:

'What undermined Russian morale more than anything else, it appeared, was the manner in which the Finns, invisible in their snow capes and silent on their skis, passed through the Soviet lines each night blowing up bridges in the rear of the enemy and tossing hand grenades into dugouts.'

The special correspondent of the *Daily Express*, Giles Romilly, a high-born communist sympathiser who had reported the Spanish Civil War, wrote:

'I have just seen a terrifying spectacle – the ruins of the 34th Soviet Tank Brigade.

General Kongratjev, Commander of that brigade, announced on January 1 that he would clear the way for the 18th Russian Division, which had been immobilised on the north-east corner of Lake Ladoga.

Stalin decorated him as a 'hero of the Soviet Union'.

Today I saw General Kongratjev's grave and the graveyard of his huge mechanised force spread out for miles in the snow like a vast car park, or, more aptly, like a huge junk yard.

At the corners of the camp the Russians had dug in and had used their tanks as pillboxes. The tanks were connected by a crude defensive works in the snow, and loopholes had been pierced in them.

But the Finnish artillery smashed the tanks by a terrific bombardment, and outside every dugout I saw a pile of dead.'

Despite the impressive Finnish resistance and superior tactics, the outcome was an inevitable victory for the huge Soviet forces. At the Treaty of Moscow on 12 March 1940, the Finns had to cede the territory and bases demanded by the Russians, but succeeded in retaining their independence.

This largely forgotten war revealed the deficiencies in the Soviet Army which Hitler was quick to read as incompetence and encouraged him to launch his Operation Barbarossa in 1941.

Chapter 3

1940 –
The Collapse of Europe

U nlike the beginning of the First World War, when fighting began almost immediately, the Second World War took months to get going. There was little of the rallying cry to enlist, instead adult men waited to receive their call-up papers, which had been implemented in April 1939, and generally carried on as usual. Although there was some tacit agreement between Britain and Germany that no civilian targets should be bombed, the cities prepared for attacks with shelters of all kinds, barrage balloons and air-raid sirens. Instead there was a sense of waiting 'for the other shoe to drop'. Watching Germany was like watching a slumbering bear, never knowing when it will awake and go on the rampage.

Germany was using the stand-off in the west to consolidate her territorial gains in the east and to prepare for her next phase of conquest. This came a little earlier than planned when Britain violated Norwegian neutrality by boarding the *Altmark* on 16 February 1940. Five days later, Hitler ordered preparations to be put in motion for the invasion of Denmark and Norway. Hitler correctly believed that Britain and France were about to send troops to cut off vital iron ore supplies at Narvik and to sow minefields in Norwegian waters to force German ships into the open sea where they could be attacked.

There was just one minor obstacle to overcome before occupying Norway. At 5.15am on 9 April, German troops crossed the border into Denmark and launched the briefest ground campaign on record. By 8.34am, Denmark surrendered to Hitler.

At the start of the war, Leland Stowe was told by his newspaper, the *New York Tribune* that he was too old to serve as a war correspondent. As he was only 39, he managed to persuade the *Chicago Daily News* and the *New York*

Post to employ him. Along with Edmund Stevens, reporting for the *Christian Science Monitor* and London's *Daily Express*, he had covered the Russo-Finnish War. On a hunch that Norway was about to be invaded, the pair arrived in Oslo on 9 April in time to witness the country's capitulation. Stowe recalled:

> *Then came the familiar roar of big bombers, but louder and nearer than I've ever heard them in Finland. It was seven forty-five a.m. I leaped to the window just as Steve [Ed. Stevens] ran in crying: "Here they are. Here they come. My God, look at them." They were five huge tri-motored planes with engines wide open, slicing down within five hundred feet of the roof tops across the park-straight toward our hotel. They roared like hungry lions. We could see the German crosses beneath their wings.*
>
> *"God help us if they let the bombs go now," I said. We twisted our necks and looked straight up, helplessly. A split-second – no we were safe. No bombs this time, but of course they'd be back. In a few moments they were, still swooping low, still roaring, still holding thousands of persons speechless and paralysed on the streets or at their windows. Next time they circled high and machine-guns began to crackle. The Nazi bombers swung steadily and disdainfully over the heart of the city and came in low once more, roaring over the Storting building and our hotel.'*

It was demonstration of the air power the Germans possessed which was overwhelming and terrifying but it did the trick; a virtual bloodless takeover. Stevens sent his report the following day:

> *The streets of Oslo today echo to the tread of German hobnailed boots. Two battalions of German soldiers, approximately 1,400 men, landed from planes yesterday afternoon and took over Norway's capital.*
>
> *From the standpoint of execution, it was one of the most remarkable feats in military history. The Germans first bombed and captured all airports and proceeded to land troops by air.*
>
> *Like the occupation of Prague, everything went with clockwork precision. The Germans encountered no resistance. No shots were fired, despite the Norwegian Government's previous announcement that the country was at war.'*

The Norwegian invasion by Germany had been a combined operation between the German Navy based in Wilhelmshaven, the Luftwaffe and the Army supplying paratroopers and specialist Alpine troops from Austria. The invasion had set sail on 6 April 1940 with the fleet heading for key ports of Trondheim, Bergen, Kristiansand and Narvik. In the Oslofjord the resistance was short but fierce with shore batteries sinking the *Blücher* (one of Germany's most modern cruisers) with about half the invasion force on board and severely damaging the pocket battleship *Lüzow*. The initial waves of aircraft were Heinkel 111 bombers used to intimidate Oslo's population. The tri-engined planes that Stowe and Stevens saw were the Junkers-52 transports that dropped paratroopers as they took Oslo's Fornebu airfield. Elsewhere, the Luftwaffe bombed strategic targets which paved the way for the completion of the invasion of southern Norway.

On 16 April, Britain and France sent their own troops to attack Narvik and Trondheim. Too few in number and supplied with inadequate equipment (no anti-aircraft guns or artillery) and paltry air cover, the Allies stood little chance against the all-round superior German forces. Any effort to reverse the German advance was doomed from the start. Reinforcements were not going to be sent with practically all men and equipment in France awaiting the German attack.

Leland Stowe continued his one-man coverage of this northern war when he travelled north through Sweden to cross into Norway to cover the fighting around Trondheim. On 25 April, he wrote this report from the Swedish border town of Gäddede:

'Here is the first and only eyewitness report on the opening chapter of the British expeditionary troops' advance in Norway north of Trondheim. It is a bitterly disillusioning and almost unbelievable story.

The British force which is supposed to sweep down from Namsos consisted of one battalion of Territorials and one battalion of the King's Own Royal (Yorkshire) Light Infantry [sic]. These totalled fewer than 1,500 men. They were dumped into Norway's deep snows and quagmires of April slush without a single anti-aircraft gun, without a squadron of supporting airplanes, without a single piece of field artillery.

They were thrown into the snows and mud of 63 degrees north latitude to fight crack German regulars – most of them veterans of the Polish invasion – and to face the most destructive of modern *weapons. The great majority of these young Britishers averaged only one year of military service. They have already paid a heavy price for a major military blunder which was not committed by their immediate command, but in London.*

Unless they receive large supplies of anti-air guns and adequate reinforcements within a few days, the remains of these two British battalions will be cut to ribbons.

Here is the astonishing story of what has happened to the gallant little handful of British expeditionaries above Trondheim:

After four days of fighting, nearly half of this initial BEF contingent has been knocked out – either killed, wounded or captured. On Monday, these comparatively inexperienced and incredibly under-armed British troops were decisively defeated. They were driven back in precipitate disorder from Vist, three miles south of the bomb-ravaged town of Steinkjer.... I was in Steinkjer Monday evening just before the British lines were blasted to pieces. I was the only newspaper correspondent to enter the burning town and the only correspondent to visit British advance headquarters and to pass beyond to the edge of the front's heavy firing zone.'

Stowe obviously relished his exclusivity as he laid on the scene of battle with a trowel:

'A score of buildings were flaming fiercely on the town's waterfront from a bombing two hours earlier. In the midst of the smoky ruin I heard machine-guns crackling at high tempo in the hills just beyond the town. Shell explosions rapped the valley regularly with angry echoes. This was the first sustained battle between German and British troops on Norwegian soil. Already the conflict was snarling hot.'

Stowe concluded his report with the observation that:

'This is merely an illustration of the tremendous initiative which has been handed to the Germans north of Trondheim by one of the costliest and most inexplicable military bungles in modern British history.'

By 3 May, the Allies had evacuated their forces from central Norway. Fighting still continued around Narvik, where the Germans suffered setbacks. There was one British correspondent who did reach Narvik: Giles Romilly of the *Daily Express*. He had covered the Winter War and moved to Stockholm when his editor asked him to travel to Narvik to cover the British intervention in Norway. Catching a train, he arrived in Narvik in time to be captured by the Germans. Romilly was not just another newspaperman; he was also Churchill's nephew. The Germans picked up on this and had him flown by seaplane to Berlin. Romilly was the first German prisoner to be classified as *Prominente* – prisoners regarded by Hitler to be of great value due to their relationships to prominent Allied military and political figures.

He was imprisoned in Oflag IV-C (Colditz Castle) in Poland, from where it was deemed impossible to escape. Although he lived in comparative comfort, he was watched 24 hours a day. He shared a room with fellow *Prominente*, Michael Alexander, who earned the status by falsely claiming to be a relative of Field Marshal Harold Alexander. Romilly used his position to cause trouble and annoyance by forever complaining. Amongst his list of complaints was the noise that the guard's hob-nailed boots made outside his door which prevented him from sleeping. Following a visit from the Red Cross, a red carpet was placed outside his room to dull the sound.

Towards the end of the war, Romilly finally made his escape. He was transferred to another heavily guarded castle in southern Bavaria, from where he abseiled down the walls and, with a Dutch officer, reached the Allied lines.

Finally, between 4 and 8 June, Narvik was secretly evacuated due to mounting pressure to prop up the collapse of France and the urgent need for the Royal Navy to support the evacuation of Dunkirk. It also spelt the end of the Chamberlain Government and the formation of a National Government. On 10 May, Winston Churchill became Prime Minister of the Government of National Unity. Although Chamberlain served in the new government, ill health forced his resignation and he died of cancer six months later.

The Norway debacle soon faded from the memory with the Fall of France and the enforced evacuation of the British Expeditionary Force. On the day of Churchill's elevation, Germany by-passed the French Maginot line and struck France through the Ardennes in a move similar to the Schlieffen Plan in 1914. The swiftly moving mechanised thrust along the Somme valley was aimed at cutting off and surrounding the Allied units that had advanced into Belgium. With the Germans to the front and on their right flank, the Allies fought a number of rearguard actions at the rivers and canals that ran down through Belgium and France, but always the momentum was with the enemy.

With all newspaper correspondents either in Paris or on other assignments, there were just the BBC correspondents left with the British Expeditionary Force. For much of the war, the correspondent made his report onto an acetate disc controlled by a recording engineer. These were then sent to the BBC in London for broadcasting. In what was one of the coldest winters with temperatures as low as -40° Fahrenheit, frost formed on the blank discs and engineers resorted to taking them to bed.

Arriving in October 1939 and enduring the bitterly cold winter, heavy censorship and lack of action had led a frustrated Richard Dimbleby to request a transfer to the Middle East: 'I had run out of things to say about the war.'

There was a deep unease in the military about in-theatre reporting and all correspondents were closely supervised by army conducting officers. This lack of freedom and with little to report made for bland reporting and, coupled with freezing temperatures, decided Dimbleby to request a transfer. He may have regretted doing so for he narrowly missed one of the defining moments of the war as the BEF was pushed back to the French coast.

His replacement was BBC reporter, Bernard Stubbs, who reported on the BEF's move into Belgium on 10 May 1940. The Allies advanced to the River Dyle, east of Brussels but the Germans made great gains to the south which threatened to outflank them. With their perimeter shrinking, the Allies began the long retreat to Dunkirk on roads clogged with escaping refugees.

Stubbs managed to return to London via Paris on 19 May. On 31 May, he reported from Dover and described returning troops as tired, exhausted but still cheerful. In fact morale was very low and no amount of rejoicing of a great escape could disguise the disaster it had been. As Winston Churchill remarked: 'We must be very careful not to assign to this deliverance the attributes of victory. Wars are not won by evacuations.'

Soon after, Bernard Stubbs left the BBC and enlisted as an officer in the Royal Navy Volunteer Reserve (RNVR). A year later, he was killed when HMS *Hood* was blown up by the *Bismarck* in the Denmark Straight on 24 May 1941.

A freelance journalist named David Divine did take part in the little boats rescue efforts at Dunkirk. The evacuation had started on 26 May but by 28 May there was still a lack of shallow draft small craft to collect men from the beaches. A call went out to commandeer all available craft from the

Thames area. Divine found a 30-foot twin-screw Thames motor cruiser called *White Wing* and on 2 June reported to Sheerness, where the Small Vessels Pool was overseen by Rear Admiral Arthur Taylor. The admiral, completing his work ashore, decided to go and supervise the rescue of a small pocket of soldiers who couldn't reach Dunkirk but were holding out at Malo-les-Bains to the east of the port. Divine was ordered to take the admiral over in *White Wing* and, despite trouble with her starboard engine, arrived by nightfall. Divine wrote an account soon after:

'Having the Admiral on board, we were not actually working the beaches but were in control of small boat operations. We moved about as necessary and, after we had spent some time putting boats in touch with their towing ships, the 5.9 battery over Nieuport way began to drop shells on us. It seemed pure spite. The nearest salvo was about twenty yards astern, which was close enough.

We stayed there until everybody had been sent back and then went pottering about looking for stragglers. While we were doing that, a salvo of shells got one of the ships alongside the Mole. She was hit clean in the boilers and exploded in one terrific crash. There were then, I suppose, about 1,000 Frenchmen on the Mole. We had seen them crowding along its narrow crest, outlined against the flames. They had gone out under shellfire to board the boat, and now they had to go back again, still being shelled. It was quite the most tragic thing I have ever seen in my life. We could do nothing with our little dinghy.

While we were still filing back to the beach and the dawn was breaking with uncomfortable brilliance, we found one of our stragglers – a Navy whaler. We told her people to come aboard, but they said that there was a white motor-boat aground and they would have to fetch off the crew. They went in, and we waited. It was the longest wait – ever. For various reasons they were terribly slow. When they found the captain of the motor-boat, they stood and argued with him. And he wouldn't come off anyway – damned plucky chap.'[4]

For his efforts, David Divine received the Navy's Distinguished Service Medal.[5] He used his experience to write a successful novel which was later made into the film, *Dunkirk*. After the war, he became *The Sunday Times* defence correspondent.

Operation Dynamo had successfully saved 308,888 British soldiers and 122,000 French troops, but practically all equipment had been destroyed.[6]

Although many soldiers were critical of the RAF, they had shot down forty-two bombers and thirty-six fighters over Dunkirk at the cost of eighty-four fighters. This had, however, considerably weakened Fighter Command's front-line strength.

Neutral America was still able to report from the German perspective. John Fisher of *Life Magazine* wrote of driving with other correspondents in a convoy of seven Mercedes-Benz staff cars from Cologne to view the Allies' retreat to the coast. In a tour that took in Arras, Lille, Brussels and Ostend, Fisher wrote about Dunkirk, which was still under attack:

'We started back down the Channel coast towards Dunkerque, passing ever-longer returning German supply trains, which told us that the battle of Dunkerque was almost over. We drove along the Moëres Canal, filled with burning barges, and passed fields where hundreds of Allied trucks stretched in lines as far as the eye could see. Equipment, supplies, coats, helmets were lying about in heaps and mounds – an immense booty for the Germans. The attack upon Dunkerque was mainly carried out by infantry and artillery, not tanks, as retreating French had flooded the area by opening the sluices of the Moëres Canal. German infantry, I was told, had to advance through water up to their necks. I saw many of them wearing Allied khaki uniforms until their own were dry again.

Before us lay Dunkerque resting at last after seven solid days of the most terrific bombardment by artillery and planes. A few hours after 40,000 French defenders gave up, I entered this last foothold of the Allied army in Flanders. The city was a pile of rubbish. Every building was destroyed, not a wall intact. Bricks and stones, many feet deep, jammed the streets. Flames were still crackling and smoke swirled through the town as fire spread unchecked. I stumbled through the smoke over twisted iron girders, dodged hanging wires still red hot, jumped across pools of molten tin and piles of glass, walked over boulders weighing hundreds of pounds...

At Dunkerque harbour Frenchmen lay where they fell, their bodies bloated, legs and arms blown off, guts hanging out. Sprawled in groups, they fell behind their machine guns, the gunner still holding the trigger. The horrid stench of the dead was overpoweringly nauseating. Rows of British trucks unable to be loaded aboard ship stood burned on a dock. Piles of bullets and munitions filled the path.

At one of the smouldering docks a French tanker named Salomé
*caught fire, its smoke choking us within a few minutes. Distant oil
tanks exploded, throwing flames 100ft into the air.'*

Another correspondent who left it late in leaving France was *The Times*
correspondent, Kim Philby, attached to the BEF headquarters. On 19 May,
he lost all his kit during the chaotic retreat from Amiens just a day ahead of
the Germans, but managed to get evacuated on 21 May from Boulogne. He
returned to France in mid-June and briefly reported from Cherbourg and
Brest before sailing for Plymouth just before the French surrender. Philby
put in a claim for his lost kit, including a 'Dunhill pipe and pouch (six years
old but all the better for it)'. The total amounted to £100.16.0, but the
accountants at *The Times* managed to knock it down to £70.

Attention now focused on Paris, where the Germans were fast approaching.

Virginia Cowles managed to catch one of the last planes leaving England
for France. Landing at Tours, she found it crammed with Parisian refugees.
She then caught a train to Paris and survived a wild scramble to get aboard
by hundreds of people. The congestion lasted for 20 miles as the whole train
disembarked to catch a connection to Bordeaux. She then had the strange
experience of riding to Paris in an empty train. On arrival the reason became
apparent with most of the population having abandoned the capital.

The Germans refrained from any bombing but the sound of artillery could
be clearly heard as Cowles sought any reporters she knew. To her dismay,
she found they had already left. Finally, she made contact with Walter Kerr
of the *New York Herald Tribune* and Henry Cassidy of Associated Press,
neither of whom had a car. Fortunately, they ran into Tom Healy of the *Daily
Mirror*, who had just driven in from Italy. Piling into the car they made their
escape on 14 June just as the Germans entered the city.

Returning to Tours was a nightmare, with vehicles of all kinds blocking
the main roads. In the end, the quartet turned on to country roads, which
were clear but offered their own hazards. Virginia Cowles wrote:

*'Tours was bedlam. The French High Command had announced that
the River Loire was to be the next line of defence and all sorts of wild
rumours were circulating... . German motor-cycle units had reached
Le Mans only thirty miles away, and were likely to come thundering
through the streets at any moment now. The Government had already
left for Bordeaux and the refugees who had scrambled into Tours in a
panic were now trying to scramble out again in still more of a panic.'*

Cowles ran into Eddy Ward, the BBC correspondent, who had left Paris just before her. In Finland he had been the first correspondent in history to take a microphone and recording equipment into a front line.

Cowles and Ward, together with four other correspondents, pooled their resources and made for Bordeaux. Once again avoiding the main roads *'choked with terror and misery, with the smell of petrol and the roll of gun-wheels, the country lanes belonged to another world.'* The country dwellers *'seemed so detached from the turmoil around them we began to wonder if they even knew a war was going on.'*

When they arrived at the port of Le Verdon to catch their ship, they heard Marshal Philippe Pétain announce that France had sued for peace and had ceased to fight. Ward recalled:

'The effect of his words was terrible. A Frenchman lunching at the next table broke down and covered his face with his hands.'

Pétain, the hero of Verdun in 1916, judged that Britain appeared on the point of collapse and it was in France's best interests to cease resistance. From being an ally in the Norway campaign and Dunkirk evacuation, Britain was now, de facto, an enemy. Instead of the French military siding with Britain, they chose armed neutrality. The armistice divided France into occupied and unoccupied zones. The Germans occupied northern and western France and the entire Atlantic seaboard, while the remaining two-fifths were controlled by the French government from the spa town of Vichy.

Viewed from this distance, it seems inexplicable that Vichy was acknowledged as the official government of France by the USA until 23 October 1944. Also Canada and Australia gave initial recognition. The USSR, Germany's fair-weather ally, broke off diplomatic relations when Vichy supported the German invasion of Russia on 30 June 1941.

An action that added to the resentment the French felt against her erstwhile ally came in July 1940 when Britain sought the surrender of the French Mediterranean Fleet at the Algerian port of Mers-el-Kébir. When this was rejected, the Royal Navy bombarded the French ships into submission, resulting in the death of 1,297 French sailors and the wounding of 350 others. With all hope of support from mainland France gone, Churchill gave wary support for General Charles de Gaulle's Free French Forces based in London.[7]

Chapter 4

1940–41 – Britain Alone

'What General Weygand has called the Battle of France is over. . . the Battle of Britain is about to begin,' so declared Winston Churchill in the House of Commons. This referred, of course, to the air war that was about to be fought over the skies of England. The battle began on 10 July with all fighting concentrated over the Channel. The Germans sought to disrupt the convoy system of colliers and escort ships that sailed close to the British coast, bringing coal from the north-east of England to the ports in the south.[8] The nearest thing to a front line for a correspondent was a cliff top overlooking the English Channel. Probably the most celebrated report of this period was made on 14 July by the BBC correspondent, Charles Gardner who recalled:

'It was a piece of luck that we (the recording team) were there as we had gone down to various south-coast towns in the hope of getting some action. Each time we had been unlucky, but we decided to ask permission to have another try at Dover. We were there on the Sunday morning, but nothing happened, and so we went for a very hurried lunch. No sooner had we got back to our observation post on the cliff, next door to an AA battery – than the alarm sounded.

A few minutes later we saw about twenty Junkers-87 dive-bombers coming from the direction of Calais at about 6,000ft and above them was an escort of about the same number of Messerschmitts. The Germans started a chain-bombing attack on the convoy, and there was a terrific din of AA fire all around and from the ships themselves. Our first record (recording disc) got the crash of a number of bombs and the bangs of the AA guns, together with my commentary, and we had the luck to see a Junkers shot down straight into the sea in front of us.'

Gardner's excitable report was rather like a horse race commentary and was heard the same day by millions. Describing the above action, he said:

'I can't see anything. No! We thought he had got a German one at the top then, but now the British fighters are coming up. Here they come. The Germans are coming in an absolute steep dive, and you can see their bombs actually leave the machines and come into the water. You can hear our guns going like anything now. I am looking round now. I can hear machine gun fire, but I can't see our Spitfires. They must be somewhere there. Oh! Here's one coming down.

There's one going down in flames. Somebody's hit a German and he's coming down with a long streak – coming down completely out of control – a long streak of smoke – and now a man's baled out by parachute. The pilot's baled out by parachute. He's a Junkers 87, and he's going slap into the sea – and there he goes. SMASH! A terrific column of water and there was a Junkers 87. Only one man got out by parachute, so presumably there was only a crew of one in it.'

Gardner went on to complete his recollection of this day's report:

'Then the German bombers turned for home, and a series of dog-fights broke out all round us between the Messerschmitts, Hurricanes and Spitfires. These were very difficult to follow, but we were able to describe some of them and to see two more German machines crash.

As soon as the battle was over we rang up the BBC and told them that we were on our way back. Censors were good enough to come straight away to Broadcasting House to pass the records, and just over an hour after our return they were broadcast.'

One wonders if the censors would have been so co-operative if Gardner had correctly identified the downed aircraft he vividly described. In fact the Junkers 87 was a Hurricane and the pilot baling out was Pilot Officer M. Mudie, who was picked up by the Navy but died the following day.

Many listeners complained that Gardner's tone was unsuitable as he appeared to get carried away with excitement. Whether it was these criticisms or his admiration for the British pilots, Charles Gardner left the BBC the following month and joined the RAF.

From 12 August to 6 September, the Germans began targeting the coastal airfields before moving inland towards London. Virginia Cowles joined hundreds of other journalists and camera men as they flocked to Dover, the world's current news centre: *'for the fierce and terrible battles taking place above the coast... .*

'I had seen the same journalists in hotels in Prague, Berlin, Warsaw, Helsinki and Paris, but this time it was different; this was the last stop. After this, there would be no other hotels to move on to.

Some of us used to climb to the top of Shakespeare Cliff about a mile from the town, and watch from there. The setting was majestic. In front of you stretched the blue water of the Channel and in the distance you could distinguish the hazy outline of the coast of France... . You lay in the tall grass with the wind blowing gently across you and watched the hundreds of silver planes swarming through the heavens like clouds of gnats. All around you, anti-aircraft guns were shuddering and coughing, stabbing the sky with small white bursts. You could see the flash of wings and the plumes from the exhausts; you could hear the whine of engines and the rattle of machine-gun bullets. You knew the fate of civilisation was being decided fifteen thousand feet above your head in a world of sun, wind and sky.

'Sometimes the planes came lower, twisting, turning, darting and diving with a moaning noise that made your stomach drop; sometimes you saw them falling earthwards, a mass of flames, leaving their last testament a long black smudge against the sky.'

Now that Britain stood alone – the only country left to confront the spread of Nazism – she was a magnet for foreign correspondents. The Americans were well represented and it was their reports on Britain's lone stand that went a long way to create sympathy and support in America. The Battle of Britain marked the first defeat for the Nazis, with the RAF the key to the victory. With the glowing reports from the American contingent of journalists, there was a significant shift in opinion in the USA.

By the end of the battle on 15 September, Germany had lost so many aircraft the Luftwaffe was forced to switch from daylight to night time bombing. She was also ordered to target civilian centres and Hermann Goering vowed that London would be bombed daily. At 5.30pm, on 7 September, some 348 bombers and 617 fighters targeted the docks in London's East End, the first of seventy-six consecutive nights of raids. It was the first sustained attempt to terrorise its citizens in what became known simply as the Blitz.

The controversial American ambassador, Joseph Kennedy, had reported that Britain could not survive.[9] President Roosevelt was not convinced and sent an informal emissary, General Bill Donovan, to assess the situation. He reported back that he was confident of Britain's chances of survival and the country should be supported in every possible way.

The focus now centred on London and how the population would cope with the incessant raids. Helen Kirkpatrick, of the *Chicago Daily News*, wrote of 9 September:

'London still stood this morning, which was the greatest surprise to me as I cycled home in the light of early dawn after the most frightening night I have ever spent. But not all London was still there, and some of the things I saw this morning would scare the wits out of anyone... . The whole night was one of moving from the basement to the first floor, with occasional sallies to make sure that no incendiaries had landed on the rooftop. That was probably more frightening than the sound of constant bombs punctuated by guns near and far. For the London air was heavy with the burning smell. The smoke sometimes brought tears to the eyes, and the glow around the horizon certainly looked as though the entire city might be up in flames any minute.'

The correspondent most associated with the Blitz was without a doubt the American broadcaster, Ed Murrow. He was born Egbert Roscoe Murrow in the 'Lil' Abner-sounding' Polecat Creek, North Carolina in 1908. He was the youngest of three sons born to Quaker dirt farmers. The family later moved to Washington State where their circumstances improved to the extent they could afford indoor plumbing. He attended Washington State College and in the holidays worked as a lumberjack. After being ragged about his name by the loggers, he unofficially changed it from Egbert to Edward.

In September 1935, he joined the Columbia Broadcasting System (CBS) and in 1937 was sent to London as director of CBS's European operations. When the Blitz began, he broadcast each evening in a programme entitled 'London After Dark', introducing his reports with what became his signature opening: 'This...is London'. He later signed off with another catchphrase that he had overheard Londoners use: 'Good night, and good luck'.

The Blitz was the perfect event for radio journalists, with its immediacy and drama accompanied by the sound of sirens, bombs and anti-aircraft guns. In Murrow they had the perfect interpreter, honest and accurate. On 10 September he broadcast:

'When you hear that London has been bombed and hammered for ten to twelve hours during the night, you should remember that this is a huge, sprawling city, that there is nothing like a continuous rain of bombs – at least there hasn't been so far. Often there is a period of ten or twenty minutes when no sound can be heard, no searchlights seen. Then a few bombs will come whistling down. Then silence again. A hundred planes over London doesn't mean they are here all at the same time. They generally come singly or in pairs, circle around over the searchlights two or three times, and then you can hear them start their bombing runs, generally a shallow dive, and those bombs take a long time to fall.

Once I saw "The Damnation of Faust" presented in the open air at Salzburg. London reminds me of that tonight, only the stage is much larger. Once tonight an anti-aircraft battery opened fire just as I drove past. It lifted me from my seat and a hot wind swept over the car. It was impossible to see. When I drove on, the streets of London reminded me of a ghost town in Nevada – not a soul to be seen... .

And so London is waiting for dawn. We ought to get the 'all-clear' in about another two hours. Then those big German bombers that have been lumbering and mumbling about overhead all night will have to go home.'

On 18 September, he reflected:

'I'd like to say one or two things about reporting of this air war against London. No one person can see it all. The communiqués are sparing of information because details of damage would assist the Germans... . It would take a lifetime to traverse the streets of this city, but there's a greater problem involved; it's one of language.

There are no words to describe the thing that is happening. Today I talked with eight American correspondents in London. Six of them had been forced to move – all had stories of bombs and all agreed that they were unable to convey through print or the spoken word an accurate impression of what's happening in London these days and nights.'

Murrow was one whose own office had been bombed out three times.

His broadcasts electrified radio audiences. Previous war coverage had been mostly provided by newspaper reports, newsreels or a radio announcer reading wire service reports. This was the first personalised reporting from a witness to a major event.[10] Murrow had the gift of dramatising whatever he reported, but by understatement and with a calm and highly descriptive radio style:

> *'I walked home at seven in the morning, the windows in the West End were red with reflected fire, and the raindrops were like blood on the panes.'*
>
> *There was a rainbow bending over the battered and smoking East End of London when the 'all-clear' sounded one afternoon.'*
>
> *One night I stood in front of a smashed grocery store and heard dripping inside. It was the only sound in London. Two cans of peaches had been drilled clean through by flying glass and the juice was dripping down onto the floor...'*

On the night of 25 September, he was accompanied by a young bomber pilot who had flown twenty-five missions over Germany. As they made their way through the dark streets, they were caught in a raid:

> *'As we lay on the sidewalk waiting for it to thump, he said: "I'd feel better up there than down here. London is dangerous. I wonder how long it takes to get used to this sort of thing. I've seen enough of this. I hope we haven't been doing the same thing in the Ruhr and Rhineland for the last three months."'*

In fact, CBS had a correspondent in Berlin, who also broadcast a nightly report on the bombings of that city. Ed Murrow hired a 33-year-old veteran foreign correspondent named William Shirer to expand the network's European operations. He had covered the German annexation of Austria and when war broke out in France he travelled to Paris with the German forces.

With the help of a German officer, who despised Hitler, Shirer managed to avoid being returned to Berlin with the other foreign correspondents and hitched a ride to Compiègne to witness France's final humiliation. In the same railway carriage that the France laid down armistice terms to Germany in 1918, Hitler was able to hand his terms to France. Shirer recalled:

'Then he [Hitler] *strode slowly towards us, towards the little clearing in the woods. I observed his face. It was grave, solemn, yet brimming with revenge. There was also in it, as in his springy step, a note of the triumphant conqueror, the defier of the world. There was something else, difficult to describe, in his expression, a sort of scornful, inner joy at being present at this great reversal of fate – a reversal he himself had wrought.'*

The day that the Luftwaffe switched from attacking airfields and began to bomb London, led to a swift retaliation by Britain. The following night, the RAF mounted an attack on the German capital, which was more of a statement that an effective raid.

As Shirer noted in his diary:

'Actually, the British bombings have not been very deadly. The British are using too few planes – fifteen or twenty a night – and they have come too far to carry really effective, heavy loads of bombs. Main effect is a moral one, and if the British are smart they'll keep them up every night.'

As the raids continued, foreign correspondents were forbidden to send reports on the British bombing of Berlin. Shirer was pressed by the Propaganda Ministry only to broadcast official accounts which he was loath to do. Realising that he was wasting his time in Germany, he begged CBS for a transfer. Getting little reaction, he made arrangements to leave citing that the Gestapo was building an espionage case against him.[11] Shirer managed to smuggle out his diaries and notes which he published as *Berlin Diaries* in 1941.

Another American journalist who found Berlin increasingly unhealthy was American-born Sigrid Schultz. In 1925 she had been appointed head of the *Chicago Tribune*'s Berlin bureau. Fiercely anti-Nazi, she made herself unpopular with the regime by reporting the increasing violence and cruel anti-Semitic laws decreed by Nazi rule. This earned her paper's somewhat colourful soubriquet: 'Hitler's greatest enemy'. She got round this by publishing her stories under the name of 'John Dickson', a fictitious journalist operating out of Paris. It was under this name that she broke the news that German negotiators had flown to Moscow to pave the way for the non-aggression pact. Schultz had been tipped off by an astrologer that Hitler regularly consulted.

By 1940, it was becoming too dangerous for Schultz to remain in Berlin and she returned to America. She did return in 1945 and was among the journalists who reported the reaction of the residents of Buchenwald as they were ordered through the liberated camp by General George Patton.

Another American correspondent who emerged from the war as the most celebrated was Ernest Taylor 'Ernie' Pyle. Representing the Scripps-Hearst group, he cut his war reporting teeth on the London Blitz. On 30 December 1941, he wrote in his conversational style about one of the iconic images of the Blitz; the sparing of St Paul's Cathedral:

'Half an hour after the firing started I gathered a couple of friends and went to a high, darkened balcony that gave us a view of one-third of the entire circle of London.

As we stepped out onto the balcony a vast inner excitement came over all of us – an excitement that had neither fear nor horror, because it was too full of awe.

You have all seen big fires, but I doubt if you have ever seen the whole horizon of a city lined with great fires – scores of them, perhaps hundreds. The closest fires were near enough for us to hear the crackling flames and the yells of firemen. Little fires grew into big ones as we watched. Big ones died down under the firemen's valour only to break out again later.

About every two minutes a new wave of planes would be over. The motors seemed to grind rather than roar, and to have an angry pulsation like a bee buzzing in blind fury…

The greatest of all the fires was directly in front of us. Flames seemed to whip hundreds of feet into the air. Pinkish-white smoke ballooned upward in a great cloud, and out of this cloud there gradually took shape – so faintly at first that we weren't sure we saw correctly – the gigantic dome and spires of St Paul's Cathedral.

St Paul's was surrounded by fire, but it came through. It stood there in its enormous proportions – growing slowly clearer and clearer, the way objects take shape at dawn. It was like a picture of some miraculous figure that appears before peace-hungry soldiers on a battlefield.'

The Blitz continued into 1941. Robert Post of *The New York Times* witnessed the heaviest air raid which took place on 10-11 May. The bombing lasted seven hours and was one of the most destructive of the war. Amongst the casualties were Westminster Abbey and the House of Commons, which was set alight by incendiary bombs causing the roof to collapse.

> *'The sun rose red over London yesterday after one of the worst air raids that London has experienced. Weary and drawn after a night of horror and fire – a night that even women living alone spent in putting out incendiaries – London began to make a preliminary reckoning of what happened... .But Londoners recovering from this raid felt a savage satisfaction... that thirty-three raiders had been shot down, four by anti-aircraft fire and twenty-nine by fighters.'*

This marked the last major raid of the Blitz until January 1944 when night bombing was resumed.

Chapter 5

Propaganda and the Media

With war declared, the First World War's censorship and propaganda behemoth, the Ministry of Information (MOI), was resurrected. In fact, wheels had been put in motion as early as 1936 but the journalist's nemesis was not implemented until 4 September. Housed in Senate House at the University of London near the British Museum, its function was: 'To promote the national case to the public at home and abroad in time of war by issuing national propaganda and controlling news and information.'

Naturally the press reacted negatively to this straight-jacket, and the appointment of an official known as 'Eye-witness' brought back bad memories of the First World War with the subsequent decline of the war reporter. This time 'Eye-witness' was not an army officer, as in the Great War, but journalist Alexander Clifford, the former Reuters correspondent who had covered the Spanish Civil War.[12] Regarded as a thoroughly competent journalist, Clifford stuck the appointment for just three months observing the 'Phoney War' in France. With little to report, he resigned, joined the *Daily Mail* and was sent to cover the events in the Middle East.

The revival of MOI was met with some resistance from other government bodies reluctant to give up their public relations divisions to a central control. In particular, the Foreign Office News Department was insistent in keeping control of its output. At a meeting of the Committee for Imperial Defence proposals were considered for the abandonment of plans for the MOI. In the end, it was Prime Minister Neville Chamberlain who backed plans for the establishment of this far-reaching Ministry.

In the first eight months, there were three Ministers of Information. The third appointment was Churchill's choice of Alfred Duff-Cooper, whose initial impression was of an organisation and staff that was unmanageable and described as 'moneyed amateurs'. He remarked that:

'On the day of the outbreak of war the vast machine came into existence and 999 officials sprang into their office chairs. The result was formidable. A monster had been created, so large, so voluminous, so amorphous, that no single man could cope with it... .Ex-ambassadors and retired Indian Civil Servants abounded, the brightest ornaments of the Bar were employed on minor duties, distinguished men of letters held their pens at the monster's service.'

He was constantly frustrated by the Foreign Office and the Service Ministries for not supplying adequate news coverage. Significantly, he failed to gain the trust of the press, whom he disliked. When Duff-Cooper resigned in June 1941, he had made a couple of useful changes in the American Division, which badly needed attention. During the interwar years, successive British governments had largely ignored America, preferring to concentrate on her Empire. Duff-Cooper recognised this and set up the British Information Services in New York in a belated effort to bolster closer ties. He also appointed Douglas Williams of *The Daily Telegraph* to head the MOI's American Division. Williams had an intimate knowledge of America and saw the need for closer ties. When the Allies invaded France in 1944, Williams returned to report for his paper.

It was not until July 1941 that the administration stabilised with the appointment of Brendan Bracken, a staunch supporter and confidant of Winston Churchill. Bracken was sometimes unfairly attacked when many of the attempts to manipulate the media came from other government departments.[13] He constantly resisted Churchill's desire to control the press and was vociferous in his support for the BBC's independence. In fact, with his experience as a newspaper proprietor, he encouraged a closer co-operation with the press and maintained that the MOI should not impinge upon the right to free speech. Whether he achieved this is open to debate.[14]

Formed in August 1941, the Political Warfare Executive (PWE) was a British clandestine body formed to produce and disseminate both black and white propaganda with the aim of damaging enemy morale and sustaining morale in occupied countries.

In *Propaganda as a Weapon of War*, Peter Ritchie Calder wrote:

'The object is to destroy the morale of the enemy and to sustain the morale of our Allies within enemy and enemy-occupied countries; we must be creating and sustaining the will to victory under

whatever pressures the enemy may exert. That is the function of the much abused word – propaganda.'

The staff came from SO1, which had been the propaganda arm of the Special Operations Executive (SOE), and from MOI and the BBC. Its headquarters was at Woburn Abbey, with London offices at BBC's Bush House. One of the aims of this secret propaganda organisation was the spreading of false stories which had a ring of truth about them. Tasked with creating rumours was the responsibility of the Underground Propaganda Committee (UPC).

The UPC was not working alone as a unit, but as a weekly gathering of former correspondents to study the various rumours proposed from the different PWE sections. The rumour mill was still using the same raw material and the same techniques used in journalism so it was second nature for the assembled correspondents seamlessly to embellish the rumours with truth. The technical term used for rumours was 'sibs', from the Latin *sibilare* meaning 'whispering'.

Some of those who contributed to this black propaganda were correspondents who had previously reported from enemy countries including:

Denis Sefton Delmer – *Daily Express*
John Raynor – *Daily Express*
Paul Bretherton – *Daily Mail*
Euan Butler – *The Times*
Ian Colvin – *The Daily Telegraph*
Richard Crossman – *New Statesman*
David Garnett – *New Statesman*
Robert Bruce Lockhart – *Evening Standard*
Ralph Murray – BBC
Peter Ritchie Calder – *Daily Herald*
Leslie Sheridan – *Daily Mirror*
Valentine Williams – *Daily Mail*

Amongst the 'sibs' was a story that General Ernst Udet, the second in command of the Luftwaffe, had quarrelled with Reichsmarshal Goering over policy regarding invading Russia. Udet was a hero from the Great War, whose victories had only been surpassed by the 'Red Baron', Manfred von Richthofen, and was greatly admired in Germany. In July 1941 the UPC began a series of press releases around the world stating that Udet had committed suicide. Headlines like the *Daily Sketch*'s: 'GOERING'S RIGHT HAND MAN KILLS HIMSELF,' and an article from *The Daily Telegraph*'s correspondent in New York dated 30 July stating:

> *'The news is contained in a secret German report which has come into my hands through diplomatic channels. The report has been smuggled from Germany, by way of Holland, by opponents of the Hitler regime. The greatest importance is attached to it by Allied official circles.'*

This was enough to provoke the Germans to deny the rumour as unfounded. Unfortunately for them, and Udet in particular, the Luftwaffe's Number Two did commit suicide on 17 November 1941. According to *The Daily Telegraph* his death occurred while under 'protective arrest'. The *Sunday Express* kept the news item going in January 1942 by echoing this rumour with the headline: 'GERMAN AIR CHIEF EXECUTED.'

A rather less plausible 'sib' was the news that the British Government had imported 200 sharks from Australia and released them in the English Channel. Apparently this was a warning to the Germans about the wisdom of invading Britain.

Another invasion warning was that Britain had a new mine that could be dropped from an aircraft but, unlike other such weapons, it did not explode but spread a very thin film of highly inflammable and volatile liquid over a wide area of the sea. The mine then ignited the liquid setting the sea on fire. This grisly news coincided with the RAF bombing the invasion barges being assembled at Calais which caused many troops to be wounded, some with severe burns. Since the Calais hospital did not have enough beds, some of the wounded were taken to Paris. Within a few hours the rumour had taken hold in the capital that the men had been burned in a foiled invasion attempt.

These 'Chinese whispers' did have a limited effect on the morale of the enemy, but it was Sefton (Tom) Delmer's propaganda broadcasts that made a greater impression. Delmer was born in Berlin, the son of an Australian Professor of English at the Berlin University. He grew up speaking fluent German and was the foreign correspondent for the *Daily Express*. In 1940, he was recruited by the Political Warfare Executive to organise black propaganda broadcasts to Germany as part of the psychological warfare campaign and joined another shadowy department called the Political Intelligence Department.

A mock radio station was set up near Milton Keynes with the intention of undermining the Nazis by pretending to be fully supportive of Hitler. Delmer's first and most notable success was a shortwave station, GSI, which stood for Gustav Siegfried Eins. It was purportedly run by 'Der Chef', an unrepentant Nazi, played by Peter Seckelmann, a former Berlin journalist. Reading Delmer's scripts, Seckelmann managed to convince the Germans that he was broadcasting from Germany. After gaining the German listener's trust, he posed as a loyal Hitler supporter who had become disillusioned with the rest of the Nazi party leadership and started spreading rumours about their deviant behaviour with accusations of rape and paedophilia. The station made some 700 broadcasts until Delmer killed it off in 1943 in dramatic fashion. To the sound of gunfire during the final broadcast, Delmer created the illusion that the Gestapo had found and shot 'Der Chef'.

Tom Delmer created several stations and, through a careful use of intelligence using gossip intercepted in German mail to neutral countries, was able to manufacture credible stories. One such was 'Soldatensender Calais' which appeared to be broadcast from France but was transmitted from a small station in the Ashdown Forest in Sussex. Amongst the popular music were inserted rumours that foreign workers were sleeping with the wives of German soldiers serving overseas.

With the end of the war, Delmer advised his journalist colleagues to say nothing of their work. Not because it was secret but lest the Germans claimed they were beaten by underhand means as the Nazis did after the First World War.

After the war, Tom Delmer returned to the *Daily Express* as chief foreign affairs correspondent until sacked by Lord Beaverbrook in 1959 over an expenses issue.

The war proved to be a tough test for the BBC News Department managers who were uncertain about the role their war correspondents should play. Richard Dimbleby, their man in the Middle East, came in for particular criticism from an appointee from the MOI, A.P. Ryan, who assumed the title of Controller News. Dimbleby had broadcast on 17 September 1941:

*'It must be admitted that the Italian advance has been very rapid....
But this does not alter the situation in general – which is causing no
anxiety; and which, it cannot be too strongly emphasised, shows no
danger to the British forces or to Egypt...'*

Ryan, as the government's man at the BBC, found this view to be in total contrast to the views expressed by his masters who considered Egypt was facing 'mortal danger', and sent a stinging rebuke to Dimbleby. Ryan had previously stated that: 'The state can require the BBC to broadcast, or to abstain from broadcasting anything it likes.' A furious Dimbleby retaliated with a trenchant cable and so began a simmering feud between the two men. In fact what Dimbleby had done was to pass on the information from the only source available – the military. This led to accusations of Dimbleby being General Auchinleck's mouthpiece.

It took until 1943, when the Allies' fortunes began to rise, for the BBC to implement a cohesive system of war reporting. In May that year, the War Reporting Unit was formed and more correspondents and support staff were recruited. By the end of the war, the BBC's stock had risen and it had become a by-word for honest and accurate reporting.

Propaganda in the Second World War was quite different from that in the Great War. With conscription, there was no need to use posters to rally recruits to enlist. The only type of recruiting poster was to encourage men to join one of the services. The nightmarish anti-German posters were not so much in evidence as they were in the previous war. Propaganda promoted important necessities that the country needed to win the war and also encouraged people to act together. The MOI distributed posters to save, make-do, send your children to the country, don't waste food, save kitchen waste for pigs and chickens, dig for victory, collect paper, metal, bones etc.[15]

Although it may appear to be 'nannyish' to present generations, there were sound reasons for such exhortations. The encouragement to grow your own vegetables in the face of the tightening U-boat blockade made good sense. One of the vegetables particularly promoted was carrots. During the height of the Blitzkrieg, the RAF employed a new and secret inboard radar system named Airborne Interception Radar (AI) which was able to pinpoint enemy bombers at night. To keep this under wraps, the MOI put the success of AI down to the consumption of carrots. The RAF night-fighter ace, John Cunningham, was nicknamed 'Cat's Eyes' for his outstanding 'kill' rate in shooting down enemy bombers. The MOI explained the success of Cunningham and his fellow night fighter pilots was down to eating carrots which gave them their superior night vision. It is not known if the Luftwaffe took note of this and started to feed carrots to their own pilots. It may not have fooled the Germans, but the British public did believe that eating carrots would help them see better in the dark and a generation of children endured this over-cooked vegetable.

Advertisements that appeared in the newspapers bore a distinctly wartime message. For instance the makers of K Shoes extolled the virtues of their footwear with this message:

Why more people buy K Shoes in Wartime
Over 900,000 men and women today wear K Shoes, for some the style and smartness are reason enough, but some people in these days of economy buy K Shoes because they know from experience that a pair of K Shoes is a comfortable long-term investment.

They know that Ks will keep their shape and smartness despite months of rigorous wartime wear.

Another product to make wartime claims drew attention to a rich breeding ground for the common cold which, with a simple addition, became something more serious:

Sirocalan Prevents Colds – The Scientific Way to Avoid 'Shelter Colds'

Another ploy was to take an altruistic stance, but make sure the company's name appeared.

Help the Bombed Hospitals now
Each Blitzkrieg is not only a battle for a city or a town; it is for Life in which our Hospitals are in the front line. Many have been bombed and the heroism of and nurses has been marvellous. Any one of us may require this essential service at any moment. Loss of every kind must be made good, so please respond at once to every appeal from Hospitals to the utmost of your means.

Beecham Pills Ltd gladly devotes this space to the Hospitals.

Other posters warned that: 'Careless Talk Costs Lives', 'Keep Mum – she's not so dumb!', 'Tittle Tattle Lost the Battle.' This and other domestic propaganda did engender a general spirit of working together towards a final victory. Although there were exceptions, the British public did pull together and that period of adversity is looked back on with admiration and some nostalgia.

The traditional wartime media forms such as newspapers and posters were joined by the newcomers of cinema, newsreels and radio.

Making films for entertainment with a strong propaganda message were extremely popular during the war. The MOI was conscious that films would further the national cause by reaching a large audience both in Britain and abroad. It depicted the enemy as wicked and evil and the Allies, including overseas resistance groups, as heroic. The war years were also British cinema's golden age.

In 1942 Graham Greene's story, *Went the Day Well?* was released. It told of the occupation of an English village by German paratroopers and played on the fears of the British public of a real invasion. In fact by the date of its release, the threat of a German invasion had receded. Instead, films were being made about the occupied countries and their resistance groups. *One of Our Aircraft is Missing* tells of Dutch civilians risking their lives to help a group of British airman get back to England.

Also released in 1943 was David Lean's first major film, an action drama about a group of Royal Navy sailors fighting the Germans in the Mediterranean. *In Which We Serve* starred Noel Coward and future British stars like John Mills and Richard Attenborough. This stirring piece of propaganda was nominated for an Oscar in 1944 but lost out to *Casablanca*. One British film that did win an Oscar that year was the MOI's film, *Desert Victory*, voted Best Documentary.[16] Amongst other British morale boosting films were *The Life and Death of Colonel Blimp* and *The Way to the Stars*.

There was one other government agency established within the MOI which followed the Great War's pattern of documenting the war through the eyes of established artists. Called the War Artist's Advisory Committee (WAAC), it was the brainchild of Sir Kenneth Clark, then Director of the National Gallery. Whilst the primary purpose was propaganda, Clark hoped that the scheme might prevent artists from being conscripted and killed on the front line. In fact most of the artist's commissions were for subjects on the Home Front, but twenty-six were given overseas commissions.

Edward Ardizzone worked as a full-time official war artist and covered much of the European war including the Fall of France, Tunisia, El Alamein, Sicily, Italy and the 1944 Invasion. Edward Bawdon also served with the BEF and witnessed the evacuation from Dunkirk, also covered the Desert War and Italy. Leslie Cole had joined the RAF but had to leave on medical grounds. He applied to be an official war artist and was sent to Malta to witness the end of the siege. He also covered Burma and Singapore, where he recorded the state of released prisoners of war. To add to this grim experience, he was one of three artists chosen to record the liberation of

Belsen Concentration Camp. It is small wonder that he began to drink heavily after the war.

Although the body of Second World War paintings have not had quite the same impact as those by artists from the Great War, there are some powerful images. For example, Leonard Rosoman's 1940 painting, 'A House Collapsing on Two Firemen, Shoe Lane, London EC4' is both horrific and disconcerting. It shows two firemen clutching a hose appearing unaware of the fate about to overtake them. Rosoman, a fellow fireman, had witnessed such a scene.

One artist who was prominent in the Great War and was to produce several memorable paintings in the Second World War was Paul Nash. Although sick with an asthmatic condition which would kill him by the end of the war, he did paint one of the best known works of the period. His large canvas, 'The Battle of Britain', produced at the time of the battle in 1941 was painted from a great height looking down on a panorama of the English Channel, with France beyond. Regimented waves of German bombers were being broken up by RAF fighters. The canvas filled the sky with vapour trails, smoke from burning planes, parachutes and doomed planes plummeting earthwards. In the foreground, the coast of England with an exaggerated meandering river, suggestive of the Thames Estuary, flowing to the Channel. The painting is an imaginative summary of the event rather than a literal one for Nash favoured symbolism and allegory over factual accuracy.

The outbreak of the war interrupted the era of great writing of the thirties. The rationing of paper affected the production of magazines and books. There was not the great body of poetry that had been produced in the Great War and no new important novelists or playwrights appeared.

Publishers feared that the war would destroy their business but the thirst for books did not diminish. This was despite paper rationing and books being printed on inferior and thinner paper. The finished appearance of British published books was not appealing and they suffered in comparison with those produced in the United States.

It became the norm for those war correspondents who had kept diaries of their assignments to a particular war theatre, to write of their experiences. Several war correspondents, like Alan Moorehead and Chester Wilmot, did write of their adventures in North Africa, which sold well when published within a few months of the campaign ending.

Chapter 6

Africa and the Eastern Mediterranean

With Britain still recovering from her military losses from the Fall of France and enduring daily bombing raids, there might reasonably be expected a period of rallying to regain her strength. Instead, a threat on the fringes of her Empire occupied the government's attention.

When a German victory over France was assured, Mussolini's Italy felt it safe to declare war on France. In a brief conflict in the Alps-Maritime regions of south-east France, the Italians fared poorly and had to settle for an advance of a modest 30 miles. Ignoring the contempt held for her tardy entrance in the war, in Il Duce's eyes this had enabled Italy to be able to sit at the peace table. As President Roosevelt succinctly put it: 'The hand that held the dagger has struck it into the back of its neighbour.'

In fact, Mussolini's ambition was set on expanding his plan for a Mediterranean and African Empire. He had already proclaimed his 'Italian East African Empire' in 1936 having occupied Ethiopia, Eritrea and Italian Somaliland which were added to his North African colony of Libya. This occupation of most of the country on the west side of the Red Sea constituted a threat to British supply routes through the Suez Canal. With Britain preoccupied with home defence, her African possessions seemed easy prey.

The general in charge of the British forces was Archibald Wavell, commander-in-chief of the Middle East Command who had a total of 86,000 British Commonwealth troops to cope with potential conflicts in Libya, Syria, Iraq, Iran and East Africa.

In the opening phase of the war, Italy conquered British Somaliland as the outnumbered British Commonwealth troops withdrew. This pallid campaign was the only victory that Italy achieved without the support of Germany. The loss of this poverty-stricken country provided Italy with a considerable propaganda coup. Churchill was highly critical of Wavell for this loss even though the British were outnumbered five to one. Wavell retorted: 'A bloody butcher's bill is not the sign of a good tactician,' an observation that infuriated Churchill and probably influenced his decision to sack Wavell the following year.

It was about this time that accredited correspondents, like their First World War predecessors, were issued with military uniforms with 'War Correspondent' shoulder flashes. They were entitled to the honorary rank of captain and wore an officer's cap with a rather unattractive bullion badge with a single letter 'C' for correspondent. It could have been worse; 'WC' was considered. The correspondents could draw army rations and use military transport complete with army drivers. The down side was that they had to be accompanied by a Conducting Officer when near the frontline.

The Italians in Libya were massing on the border and succeeded in advancing to Makitila, where they dug, fortified their positions and awaited reinforcements and supplies before marching to the Nile. The Italian newspapers announced that: *'Nothing can save Britain now'*. The odds seemed against Wavell, whose force in Egypt numbered 30,000 facing approximately 150,000.

British patrols reported that the Italian defensive positions were dispersed with fortified camps separated by large distances and not able to provide mutual support. Wavell made his preparations in the strictest secrecy and when Operation Compass was launched on 7 December 1940, most of the troops thought they were embarking on a training exercise. The thrust of the operation was to penetrate the gaps in the Italian defences with tanks and infantry and take the enemy fortified positions from the rear.

As the operation got under way, General Wavell summoned the half dozen or so war correspondents into his office and gave them the news that the long awaited offensive had started.

At that time there were a number of Australian journalists working in London, drawn by the prospect of broadening their experience and furthering their careers. They were encouraged by the attitude of Lords Northcliffe and Beaverbrook, who were happy to hire Dominion talent. Arthur Christiansen, the editor of the *Daily Express*, was particularly complimentary about Australian journalists, noting that they were: 'the best newspapermen of the overseas bunch'. Prominent amongst Australian journalists were Noel

Monks, Ronald Monson, Alan Wood and one of the most successful, Alan Moorehead, of whom Clive James wrote *'he was a far better reporter on combat than his friend Ernest Hemingway'*.

On Wavell's offensive, Moorehead wrote:

> *'Wavell revealed his game of bluff. It was vitally necessary to convince the enemy that we were much stronger than we actually were and to keep them timid and anxious.'*

He was able to tell them that the first Italian camps had been taken and that if they wished, they could travel to the front. For the correspondents it was a matter of playing catch up. Left to their own devices as to how they reached the front, they hitched lifts and scraped together what food was available. This unpromising start developed, in Alan Moorehead's case, into one that was: 'exasperating, exciting, fast moving, vivid, immense and slightly dangerous'.

> *'Following in the wake of the army while it was still hammering in the same way and at the same speed at the Tummars, we came on strange pathetic scenes at Nibeiwa [the first fortified position to be attacked]. Here and there before the breaches in the walls a dead man lay spread-eagled on the ground, or collapsed grotesquely at the entrance of his dugout under a gathering cloud of flies... .*
>
> *Extraordinary things met us wherever we turned. Officers' beds laid out with clean sheets, chests of drawers filled with linen and abundance of fine clothing of every kind. Uniforms heavy with gold lace and decked with the medals and colours of the parade ground hung upon hangers in company with polished jackboots richly spurred and pale blue sashes and belts finished with great tassels and feathered and embroidered hats and caps...We came upon great blue cavalry cloaks that swathed a man to the ankles, and dressing-tables in the officers' tents were strewn with scents and silver-mounted brushes and small arms made delicately in the romantic northern arsenals of Italy.*
>
> *We sat down on the open sand and ate from stores of bottled cherries and greengages; great tins of frozen hams and anchovies; bread that had been baked somehow here in the desert and wines from Frascati and Falerno and Chianti .'*

And much, much more. Besides food of all kinds, there was a huge booty of equipment including hundreds of lorries, hospital equipment, guns, artillery and tanks.

Moorehead read one of the thousands of letters that was found in the fort which summed up the folly of waging a war in such a fashion:

> *'We are trying to fight this war as though it is a colonial war in Africa. But it is a European war in Africa with European weapons and against a European enemy. We take too little account of this in building our stone forts and equipping ourselves with such luxury. We are not fighting the Abyssinians now.'*

Moorehead contrasted this inappropriate opulence with the British officers:

> *'In the British lines there were no sheets, no parade-ground uniforms, and certainly no scent. The brigadier dressed in khaki shorts and shirt. He got bacon for breakfast, bully stew and tinned fruit for lunch, and the same again at night. His luxuries were the radio, cigarettes and whisky with warm water.'*

The Italians were totally demoralised and surrendered in their thousands.

> *'An entire captured division was marching back into captivity. A great column of dust turned pink by the sunset light behind them rose from the prisoners' feet as they plodded four abreast in the sand either side of the metalled track. They came on, first in hundreds, then in thousands, until the stupendous crocodile of marching figures stretched away to either horizon. No one had time to count them – six, possibly seven thousand, all in dusty green uniforms and cloth caps. Outnumbered roughly five hundred to one, a handful of British privates marched alongside the two columns.'*

A week later, every Italian had been either captured or pushed out of Egypt. It was also Britain's first victory of the war.

By February 1941, Wavell's Western Desert Force, which now included the 6th Australian Division, had defeated the Italians at Beda Fomm taking 130,000 prisoners and appeared to be on the verge of overrunning the last of Mussolini's forces in Libya. To add to his list of victories, the following month Wavell's East African forces had occupied Ethiopia and Somaliland.

Richard Dimbleby made the long journey to witness the last big battle of the East African campaign at Keren. Taking a boat to Khartoum, Dimbleby and his recording engineer then drove an ancient Italian lorry to Eritrea to witness the last two weeks of the final assault against the Italians at Keren. The Anglo-Indian force, outnumbered two to one, climbed the steep and jagged approaches to the town. In an effort to get a good view, Dimbleby climbed up a rock-face in temperatures over 120 degrees and settled to look through his binoculars. There was a whine and a smack as a bullet hit the rock close to his head. As he fell back into cover, he landed on a sergeant who observed: 'Funny, they don't usually fire at this time of day. It must be your size.'

Early on 16 March, Keren was captured. Dimbleby drove into the fortress town, which was filled with the rapidly decomposing dead and the sky black with circling vultures.

In the Western Desert, Alan Moorehead made some acute observations about the British Army's temporary occupation of the desert:

> 'We made no new roads. We built no houses. We did not make the desert liveable, nor did we seek to subdue it. We found life in the desert primitive and nomadic and primitively and nomadically we lived and went to war. . .As a fighting area the desert is superb. You get there as close to a straight out trial of strength as you will on any battle front on earth... .Neither side came into the desert for conquest or loot, but simply for battle.'

Alan Moorehead, along with Alexander Clifford of the *Daily Mail*, Captain Geoffrey Keating, their conducting officer and their young driver, attached themselves to a fighting patrol of armoured cars which was heading towards Benghazi. Mile after mile they passed groups of Italian soldiers surrendering but by early evening had not reached the main enemy force.

> 'And then at last we were on the enemy. A group of Italians in green uniforms were laying mines in a bend in the road. They dropped the mines and fled in the bushes at the sound of the leading armoured car and our truck following next in line. There were two more armoured cars following immediately behind us. We could still see and hear the Italians in the bushes, but, having seen so many surrender already, it did not seem worthwhile giving them a burst of machine-gun fire... the Italians, about a dozen in all, emerged onto the road a little further

up and stood watching us. It was strange they did not surrender. "Give them a burst," someone began to say, and then from the hill ahead a long whining scream of bullets came at us down the roadway. We were ambushed.

The enemy were in force. Breda guns, two-pounders and mortars crashed their shells dead amongst us. Clifford and I made for the wooded bank on the left, but it was hopeless – the enemy were firing almost at point-blank range, two or three hundred yards away. The rest of the patrol also tried to make for cover, some of them shooting as they ran. One Breda-gun burst set the armoured car next to ours ablaze, killing the men inside. I heard the muffled scream of another man, hit half a dozen times in the legs, being gallantly dragged back along the gutter by his comrades. The enemy's tracer bullets made long crisscross sheaths of light down the road.

Then I saw Keating, full in the face of fire, running down the line of empty armoured cars trying to get a first-aid kit. Our driver had been cruelly hit on the arm by an explosive bullet as he had leapt from the truck. I ran over to him, tearing off a bandage from a sore on my knee, but he was huddled up crookedly in the shallow drainage gutter, quickly drenching in his blood. Clifford joined me, and together we tore off his greatcoat and cut away his sweater and shirt. But then the Italians creeping closer saw us – the last of the British left around the cars. They blew our truck to bits while we lay four yards away trying to stem the wounded man's flow of blood. Then Keating, who had somehow got up the roadway, joined us with a first-aid pad which we fixed in the wounded man's arm. The fire was very close and heavy and our cover not more than eighteen inches, so we had to stop and be still from time to time. Then a piece of shrapnel struck Keating in the forearm, while a bullet tore a ragged hole in his leg. He fell softly upon the driver in the shallow trench. Clifford was nicked neatly in the behind. Another bullet passed through the folds of my greatcoat and, certain I was hit, I remember waiting frigidly for the pain to come.

By now the line of cars was blazing, and although the enemy could see Clifford and me alone, trying to bind up the wounded men, they concentrated all their fire upon us. It was madness then to stay.'

With dusk falling, Moorehead and Clifford managed to drag their wounded companions back through the bushes to their own lines, where a doctor operated on them under the light of hurricane lamps.

On the point of expelling the Italians from Libya, Wavell was ordered to halt his advance and send troops to Greece, which was being threatened by the Axis. He disagreed with this decision but followed his orders. The result was disastrous.

The rush to reinforce the Greeks had deprived Wavell of 60,000 troops he could ill afford to lose. In a hasty and doomed campaign the Anzac/British force lost 15,000 killed or captured and all their equipment was destroyed. Britain's foothold in Europe was gone.

Guy Harriott of the *Sydney Morning Herald*, had arrived with the first contingent of the 2nd AIF. In the brief Greek war, he was attached to the Greek Army, who had pushed the Italian Army back across the Albanian border. When the Germans invaded, the Greeks became involved in a fighting retreat in which Harriott, in the tradition of many war correspondents, became actively involved. During particularly heavy fighting, he was anxious to take his report to the rear for dispatch. Communications with the artillery had broken down due to the enemy pinning down all attempts to send runners. Despite the danger, Harriott offered to carry the message to the supporting artillery although he knew that three runners had already been killed that day trying to get through. He managed to deliver the message, the guns got the range and the *Herald* got the story on time. For his courage under fire, the Greeks awarded him the Greek Cross of Distinguished Merit.

Harriott was involved in another scrape with death just a short while afterwards. He was on a ship carrying 400 Italian prisoners of war when it struck a mine. Harriott colourfully wrote:

'On the prisoners' deck hell had broken loose. They were screaming in wild mob panic. I heard shouted orders and the rattle of shots. I fought my way to the upper deck and saw Australian guards striving desperately to defend one of the lifeboats against a mob of 400 shrieking maniacs. The guards were ringed in, using their rifle butts with vigour, but they were cool and quite unshaken. It was a scene to be remembered. The panic-stricken crowd, trampling one another, shrieking senseless curses, and the little steady group of khaki figures. Disciplined and brave and thinking, in the midst of hell, only of their duty.

The ship gave a convulsive lurch. I jumped overboard. The water was full of prisoners, crazed with fear. They were clutching at each other and screaming, over and over, "madre, madre – mother, mother". They drowned one another and they drowned themselves, and, but for desperate use of fists and boots, they would have drowned me. I fought my way clear and looked back towards the ship. I saw something I shall never forget. Two Australian soldiers, evidently posted as sentries, were standing on that reeling deck, still and erect, their helmets on their heads, their bayoneted rifles in their hands, "sticking it out" to the bitter end.'

Another hasty evacuation from Crete soon followed and the swift advance now decided the Vichy French in neutral Syria to throw in its lot with Germany. She allowed German aircraft staging bases to assist in the overthrow of the pro-British government in Iraq. The Axis victories had encouraged a pro-Axis faction to take over the government and install the pro-Nazi, Rashid Ali, as prime minister.

Churchill saw Iraq as vital to British interests and pressurised Wavell to send a division-sized force from Palestine to relieve the besieged British air base at Habbaniya. Instead, the Indian 20th Infantry Brigade under General Claude Auchinleck landed at Basra to protect the precious oil fields. By the end of May, General Sir Edward Quinan's Anglo-Indian force had captured Baghdad and the war was over.

Many of the Australian correspondents complained that they were hampered and obstructed by British officers who favoured other foreign correspondents. Despite this, some of Australia's outstanding correspondents including ABC's Chester Wilmot, Ronald Monson and his frequent travelling companion the poet, Kenneth Slessor, established their reputations in the Middle East.

Ronald Monson, representing the *Sydney Daily Telegraph*, the *Melbourne Argus* and the London *Daily Express*, wrote an account of the Greek campaign for the British Ministry of Information and soon after published a book, *The Battle of Greece*. He joined the advance on Baghdad and was mentioned in despatches for swimming across the Euphrates River under Iraqi fire to rescue a wounded British soldier. What must have irked Monson was when the two of them almost reached safety they were helped by an officer who was later awarded the Distinguished Service Order. Similar acts performed by war correspondents going back to Queen Victoria's colonial wars were always acknowledged with a mention in despatches but never a gallantry medal.

In early June, Wavell sent a force under General Sir Henry Wilson to invade Syria and Lebanon in response to the help that Vichy France had given to the pro-Axis government in Iraq. The Vichy French forces under General Dentz put up a spirited defence, but there was little enthusiasm for the conflict. As Guy Harriott wrote:

'The melancholy war in Syria and the futile defence by General Dentz, who proved a willing tool of Vichy, cost us in Australian casualties alone 1628 good fighting men...The campaign consisted of a month's fighting against troops of a Power with whom we were not at war, troops who a year ago had been our brothers in arms against a common enemy.'[17]

Wavell's Western Desert Force, now stalled in Libya, had reached little further than Benghazi. Mussolini requested help from Hitler, who despatched a motorised force termed the Afrika Korps under the command of General Erwin Rommel. They were ordered to reinforce their Italian allies and to defend against any further British advance. Instead, Rommel discovered just how weak the British advance was and went on the offensive. By the end of April the depleted Western Desert Force had been pushed back to the Egyptian border, leaving the 9th Australian Infantry Division to defend the fortress port of Tobruk, 100 miles west of the Egyptian border.

On 15 June 1941, General Wavell launched Operation Battleaxe in an effort to clear eastern Cyrenaica of German and Italian forces. It was also hoped to relieve the siege at Tobruk. The initial assaults against Rommel's strong defensive positions resulted in the British loss of half her tanks on the first day. By the third day, the British narrowly avoided a complete disaster by withdrawing just ahead of a German encircling movement which would have cut them off from retreat. The result of this failure spelt the end for Wavell, who was replaced by General Claude Auchinleck, who had impressed Churchill with his handling of the Iraqi uprising.[18]

The Western Desert Force was reorganised, renamed the Eighth Army and placed under the command of Lieutenant General Alan Cunningham, whose brother was Admiral Andrew Cunningham, Commander-in Chief, Mediterranean Fleet. After months away on other consignments, Alan Moorehead returned to Egypt in time for the launch of Operation Crusader. As he and other journalists neared the frontline, he noted:

'The old days of small piratical raids were gone. The desert was filling up with thousands upon thousands of armed men. Two great armies… lay camped within half a day's distance of one another. As more and more guns and tanks were pressed into the desert, the days of peace were running out rapidly. The new battle when it came would no longer be a border skirmish but a full-scale test of strength between the Germans and the British.'[19]

Prepared for a long assignment, Moorehead and his companions, the *Daily Mail*'s Alexander Clifford and Richard Busvine of the *Chicago Tribune*, rode in a Humber staff car with their conducting officer. Their supplies of bedding, water, petrol and provisions filled two trucks, which followed behind. The advance started on 18 November in the face of a storm of sleet and a freezing wind from the Mediterranean. Most of the correspondents followed the 7th Armoured Division as it drove north-west towards Tobruk, in attempt to link up with the defenders who had broken out to meet them.

Unfortunately, in two days of intense fighting at Sidi Rezegh, the 7th Armoured Brigade was forced to withdraw having lost all but four of their 150 tanks.[20] Moorehouse had been joined by Edward (Eddy) Ward, the newly-arrived BBC reporter in witnessing this annihilation. On his return to England after the Fall of France, Ward had been sent out as a replacement for Richard Dimbleby, who was prostrated with diphtheria.[21]

'The airfield [at Sidi Rezegh] fell, and as my party struggled back in the mud and darkness I saw the enemy's Very lights creeping rapidly around us…. That meant we were surrounded…at least temporarily. On this night the firing did not cease and the broken burning tanks glowed fitfully and grotesquely across the damp sand of the desert.

In the morning we left Ward behind and made a bolt southward to reach rear headquarters. Even as we bumped along the uneven track German armoured cars came in again from the west and east driving in front of them, like stampeding cattle, hundreds of British lorries, ambulances and supply wagons.'

The disorganised retreat continued the following day. Having stopped briefly at the divisional headquarters, Moorehead and his companions saw hundreds of British trucks and tanks race past their stationary vehicles.

'Then another great swarm of vehicles rushed through the camp and now the shells began to fall among them. It had been a bright early morning, but now the churned-up dust had blotted out the sun and visibility became reduced to two hundred yards or less. In this semi-darkness and confusion thousands of vehicles got hopelessly mixed so that men and vehicles of entirely different units travelled along together and, since many of the drivers had no orders, they simply rushed ahead following anyone who would lead them.

All day for nine hours we ran. It was the contagion of bewilderment and fear and ignorance… . We were just a few hangers-on of the battle, the ones who were most likely to panic because we had become separated from our conducting officers and had no definite job to do. I came to understand something of the meaning of panic in this long nervous drive.'

Eddy Ward was not so lucky. He was recording the fighting with the South African Division to the left of the Armoured Division, when the Germans performed an encircling movement. As with all battles, no individual knows exactly what is going on as illustrated by Eddy Ward's recollection:

'The bombardment got nearer. I didn't worry much. I dug my slit-trench a little deeper, just to be on the safe side. So did [Godfrey] Anderson, the AP correspondent. So did Lamprecht, of the South African Radio. Harold Denny [New York Times] went on hammering away at his typewriter. Then a certain amount of stray metal began flying about. I sat on the edge of my slit-trench and ducked occasionally… . Harold continued to tap out his story. A few shells screamed over and burst two or three hundred yards away. One hit a truck and set it on fire.

Shells began arriving more regularly. Another truck on the perimeter of the widely dispersed vehicles burst into a sheet of flame and sent up a great column of black smoke. Stray machine-gun bullets began singing overhead. It didn't occur to me that anything was really wrong. It was bit unpleasant, and I wished I could persuade old Harold to get into his slit-trench. But he was getting well into his story and evidently didn't want to lose the thread of it.

I dug my slit-trench a little deeper. Just to be on the safe side. Now a shell burst eighty yards behind us. Half a dozen more came over. Getting a bit closer.

The orchestra had stopped tuning up. The symphony had started. Ah well! I'd wanted to see a tank battle. Looked as if I was going to get my wish. A plume of sand and stones shot into the air and came tumbling down all around us… . Ought I to be taking notes on all this? No, the hell with the notes! I shouldn't be likely to forget any of this.

The brass gave way to the strings. A pizzicato of machine-gun bullets followed the screaming, booming shells. I lay face down convinced that my behind was sticking up above ground-level like an ant-hill. Wished I had another tin hat to put on my behind.

The fury of the bombardment grew so intense as to be unbearable… . This could not go on. The air was too full of metal. Sooner or later with mathematical certainty a piece was bound to hit me.

The din was overpowering and then came a deep rumbling noise, which was greatly magnified through the fact of my being below ground-level. It grew louder and louder, and as the noise increased the machine-gun bullets came thicker and thicker, until they hummed a few feet over my head like a wasp's nest.

"It's the tanks! Thank God it's the tanks! We're Okay!" I heard Lamprecht cry. I raised myself on one elbow and looked. The damned things were weaving in and out of the vehicles, blazing away with their machine-guns. They were still over a hundred yards away.

"Yes, it's the tanks all right," I said, "and they've got nice, big black crosses on them."'

So Eddy Ward and his fellow correspondents went into a lengthy captivity during which they were frequently moved through Italy and into Germany as Allies advanced.

Another trio of correspondents caught up in the chaotic retreat were Alaric Jacob of the *Daily Express*, Matt Halton of the *Toronto Star* and Sam Brewer of the *Chicago Tribune*. They had the nerve-wracking experience of a burst tyre as a stream of vehicles shot past in full flight. Jacob recalled:

'Now we found ourselves left entirely behind. The desert had emptied. As we strained and sweated over the wheel we looked ever and anon over our shoulders and noted the shell bursts creeping up on us… . "Surely we are not going to stand here impotently and let ourselves be captured." Our driver looked up from the wheel and

with a loud whoop of triumph called out, "It's on!" We tore off eastwards and a mile or so further we overtook the two best cinematographers in the desert, Ronnie Noble and Freddie Bayliss. They were in a desperate situation as their car had a serious breakdown, so they just jumped on our running-board and hung on for dear life.'

The correspondents had taken a bad beating with the capture of Ward, Anderson, Denny and a half a dozen South African reporters. The mood in the correspondents' camp further deepened when they learned that Alexander Massy Anderson, Reuter's naval war correspondent, had been killed.

Anderson had served as the Reuters manager in Alexandria for ten years. At the outbreak of the war, despite not being a journalist, he was appointed a naval war correspondent, probably because of the naval connections he had made in the port of Alexandria. His reporting style was described as 'clear and sober', and he covered many naval operations by the British Mediterranean Fleet, including the successful Battle of Taranto.

It was, however, his account of the dive-bombing of the aircraft carrier HMS *Illustrious* that sealed his reputation. On 10 January 1941, the ship was attacked about 85 miles west of Malta in what at that time was the heaviest mass dive-bombing attack on a single ship. Massy Anderson managed to send off his report when the carrier managed to reach Malta:

'Battle-scarred but triumphant, the giant Illustrious *made port yesterday after furiously fighting waves of German dive bombers at intervals for seven hours in the narrow channel off Sicily where the Luftwaffe, swooping down in its first Mediterranean action, struck the severest blows ever delivered from the air against a single warship.*

The gallant crew of this British aircraft carrier hit back with a coolness and precision that are beyond praise and the terrific fire erupted by the multiple-barrelled guns of the Illustrious *sent some of Adolf Hitler's 'serial destroyers' plummeting crazily into the sea... .*

It was shortly after noon when two torpedo-carrying planes appeared, but the long, sleek missiles they launched passed harmlessly astern of the 23,000-ton carrier.

Soon afterward the main assault began. Three Junkers-87 Stukas approached from the clouds and the guns of the Illustrious *and all the other ships opened up with a terrific barrage fire.*

Four more Junkers quickly joined in and the sky became filled with a confused mass of bursting shells and twisting planes. The noise was appalling.

The leading German plane dived through the inferno straight at us. I watched this Stuka release a single 1,000lb bomb, which fell into the sea slightly astern of us. Then I saw fifteen bombers diving at the British warships. But, while watching the Nazi attackers overhead, my attention was diverted by several of our own planes which were taking off from the flight deck of Illustrious.

A few minutes after the last British fighter took off, one of the German bombers, diving low, scored a direct hit on the Illustrious *with 1,000-pound bomb. A tremendous explosion shook the whole ship.*

The next thing I saw was the wing of a German plane drop from the sky and fall across the after-deck of the Illustrious.

The air was filled with over-powering fumes of explosive chemicals, but the guns of the Illustrious *roared continuously. The chatter of the pom-poms mingled with the harsher crack of the heavier anti-aircraft cannon in a steady thunder.*

I could see that the Illustrious *had been hit immediately below the bridge. Fortunately, the damage was slight. Casualties were suffered, but the wounded received only minor injuries.*

The Stukas appeared to converge upon us from all sides, then to dive one after another into the blazing gunfire. They held their bombs until the last minute, then released them and quickly swerved off.

After what seemed to be an eternity, though it only lasted five minutes, the gunfire ceased. The decks were covered with the foam of fire extinguishers. Riddled and splintered fragments of steel pipes were piled where I had been standing a moment before.'

In fact the damage was considerable. Two lifts, each weighing 300 tons were wrecked and welded into different shapes by the intense heat of the fires that raged below. As the fires were brought under control, another 1,000lb bomb penetrated a damaged lift shaft and reignited some of the fires. Fortunately the boilers were untouched and serviced by stokers working in temperatures of 130°F. Anderson was not just a detached watcher for he joined in tending the wounded during the seven-hour attack and received high praise from the officers.[22]

Another correspondent, who was awarded the Pulitzer Prize for his account of the bombing of *Illustrious*, was Laurence Allen of Associated Press (AP). He was also with Anderson when the latter met his death. On 15 December, while returning to Alexandria on the light-cruiser HMS *Galatea* after a sweep along the Libyan coast, Anderson's luck ran out. Shadowed by the German submarine, *U-557*, *Galatea* was hit with two torpedoes and sank in three minutes. Massy Anderson was one of the 469 crew members who died.[23]

Allen had an incident-filled war. On 14 September 1942, he was onboard the destroyer HMS *Sikh*, covering a commando raid on Tobruk, when it was hit and sunk by anti-aircraft batteries. Allen again survived and was taken prisoner. During his twenty-two months as a PoW, Allen made three escape attempts. On 20 May 1944 he was repatriated in a prisoner exchange.

After his capture, Larry Allen was succeeded by Edward Crockett, who covered the North African campaign from El Alamein to Tunis. His war reporting career was, alas, brief. On 5 February 1943, he was drowned when the Royal Navy mine-layer he was on was torpedoed by a U-boat and sank.

Not all fellow correspondents were moved by the tributes paid to the fallen correspondents. Richard Dimbleby, who resented the BBC's habit of combining his reports with those of the news agencies, was critical of the fulsome tributes paid to two members who had died at sea: '*Wish Reuters hadn't put out such a long splurge...saying, "There is something in the courage of a war correspondent that transcends the courage of a soldier!" For God's sake!*'

On 23 November, Rommel launched his own attack towards Egypt with the intention of further scattering and destroying the Allies. By 4 December, it was clear that Rommel was not going to succeed so he decided to narrow his front by abandoning the Tobruk front and retiring to the prepared defences at El Agheila, thus ceding to the Allies the whole of Cyrenaica. On the face of it, Operation Crusader could be called a victory, albeit a pyrrhic one. Certainly the claims in the newspapers gave the impression of a total victory with such headlines as 'ROMMEL SURROUNDED', 'ROMMEL IN ROUT' and 'GERMANS DESPERATELY TRYING TO ESCAPE BRITISH NET'.

Now it was the turn of the British supply line to be extended to breaking point. Benghazi port had been so bombed and mined to make it practically unusable, so supplies had to be carried by lorry over 500 miles in the winter rain that was described as the worst in living memory. Movement became almost impossible with the RAF grounded in flooded airfields and isolated groups of men strung across the sodden desert.

As Alan Moorehead observed: '*The trouble was that the further you got away from your base, the nearer the retreating enemy got to his. Consequently, as you got weaker, the enemy got stronger.*'

In January 1942, Rommel began to probe the Allied line and, finding little opposition, began a limited offensive. Auchinleck and General Neil Ritchie, who had replaced Cunningham, pulled back to a new position west of Tobruk which was called the Gazala Line and both sides reorganised and built up their men and equipment. The lull between February and June incensed Churchill, who urged Auchinleck to be more aggressive and bring the British a much needed victory. There was also the very real danger that Malta would be invaded and the Germans would then have a near free-hand in supplying the Afrika Korps without being harried by the RAF.

A correspondent who had reported on the air attacks on Malta was Bernard Gray of the *Sunday Pictorial*. He was probably the last newspaper reporter to cover the retreat to Dunkirk with a reputation described as 'richly piratical'. Having witnessed the repeated bombing of Malta, he was anxious to leave and cover the North African campaign.

Using well-placed friends, which may have included the newly-arrived governor of Malta, General Lord Gort, Gray managed to wangle his way aboard the submarine HMS *Urge*, which was due to sail for Alexandria. The Royal Navy strictly forbade civilians, especially newspapermen, from sailing in their submarines. Gray was using the *Urge* for a passage to Egypt and not as an assignment. Although his name did not appear amongst the list of crew members, he was the only 'unofficial submariner' and journalist known to have perished in a submarine. On 28 April 1942, *Urge* left Malta and disappeared en-route to Alexandra. All 43 crew, including Bernard Gray, drowned, most likely striking an Axis mine. For years, an embarrassed Royal Navy refused to acknowledge that Gray had been on board. Finally, a letter from the Admiralty admitted that Gray had died on HMS *Urge*.

Rommel attacked on 26 May 1942, and after some intense tank battles, made great inroads that threatened to overwhelm the defenders. His success was nearly his downfall, for his armoured units had moved too far from his fuel supplies. Rommel even contemplated surrender and it was at this point that Ritchie should have gone on the offensive. Instead, Rommel was allowed to withdraw without further significant losses. Again Churchill was furious at the hesitancy displayed by Ritchie and, to borrow Abraham

Lincoln's damning comment about one of his Civil War generals, 'he snatched defeat from the jaws of victory'. Rommel was again allowed to take the offensive on 3 June.

Moorehead, Clifford and other correspondents arrived too late for the first few days of the battle but the fighting soon caught up with them. Again, sensing a retreat, the correspondents quickly packed up and, driving through the night, arrived in Tobruk in time for a heavy air raid. By 16 June, nearly all the British positions west of Tobruk had fallen and the Gazala Line was broken.

Having driven once more to Gazala, Moorehead and his colleagues returned via Tobruk, which they found preparing for another siege, this time defended by the South Africans. Loading up with supplies and petrol, they exited towards the east: *'It was always a relief to get out of Tobruk. I think we knew that the place was doomed.'* Moorehead's pessimism was shared by the BBC who, during the following siege, made an unforgivable error of judgement by suggesting that Tobruk was not after all vital and might be lost. The effect it must have made on the isolated defenders can be imagined. The South African commander, General Klopper and his staff heard it, and sent almost the last message from the surrounded perimeter: 'I cannot carry on if the BBC is allowed to make these statements.' Shortly after, Klopper surrendered.

Moorehead added:

> *'The old faith in the BBC began to dissipate around this period and soldiers began to ridicule the broadcasts. Unquestionably, the same bitter criticism would have fallen on the newspapers had the men seen them, for there were at this time many London commentators who were taking wild guesses at the situation in the absence of any real news. But the BBC came in for all the blame. Two months before it was alleged the BBC had revealed future British plans, and Auchinleck protested personally to Churchill.*
>
> *At the moment it was the Tobruk broadcast that counted. Presumably it was thought to be more important "to prepare the public for defeat", than try to hold Tobruk itself... .*
>
> *'To the defenders in Tobruk it seemed an outrage.'*

Churchill was in Washington conferring with President Roosevelt when the news of the Tobruk surrender came through. He later wrote: *'This was one of the heaviest blows I can recall during the war. Not only were the military effects grim, but it affected the reputation of British arms… .Defeat is one thing; disgrace is another.'*

The British had fallen back to a new defence line at El Alamein and the way to the Nile seemed wide open to Rommel. But the Afrika Korps, like the Allies, was totally exhausted after three weeks continuous fighting and travelling. The British did have a distinct advantage in that they were able to replace most of their exhausted men with fresh troops, like the Australians, and the RAF held the mastery of the skies.

Moorehead explained:

'There were also excellent tactical reasons for falling back on the Alamein Line. The line was unique in the desert; no other line had a top and a bottom. Every other line, British or Axis, had been turned because its southern end lay in the open desert. The Alamein Line was based at its northern end on salt lakes by the sea and at its southern end on the Qattara quicksands. It was only forty miles in length… .

The Alamein Line, of course, was a reporter's paradise. It was so short and compact that you could visit the whole front in the course of a day…if an engagement flared up anywhere we heard about it within a few hours and were able to get to the spot at once.'

The correspondents received their mail by despatch rider, which resulted in different reactions: *'I had known correspondents on opening their cables to announce that they had to go to Peru or Moscow, and half an hour later disappear out of the desert forever. Others might glower over some rebuke because they missed a story or again, with heavy modesty, reveal that they had a word of congratulations or a raise.'*

In anticipation, there were nearly 100 Allied war correspondents in the desert to give the coming battle saturation coverage. According to Robert Hughes, the correspondent for Sydney's *Daily Telegraph*: *'All correspondents reacted the same way. We were all shaken, scared and embarrassed by our need to conceal our fear by exaggerating it.'* When he came under artillery fire, he found he had broken his nails digging his fingers into the earth where he lay.

Auchinleck went on the attack on the night of 26/27 July but failed to shift the enemy and ended offensive operations on 31 July. A few days later he was replaced by General Sir Harold Alexander with General Bernard Montgomery in command of the Eighth Army.

After a succession of conventional and rather uninspiring commanding officers, the appearance of General Montgomery, or 'Monty' as he was quickly dubbed, had an uplifting effect on his command. He frequently adopted an unconventional style of dress including an Australian bush hat with assorted regimental cap badges. But the one with which he was most associated was the black beret and badge of the Royal Tank Regiment to which he added his bullion general's badge. He appeared at just the right time when morale was flagging as there was yet another build up to another desert battle. On taking up command of the Eighth Army on 13 August 1942, he made one of the memorably inspiring speeches of the war, which included:

> *'I do not like the general atmosphere I find here. It is an atmosphere of doubt, of looking back to select the next place to withdraw, of loss of confidence in our ability to defeat Rommel, of desperate measures by reserves in preparing positions in Cairo and the Delta. All that must cease. Let us have a new atmosphere...*
>
> *Here we will stand and fight; there will be no further withdrawal. I have ordered that all plans and instructions dealing with further withdrawal are to be burned at once. We will stand and fight here. If we can't stay here alive, then let us stay here dead.'*

After a three-month hiatus in which there was much training, re-equipment and a build up of materials, the long-expected battle began at 10pm on 23 October with attacks to the north and south of the line. On hand to record the start of this great battle was BBC's debutant commentator, Godfrey Talbot, whose series of recordings of the sounds of battle and interviews established his reputation.

Talbot had been sent to Cairo to replace Richard Dimbleby, who had displeased the BBC in London for spending too much time in Cairo and living a rather grandiose lifestyle, with a liveried chauffeur and a house-boat on the Nile. He was also criticised for putting out optimistic reports of the situation in Egypt which were soon disproved. Dimbleby's reports were therefore 'causing acute embarrassment at the BBC', and one wonders if the infamous 'Tobruk' broadcast emanated from the same source. Dimbleby was also perceived as being too close to Auchinlech and his staff at a time when Churchill was highly critical of his Middle East commander.

Instead of departing under a cloud, Dimbleby was: *'feted throughout Cairo by friends and officials. Government ministers, ambassadors, and*

Army commanders.' Talbot was astonished by the affection and respect in which Dimbleby was held:

> *'I was a journalist succeeding a personality. There were war correspondents and there was Richard Dimbleby. He had made a quite extraordinary impression in the Middle East.'*

In fact Godfrey Talbot disliked the life in the desert as much as Richard Dimbleby and took every opportunity to return to the comforts of Cairo. For the period of the El Alamein Battle, he did stick with the advancing Allies and sent this sample report complete with noise of tanks and gunfire:

> *'This is Godfrey Talbot recording in the desert. The sound you can hear now is the sound of British tanks moving into battle. It's the night of Sunday/Monday 1-2 November and it's the early hours of the morning, and now on this desert, with the sand clouds whirling up behind each vehicle, British tanks in large numbers are moving into battle.*
>
> *Shells by the thousand are being pumped into the enemy, and here we are at the side of one of these desert tracks watching the armed might of the Eighth Army go forward to engage the enemy. The moon, just half a moon, is shining down here, and overhead there is not only the moon, but the flares that have been dropped which are shining down on the desert and illuminating this battlefield. Tank after tank is going past, just as I speak now.*
>
> *One can't see very clearly, because of the fog, it is indeed a fog, but a fog of sand, very soft here, and each tank as it goes past throws up a great cloud.'*

Broadcasts like these were sent back to Cairo, where they were listened to by four separate censors: Army, Navy, RAF and Egyptian Government, all of whom could make crude cuts that might damage the rest of the disc. The Egyptian State Broadcasting sent them by commercial beam radio to London, where reception might or not be reasonably good. The whole despatch was then re-recorded and broadcast to the British listening public. Soon, Talbot's voice became familiar to thousands of listeners. Although in the transcribed word the broadcasts don't compare with newspaper reporting, the immediacy of the broadcast excited the public.

By 4 November, Monty's Eighth Army had achieved their breakthrough and the Afrika Corps began the long fighting retreat back across Libya.[24]

Four days later, Operation Torch, the British-American invasion of Vichy French Morocco and Algeria, began with the intention of catching the Axis in North Africa in a pincer movement. Once the landing had successfully been accomplished, then the combined forces were to advance eastwards towards Tunisia and occupy the country before the Axis could react. This was the priority rather than rid the territories of the large Fascist element still in control of much of the region. A disgusted Ernie Pyle wrote on 4 January 1943:

'There are an astonishing number of Axis sympathisers among the French in North Africa. This is a great puzzle to me. I can't fathom the thought process of a Frenchman who prefers a German victory and perpetual domination rather than a temporary occupation resulting in eventual French freedom.

But there are such people, and they are hindering us, but that a strange, illogical stratum is against us. And that our fundamental policy still is one of soft-gloving snakes in our midst.'

Although the Allies came within a short distance of Tunis, there was not enough manpower to carry it through, because the Axis, supplied from nearby Sicily, had arrived in great numbers. The terrain helped the Axis, being mountainous with a few easily defended passes and the fortified Mareth Line. The Allies, now advancing in the mid-winter rain and cold, suffered several defeats. By January, Rommel had planned that his final retreat from Libya would enable his Afrika Korps to take a prepared position in the formidable Mareth Line.

With the British holding the north and south, Rommel decided to attack what he considered a softer target in the centre held by the inexperienced Americans at Kasserine Pass. His first attack was repulsed but with tank reinforcements Rommel broke through on 20 February, killing more than 1,000 American soldiers. In their hasty retreat, they left behind most of their equipment. It was America's first taste of defeat in battle. Ernie Pyle was on hand to witness the event:

'That Sunday morning hordes of German tanks and troops came swarming out from behind the mountains around Faïd Pass. We didn't know so many tanks were back there, and didn't know so many Germans were either, for our patrols had been bringing in mostly Italian prisoners from their raids.

The attack was so sudden nobody could believe it was in full force. Our forward troops were overrun before they knew what was happening. The command post itself didn't start moving back till after lunch. By then it was too late – or almost too late.

Command cars, half tracks and Jeeps started west across the fields of semi-cultivated desert, for by then the good road to the north was already cut off. The column had moved back about eight miles when German tanks came charging in upon the helpless vehicles from both sides.

It was a complete melee. Every Jeep was on its own… . The Germans just overran our troops that afternoon. They used tanks, artillery, infantry, and planes dive-bombing our troops continuously. Our artillery was run over in the first rush. We were swamped, scattered, consumed, by the German surprise.'

Further to the north, Alan Moorehead, returned to North Africa after assignments in India and Washington, was reporting in the British sector. He wrote poignantly of the casualness and randomness of death:

'As the fighting died down we came back to El Aroussa village, which was much cut about with bombing, and the usual argument broke out about where we were going to sleep. One group favoured a great barn-like building in the centre of the village despite the fact it had had its roof torn off and was now filled with coils of barbed wire. The other group favoured the open countryside away from bomb targets. In the end we compromised with a verandah of a villa on the outskirts.

The morning broke unusually clear and I wandered into the village. In the main street half a dozen Tommies were washing in the horse-trough and I fell into conversation with them. They were Londoners, adolescent boys on their first campaign and enjoying a good deal of it… . They were friendly and shy and very determined to do well in the war...

As I walked back to my camp the Stukas came over. They came very slowly and I suppose about eight hundred feet up, just a dozen of them with one or two fighters up above. There was ample time to run a few yards into the fields and throw myself into the first available hollow.

It seemed for a moment they were going to sail by the village but at the last moment they altered direction, opened their flaps, and dived. The bombs tumbled out lazily, turning over and over in the morning sunshine. Then with that graceful little jump and flick each aircraft turned upward and out of its dive and wheeled away. It all happened very slowly. They could scarcely have missed the centre of the village but they were very lucky to have hit a large truck filled with ammunition. The truck caught fire and the bullets kept blowing off in all directions, red for the tracers and white for the others... . One of the explosions performed the remarkable feat of killing a dove which flew through the air and struck down an officer who was in the act of talking to me.

I walked over to the centre of the village keeping care to stay away from the exploding ammunition lorry... . The barn-like building in which we proposed to spend the night had taken another direct hit and the coiled barbed wire had threshed wildly in a thousand murderous tentacles. The blast had carried these fragments across to the water trough and now my six young friends were curiously huddled up and twisted over one another. It is the stillness of the dead that is so shocking. Even their boots don't seem to lie on the ground as those of a sleeping man would. They don't move at all. They seem to slump into the earth with such unnatural overwhelming tiredness; and I will never grow used to the sight of the dead.'

After many hard-fought months, Tunis fell on 7 May and the Tunisian Campaign was finally won. The last Axis resistance ended with the surrender of over 230,000 prisoners of war.

Chapter 7

The First Assaults on Mainland Europe

Sicily

The huge loss of manpower and new equipment that Hitler belatedly poured into North Africa seriously depleted other Axis-held territories in the Mediterranean. This included Sicily which lay just 80 miles from Tunisia. Determined not make the mistake of committing anything but a huge air and sea landing force, the Allies sent 150,000 troops in the initial landings – more than took part in the Normandy landings the following year. The air was dominated by 4,000 Allied airplanes and over 3,000 ships and landing craft, which saw the landing successfully accomplished in the face of token opposition.

The invasion, codenamed Operation Husky, was under the overall command of General Dwight Eisenhower, with the American Seventh Army, commanded by General George Patton, and the British Eighth Army under General Montgomery. The two armies landed at adjacent beaches in the south-east of the island, with war correspondents in force. Michael Chinigo of International News Service (INS) waded ashore with the first group of assault troops having been assigned to the 3rd Infantry Division. Despite being wounded in the wrist and arm by shellfire, he accompanied a patrol which entered the capital, Palermo, in advance of the occupation. Fluent in Italian, he informed the Chief of Police that the Americans were about to capture Palermo and resistance was fruitless, thus enabling the city to be taken without a fight.

Another American correspondent who chose to be in the forefront of action was *Chicago Tribune*'s John Thompson. He flew with the airborne troops and parachuted on the night of 9-10 July. Unfortunately, this heroic and daring attempt to obtain a scoop came to naught, when he landed in an olive tree receiving a twisted knee and a cracked rib. At least the Army recognised his effort by later awarding him the Purple Heart.

The Reuters senior correspondent in Washington, South African-born Kenneth Stonehouse, was anxious to cover the war in Europe and volunteered to become a war reporter. In order to return to Europe, Stonehouse and his wife sailed on a neutral Portuguese ship to Lisbon, from where they caught Flight 777 to London. There was an informal agreement on both sides to respect the neutrality of civilian planes from countries not involved in the war. Despite this, the agreement was broken on 1 June 1943. Flying over the Bay of Biscay, the defenceless Douglas DC-3 was attacked and shot down by six Junkers Ju-88 fighter bombers, killing all thirteen passengers and crew. Perishing with the Stonehouses was the famous Hollywood actor, Leslie Howard.[25]

Lisbon was the scene of another fatal air crash. Frank Cuhel of Mutual Broadcasting System and Ben Robertson of the *New York Herald Tribune* were among the twenty-four passengers and crew who lost their lives aboard a Boeing 314 Clipper long-range flying boat in a landing accident on 22 February 1943.

The Americans undertook to cover Montgomery's flank as he advanced up the east coast – something Patton did not take kindly to. This was to be the first of many clashes between these two egotists. In the event Montgomery became bogged down against stubborn German defending, which gave Patton the opportunity to advance through the west of Sicily, reaching Messina, the closest port to mainland Italy, before Montgomery. Michael Chinigo again repeated his Palermo exploit by entering Messina with a patrol and returned to his lines with two truck loads of Italian prisoners.

Many of the correspondents who had covered the North African campaign continued with the Italian campaign. Amongst them was the Oxford-educated Alexander Clifford of the *Daily Mirror*. Having reached Tunis with the Eighth Army, with whom he had been since El Alamein, he followed them in the taking of the Italian island of Pantelleria, which had been a thorn in the side of the Allies with its radar installations and airfield. It was garrisoned by 15,000 Italian soldiers sited in well-entrenched pill-boxes and many gun batteries.

The island was subjected to intense aerial bombing and naval bombardment for over a month. On 11 June, after two surrender demands went unanswered, the amphibious assault went in. When the Allied invasion force was sighted, the garrison commander changed his mind and radioed Malta offering to surrender. It was too late, as Clifford reported:

> *'The attack was already underway. The whole tremendous process had been put in motion. Wave after wave of Flying Fortresses (B-17s) was approaching the target. Fifty, eighty... and when their number got into three figures the men in the assault craft, rapidly approaching the island, stopped counting. They had never seen anything like the bombing. At last the planes flew away. The British cruisers were still firing, but the one brave Italian gun which had been replying was silent now. At noon, zero hour, the attackers disembarked. On one of the beaches there were a few bursts of machine-gun fire, but they were short and ineffectual. Not a shot was fired in the harbour. As an assault craft came skimming in, shabby, dusty Italian troops began popping out of ruined houses and hoisting white flags. They were waiting to surrender... .'*

Winston Churchill wrote in his memoirs that in the capture of Pantelleria: *'the only British casualty was man bitten by a mule.'*

Alexander Clifford had previously been mentioned in despatches for his part in the rescue of two wounded soldiers in the Libyan ambush that was related by his friend Alan Moorehead. He was again recognised by the military during the Sicily campaign. Flying over Sicily on a bombing mission, he took the place of an air-gunner who had been wounded during an attack by enemy aircraft. Despite being untrained, Clifford managed to shoot down an enemy fighter, something that was covered up as war correspondents were not supposed to take up arms against the enemy.

Back on terra firma, Clifford followed the fortunes of Patton's Seventh Army and ran into an incident that he refrained from reporting. About three days after the landings, the American 45th Infantry Division took the airfield at Comiso. The defenders, a mixture of Italian and Germans, surrendered. Clifford was appalled when he witnessed 110 prisoners machine-gunned by members of the newly-arrived 180th Regiment in two separate incidents. The following day, Sergeant Horace West of the same regiment, single-handedly shot and killed 37 PoWs captured at the Biscari airfield. Later that day, Captain John Compton of the 45th Division, executed 37 Italian prisoners.[26]

Clifford reported these incidents to Patton, who promised that culprits would be punished, but there was no investigation or trial. The journalist blamed the shootings on: '*Patton's bloodthirsty way of talking, and wording of his instructions, before the landing in Sicily, was taken too literally.*'

In fact, Patton's message relayed by loudspeaker to his men before the invasion was quite unequivocal:

> '*If your company officers in leading your men against the enemy find him shooting at you and when you get within two hundred yards of him he wishes to surrender – oh no! That bastard will die. You will kill him. Stick him between the third and fourth ribs. You will tell your men that. They must have the killer instinct. Tell them to stick him. Stick him in the liver. We will get the name of the killers and killers are immortal. When word reaches him that he is being faced by a killer battalion he will fight less. We must build up that name as killers.*'

While the names Patton and Montgomery are forever linked through their total belief in their infallibility and a taste in showmanship, their personalities were quite different. Montgomery was a strategist, waspish, boastful and pedantic. Patton was dynamic, undiplomatic, a loose cannon and a real problem for General Eisenhower.

The execution of the PoWs was fairly common knowledge amongst the Allies but had not been made public through the newspapers. Around the same time as the shootings, another couple of incidents involving Patton were initially successfully hushed up until it could no longer be kept secret. It was a broadcast in November by Drew Pearson on a radio programme called 'Washington Sunday Night', which revealed that General Patton had been severely reprimanded by Eisenhower. The way was now open to reveal the story of a general who slapped a shell-shocked soldier in a hospital.

Early in the Sicilian campaign, Patton visited the evacuation hospital and went among the wounded, trying to cheer them up. Edward Kennedy of AP wrote:

> '*He patted some on the back, sympathising with them. He then came upon a 24-year old soldier sitting on a cot with his head buried in his hands, weeping.*
>
> "*What's the matter with you?*" *Patton asked, according to persons who were in the hospital tent at the time. The soldier mumbled a reply which was inaudible to the General. Patton repeated his question.*

"It's my nerves. I guess I can't stand shelling," the soldier was quoted as replying.

Patton thereon burst into a rage. Employing much profanity, he called the soldier a "coward", "yellow belly" and numerous other epithets, according to those present. He ordered the soldier back to the front.

The scene attracted several persons, including the commanding officer of the hospital, the doctor who had admitted the soldier and a nurse.

In a fit of fury in which he expressed sympathy for men really wounded but made it plain that he did not believe that the soldier before him was in that class, the General struck the youth in the rear of the head with the back of his hand.

The soldier fell over slightly and the liner of his helmet which he was wearing fell off and rolled over the floor of the tent. The nurse, intent on protecting the patient, made a dive toward Patton but was pulled back by the doctor. The commander of the hospital then intervened.

Patton then went before other patients, still in high temper, expressing his views. He returned to the shell-shocked soldier and berated him again… . Patton left the hospital without making further investigation of the case.'

This incident took place on 10 August 1943. The unfortunate patient was Private Paul Bennett, a four-year veteran in the Field Artillery who was suffering from shell-shock. The man-handling of Bennett by Patton ended when the general pulled out his famous pearl-handled pistol and threatened the patient. It took the intervention of the hospital's commander to physically separate the two. In fact this was the second such incident. On 3 August, Patton visited another evacuation hospital and came upon Private Charles Kuhl, an infantryman, who had been diagnosed with exhaustion and suffering from malarial parasites. Patton slapped him with his gloves, grabbed him by the collar and kicked him out of the tent. Kuhl was quite forgiving saying that Patton was pretty worn out… . 'I think he was suffering a little battle fatigue himself'. Patton was overheard by Noel Monk angrily denying the reality of shell shock claiming the condition was 'an invention of the Jews'.

The story made headlines around the world with the exception of Britain. In a rare example of self-censorship, *The Times* downplayed the news in a small item blandly headed with AN UNFORTUNATE INCIDENT. Its correspondent at Allied HQ in Algiers, Philip Ure, explained to Eisenhower that: 'General Patton is too great a commander to be anywhere but in the field of active service.'

The conquest of Sicily had not been a pushover, claiming 11,848 British and 8,781 Americans killed, wounded or captured. It had been the first assault by the Anglo-American forces on mainland Europe and an invaluable experience in coalition planning.

It was not only the soldiers who were feeling the strain. In his report of 25 August 1943, Ernie Pyle remarked on the fact that it was not only the overworked soldier who was overwhelmed by exhaustion:

'I've noticed this feeling has begun to overtake the war correspondents themselves. It is true we don't fight and, unlike the infantry, that we are usually under fire only briefly and, indeed, we live better than the average soldier. Yet our lives are strangely consuming in that we do live primitively and at the same time must delve into ourselves and do creative writing.

That statement may lay me open to wisecracks, but however it may seem to you, writing is an exhausting and tiring thing. Most of the correspondents actually work like slaves. Especially is this true of the press association men. A great part of the time they go from dawn until midnight or 2am.

I'm sure they turn in as much toil in a week as any newspaperman at home does in two weeks. We travel continuously, move camp every few days, eat out, sleep out, write wherever we can and just never catch up on sleep, rest, cleanliness, or anything else normal.

The result is that all of us who have been with the thing for more than a year have finally grown befogged. We are grimy, mentally as well as physically. We've drained our emotions until they cringe from being called out from hiding. We look at bravery and death and battlefield waste and new countries almost as blind men, seeing only faintly and not really wanting to see at all.

Just in the past month the old-timers among the correspondents have been talking for the first time about wanting to go home for a while. They want a change, something to freshen their outlook. They feel they have lost their perspective by being too close for too long.

I am not writing this to make heroes of the correspondents, because only a few look upon themselves in any dramatic light whatever. I am writing it merely to let you know that correspondents too can get damn sick of war – and deadly tired.'

Dieppe

While the invasion of Sicily had been a success, another smaller assault closer to England was not. In the early hours of 19 August 1942, a force of about 6,000 pre-dominantly Canadian troops launched a raid on the French port of Dieppe, 65 miles across the Channel.

Churchill had returned from a meeting with Joseph Stalin in Moscow, where the Russian leader urged the Allies to open a second front to divert German troops to the west. Unwilling and unready for a full-scale invasion of France, Churchill was persuaded by the Director of Combined Operations, Admiral Lord Louis Mountbatten, of his plan for a 'reconnaissance in force' on Dieppe. Mountbatten had been in charge of the 26 March raid on St Nazaire, which had rendered the huge dry dock inoperable for Germany's last remaining battleship *Tirpitz*. The raid had succeeded in its object and Mountbatten was encouraged to launch another Combined Operation's assault on mainland Europe.[27]

With Churchill's blessing, Mountbatten pushed through the raid over the objections of other senior officers who thought the plan was ill-advised and flawed. The idea of landing such a small force on the beaches of Dieppe, have them destroy some coastal defences, hold the town for two tides and then withdraw seemed not only foolhardy but would in no way alleviate the pressure on Russia.

The amphibious landing would be the greatest since Gallipoli in 1915 and would match it as a disaster. Under pressure from the Canadian Government to ensure their troops saw some action, 5,000 men of the 2nd Canadian Infantry division made up the bulk of the operation with 1,000 British commandos and fifty US Rangers. Twenty-one correspondents and photographers, mostly Canadian, were also allowed to accompany the raid. All the key newspapers in Ontario and English-speaking Quebec were represented.

Intelligence of the area was poor; the German gun positions on the cliffs had not been detected and the town was deemed to be lightly defended. In fact the Germans were forewarned, having been alerted by the British showing interest in the area and the build-up of landing craft in southern English ports.

As the Allies approached their separate landing points, the British commandos ran into a German tanker escorted by E-boats. The exchange of fire further alerted the Germans and all hopes of a surprise attack had vanished. The bombardment from the Royal Navy destroyers was inadequate as the landing craft made their way to the shingle beaches, which were steeper than expected.

Ross Munro of the Canadian Broadcasting Corporation was with the men of the Royal Regiment of Canada. Years later he told the truth about the landing:

'They plunged into about two feet of water and machine-gun bullets laced into them. Bodies piled up on the ramp. Some staggered to the beach and fell. Looking out of the open bow over bodies on the ramp, I saw the slope leading up to a stone wall littered with Royal Regiment casualties. They had been cut down before they had a chance to fire a shot. It was brutal and terrible and shocked you almost to insensibility to see piles of dead and feel the hopelessness of the attack at this point. The beach was khaki-coloured with the bodies of the boys from Central Ontario.'

Munro, along with the other correspondents, had their copy thoroughly vetted by Mountbatten's censors until it read like a gung-ho piece of fiction. After the war, the pragmatic Munro said that he had a few regrets about how his reporting had been distorted by the censors but added: *'You get very deft and skilled at telling the story honestly and validly despite the censorship.'* The *Toronto Star* of 22 August headlined its report with 'LIKE FIREWORKS SAYS ROYAL'S SERGEANT OF BATTLE OF DIEPPE.' It was followed with:

'In the grimmest and fiercest operation of the war since British troops swarmed out of Dunkirk, the Canadians assaulting Dieppe gave the German elite coastal defensemen a sample of the courage the Dominion's fighting men display when they are assigned to battle.'

Wallace Reyburn of the *Montreal Star* was the only correspondent who landed and waded ashore with the South Saskatchewan Regiment. He was the tenth man to go ashore at Green Beach, Pourville, west of Dieppe, where he witnessed the heavy fighting for six hours. He managed to escape back to England in a destroyer which he only reached after two of the landing craft in which he had set out had been sunk. He was fortunate to escape with minor injuries.[28]

Frank Gillard observed the raid from the Royal Navy destroyer HMS *Calpe*, which acted as the raid's command ship. She also acted as a hospital ship despite losing a quarter of her crew to bombardment. Gillard was the only BBC correspondent with the Dieppe raid because he had been the regional correspondent closest to Portsmouth. He was highly praised by the BBC and Mountbatten's staff for his outstanding coverage. Possibly it was because he broadcast the extraordinary line: 'As a combined operation this was an all time model.' Forty years later, he wrote:

'I am almost ashamed to read my report, but it was that or nothing. It was a day of wrangling, first with one censor and then with another, until our mutilated and emasculated texts, rendered almost bland under relentless pressure, was released twenty-four hours after our return. It was so stupidly frustrating. There was sheer folly at Dieppe, but that was at the planning level. Those who had to execute these misguided orders against impossible odds showed gallantry and heroism of the highest order. Given half a chance, we could have presented Dieppe in terms that would have evoked pride along with sorrow. But PR handling of Dieppe was as great a disaster as the operation itself.'

Another correspondent on the *Calpe* was Quentin Reynolds of *Collier's Weekly*. He was well-regarded in London and by the MOI in particular for his contribution to the GPO film about the blitz '*London Can Take It*.' He wrote:'*The correspondents of the Second World War were a curious, crazy, yet responsible crew. For the sake of the war effort, and because the war against Hitler was considered a just one, they did what was required of them.*' In Reynolds case, for the sake of the war effort, he reported what senior officers told him with little or no question.

Fleet Street had only one pool contributor at Dieppe. To the consternation of Max Aitken's *Daily Express*, Alexander Austin of the worthy but uninspiring *Daily Herald* was chosen. In common with his fellow correspondents, he wrote gushingly of Mountbatten and success of operation. Based on his report, this item appeared in the *Glasgow Herald* from sources in neutral Turkey:

Istanbul, Sunday, 24 August 1943

'German local propaganda is doing its utmost to convince Turkish opinion that the Dieppe raid was an abortive attempt at invasion of the Continent. Turkish commentators, however, after a careful perusal of both the British and German official communiqués, have reached the conclusion that it was a raid on a larger scale than any preceding ones, which might be considered as a rehearsal for a second-front landing... .

Turkish experts point out that in spite of enormous difficulties, the raiders succeeded in landing tanks, as was admitted by the Germans themselves, which was very encouraging from an invader's point of view.[29]

Taking all into consideration, Turkish commentators consider the operation successful because of its immediate results, of the psychological effect on Europe, especially in Germany and France, and of the consequent necessity for the Germans to reinforce their air and probably their land forces in France at the expense of other fronts.'

After ten hours, the survivors of the debacle withdrew from the beaches, where 1,380 had been killed and 2,000 taken prisoner – a loss of over fifty per cent.

Mountbatten immediately hailed the raid as a tactical triumph: *'The raid has gone off very satisfactorily. The planning has been excellent, air support faultless and naval losses extremely light. Of the 6,000 men involved, two thirds returned to Britain and all I have seen are in great form.'*

The raid began to be described at a 'reconnaissance raid' and a dress rehearsal for a future invasion. In fact both Quentin Reynolds and Wallace Reyburn used the term as titles for the books they wrote after the raid: *D-Day Dress Rehearsal – the story of Dieppe* and *Rehearsal for Invasion*, respectively.

An official report into the raid came down on Mountbatten's side and he was given a clean bill of health. For the war correspondents, they later acknowledged that Dieppe had not been their finest hour.

Chapter 8

The Russian and Pacific Fronts 1941–42

T he war went global in 1941 and was then rightly referred to as World War. On 22 June, Germany put into motion Operation Barbarossa for invading Russia, its erstwhile ally in the division of Poland in 1939. Despite their ongoing economic relations – German supplied military and industrial equipment in exchange for raw materials – each side was suspicious of the other's intentions. Nonetheless, after Germany entered the Axis Pact with Italy and Japan, she began negotiations for the Soviet Union also to join. Predictably, these came to nought as conflict became increasingly likely.

The scene was set for a clash of two of the greatest armies the world had seen. The Western newspapers carried stories about the anticipated attack but, when it came, they were caught unprepared. On 22 June there were just seven Western correspondents in Russia, none of whom was first with news of an invasion. The announcement came from von Ribbentrop at a press conference in Berlin and was quickly relayed via the American correspondents.

The Americans, whose government was still nominally neutral, had correspondents in Berlin like Howard K. Smith, one of 'Murrow's Boys', who had succeeded William Shirer at CBS. He recalled that life was not pleasant, with harassment in the streets and restaurants, phones tapped and offices watched. One of their number, Richard C. Hottelet of UP, was arrested by the Gestapo in March and accused of espionage. After nearly six months imprisonment, he was suddenly released in a prisoner exchange. With the help of an American official from the embassy, he managed to be spirited out of Germany, through France and over the Spanish border. He later joined CBS and reported the D-Day landings.

Two of the correspondents already in the Soviet Union were the novelist Erskine Caldwell and his wife, the photographer Margaret Bourke-White, writing and photographing a feature about the Russian countryside for *Life* magazine. In order to see the Red Army, the correspondents had to wait for a specially arranged visit in September. They were all taken as a sort of tourist group to recently retaken towns and battlefields like Yelnya, where Russian soldiers posed in front of the ruined cathedral or the wasteland of Ushakovo where it was claimed 50,000 Germans were killed.

The Russians were highly suspicious of Western correspondents for several good reasons. In 1919 both Britain and America became briefly involved with the anti-Bolshevik forces in the Russian Civil War. Then there was the tacit support of Finland against the Russians in the recent Winter War. Finally, Britain banned the communist newspaper, the *Daily Worker*, in January 1941. There had always been correspondents who acted as part-time intelligence agents and this was another reason for the Russians to be wary of letting Western newsmen anywhere near the fighting. In fact many of the correspondents were left-leaning and some were avowed communists; among them were Alexander Werth of the *Guardian*, Erskine Caldwell, Margaret Bourke-White, Quentin Reynolds, Ralph Parker of the *New York Times* and Alaric Jacob of the *Daily Express*.

Ralph Parker had been *The Times* correspondent in Czechoslovakia in 1938. He was recruited by the SOE at the start of the war but his commitment was suspect and he became a freelance correspondent in Moscow for several journals. He later defected to the Soviet Union and married an Intourist guide who was a suspected KGB agent. After the war, Parker had contact with the defectors Guy Burgess and Donald Maclean.

Alaric Jacob was the son of an Indian Army colonel and a Norwegian mother.[30] He was a childhood friend of Kim Philby and educated at the same school as Cyril Connolly and George Orwell. His mentor was Margaret Asquith, wife of the former prime minister, who managed to arrange a job for him at Reuters. For two years he covered the North African campaign as well as a four-month assignment in Russia for the *Daily Express*. At the end of 1943, he and his wife left England for Russia choosing to take a highly perilous return journey by sailing in a ship of the Arctic Convoy. Jacob's obituary in 1995 described an archetypical champagne socialist: '*He processed the grand manner of an Edwardian foreign correspondent with an Alan-Clark-like taste for vintage claret, a good cigar and fine brandy*'.

The invasion had totally overwhelmed the Soviets who retreated in confusion. In the first few days a greater part of the air force had been destroyed, half a million men killed and a million captured. The Soviet leaders imposed a strict embargo on any news from the front which virtually made redundant the job of the war correspondent. The only news that could be reported was official news, which at times was grossly exaggerated. For instance it was claimed that two million Germans had been killed, wounded or captured, which was the total strength of the whole German army on the Eastern Front.

In October, as the Germans began to approach Moscow, government departments, the diplomatic corps and all the foreign correspondents were moved 1,000 miles east to Kuibyshev (formerly Samara) on the banks of the Volga River. Here the war correspondents were marooned until the threat receded and everything moved back to Moscow. Many foreign correspondents, despairing of ever overcoming the Soviets' distrust, moved off to cover the war in North Africa where censorship in comparison seemed so much more lax. Yet, despite the draconian censorship and restriction of movement, more correspondents arrived to cover the front where the war was going to be won.

Bill Downs arrived to take over from Larry LeSueur as CBS Russian correspondent. Although Downs found the assignment no easier than did LeSueur, he was taken to see the newly-captured city of Stalingrad. Downs told his listeners:

> *'Try and imagine what four and a half months of the world's heaviest bombing would do to a city the size of Providence, Rhode Island, or Minneapolis or Oklahoma City. It was utter and complete and absolute devastation. In a 50-mile radius one could see only piles of bricks and rubble and corpses. There are sights and smells and sounds in and around Stalingrad that make you want to weep and make you want to shout and make you just plain sick to your stomach.'*

Another communist-sympathiser was the CBS correspondent, Winston Burdett. He had joined the Party in 1937 and in 1939, agreed to spy for the Soviet Union. Using his press credentials as a roving reporter, he fed information on the morale of the Finnish population and troops during the Winter War. He then spied intermittently for two more years but, becoming disillusioned with the Soviets, quit in March 1942. He was hired by CBS in 1940, who knew nothing of his spying activities until the 1950s.

It was while he was working in India that he learned that his Italian wife, Lea Schiavi, had been murdered in Soviet-occupied Iran. The story he learned was that on 24 April 1942, she was travelling with another woman and two Kurds, when they were stopped by Kurdish gendarmes. On learning her name, one of the guards poked his rifle through the car window and shot Lea Schiavi point blank. She was shot again as the car accelerated away. The suggestion was that the anti-Fascist journalist had been killed on the orders of either the Italians or Germans. Indeed, the guard who fired the shot was arrested and imprisoned for life.

It was fifteen years later that Burdett told a Senate Internal Security Subcommittee another version of what had happened. His wife's car had been halted by a truck full of Russian troops who, upon identifying her, killed her. Burdett believed it was because she had uncovered links between military training camps in Iran and an upcoming communist coup in Yugoslavia. Also, he attributed her murder to his decision to leave the Communist Party and stop spying for them.[31]

Pacific

Just six months after Germany launched Operation Barbarossa, the Japanese launched their attack on the home of America's Pacific Fleet at Pearl Harbor in Hawaii. Ed Murrow and his wife had been invited to dinner with the Roosevelts at the White House on 7 December. When news of the attack was learned, Mrs Roosevelt phoned to say that the invitation still stood. Although the president did not dine with them, he requested Murrow to remain behind and to join him in the Oval Office and confided in him how damaging the attack had been. The Pacific fleet had suffered eight battleships either sunk or damaged, seventy-five per cent of warplanes destroyed and about 3,500 servicemen killed or wounded. It was an indication of the trust Roosevelt had in Murrow to disclose this information and, tempting as it was to break the news, Murrow kept the president's assessment to himself.

His fellow CBS correspondent, Eric Sevareid, also learned the truth from high placed officials and was not so reticent in broadcasting the details. This was just before a heavy censorship blanket descended on all news from Hawaii. UP's telephone call to its office in San Francisco was cut off mid-report and all non-official communications were stopped for four days. When news was released it was grossly distorted. The censors allowed that the damage was one 'old' battleship and destroyer sunk with a few other ships damaged, whereas the Japanese had suffered heavy casualties.

It is not known just how many hands the following news went through to reach the *Daily Express* in London:

'The main US Pacific Fleet is heavily engaged with a Japanese battle fleet, which includes several carriers, just off Pearl Harbor, its Hawaii base. Washington reports late tonight that one Japanese carrier and four submarines have already been destroyed by the American forces off Hawaii.'

The American newspapers were no better informed and relied on speculation. The *New York Times* wrote on 8 December:

'The crash of exploding bombs in the Hawaiian Islands, Guam and possibly the Philippines, the roar of anti-aircraft guns and the twisted skeletons of wrecked planes heralded the war in the Pacific, with the principal antagonists the United States and Japan – a war that has long been brewing, a conflict often predicted but previously avoided. But the Japanese aggression yesterday did more than start a Pacific war. It broadened the conflicts already raging into a world-wide struggle whose end no man can know.'

One Hawaiian resident who was a witness to the attack was the creator of Tarzan, Edgar Rice Burroughs. Encouraged by what he had seen, he applied to become a war correspondent with UP at the age of 67, the oldest accredited correspondent in the Pacific Theatre. Rather in the style of Ernie Pyle, he interviewed GIs and sent the interviews to their home town papers so their families and friends could read about their local heroes. He had several near misses and in 1945 was on a ship that was attacked by a kamikaze plane. On 9 December, he wrote an open letter describing the Pearl Harbor attack:

'To Whoever Gives a Damn
When we awoke on Sunday morning, 7 December, we heard a great deal of firing, some of it very loud, but we hear a great deal of firing here and had been informed by the newspapers the day before that heavy guns would be fired from various parts of the island during the ensuing several days; so we thought nothing of it and went to breakfast.

After breakfast we dressed for tennis and went on court…. Soon many of the hotel guests were congregated there watching the show. Bombs were falling on Pearl Harbor. We could hear the detonations and see the bursts quite plainly. Anti-aircraft shells were bursting and fighting ships at sea were firing. We could see them plainly. Bombs were falling not far from us. One nearly hit a large freighter or supply ship lying off coast perhaps a mile or so from us. It got out of there in a hurry. Black smoke was billowing up from Pearl Harbor…. It was either an oil tank or a tanker or our burning fighting ships. We don't know yet.

For several hours we alternated tennis while watching the show they were putting on before we learned that it was the real McCoy. Even the truth did not interfere with our tennis. . .

Bombs fell on the city not far from us, smoke rising from several fires. Ambulance, police and fire sirens were screaming almost continuously. Anti-aircraft shells were bursting all over the place. I think that many of our civilian casualties, and there were a great many, were caused by our own fire.'

The Japanese were simultaneously attacking on several fronts: Hong Kong, French Indo-China, Thailand and the Philippines. On 23 December, Manila correspondent, Raymond Clapper of the Scripps-Howard media company, wrote of the meagre local forces and lack of equipment:

'Read it and weep. Marines on Wake Island fighting off the Japanese with only four planes, then only two, and finally with only one plane. American soldiers in the Philippines defending bridges with rifles and hand grenades.

It won't be our men out there that will lose the Philippines. If the islands are lost they will have been lost here, by our lagging war production.'

Another of the correspondents covering the invasion of the Philippines was Melville (Mel) Jacoby of *Time-Life* magazine. He had been in China, but was transferred to Manila in October 1941. Soon after he married Annalee Whitmore, one of America's first accredited female war correspondents, and together they reported the incessant bombing of Manila and the final pockets of opposition to the overwhelming Japanese forces who outnumbered the Americans by six to one.

When Manila fell, Mel and Annalee Jacoby barely made it out of the city alive. The couple jumped from a burning dock into a tiny boat that took them to the Bataan Peninsula where he covered the last days of American resistance.[32] Limited wireless facilities prevented him from filing detailed reports, but those he did send were the most vivid read by the American public. In the 9 February 1942 edition of *Time* he wrote:

> *'The paramount topic is guessing when help will arrive, betting on when they will return to Manila. The men have seen action and tell plenty of stories about the Japanese: how, across the barbed wire on the firing line, the Nipponese dead are piled high. They say the stench of rotting bodies is terrific, though the Japanese have been removing their dead by the truckload, taking them to Manila where they have taken over all the morgues.*
>
> *Our men show wounds from the light-calibre Japanese rifles. One sergeant who was shot through the neck, the bullet coming out the other side, merely put Band-Aids on each side and continued fighting. The men like to repeat stories of unusual nature which pass up and down the lines.'*

Jacoby and Clark Lee of AP advised each other to get out while they could:

> *'I said to Mel, "It looks like everything is folding up, fast. Time to get moving somewhere. Especially you, as you are on their black list for your work for the Chinese government in Chungking."*
>
> *Jacoby replied: "I hear that your name is about third on their Navy's black list. You better not stick around too long either."'*

The Jacobys made their final escape and followed General Douglas MacArthur to Australia, then the only safe haven in the South Pacific. Tragically, just before the couple were due to return to America, Mel Jacoby became the victim of a freak accident. He was onboard a C-40 transport plane accompanying General Hal George and a small press corps which had landed at a new airfield in the Northern Territory of Australia. The C-40 parked half way down the runway in a designated area to allow the passengers to disembark and catch the transport to take them to 49th Fighter Group's headquarters. As they waited, a couple of Kittyhawk fighters were taking off. Unfortunately, the second plane lost control and ploughed into the parked C-40. General George was mortally injured and Mel Jacoby was struck by the propeller and died immediately.

Three days after the Pearl Harbor attack, the Japanese inflicted another devastating blow on Allied naval power. Cecil Brown of CBS and O'Dowd Gallagher of the *Daily Express*, were summoned from their lunch at the Raffles Hotel by the Singapore Public Relations Office (SPRO) and invited to sail for four days with the newly-arrived battleship *Prince of Wales* and the battle-cruiser *Repulse*. Both were initially reluctant to leave Singapore as it seemed to be the place where all the action was about to take place. The prospect of sailing on the famous *Prince of Wales* was too much of a rare offer to pass and the pair quickly packed and boarded the ship. To their disappointment, they found there was no room for them and they were transferred to *Repulse*.

Setting sail on 8 December, they headed north along the east coast of Malaya looking for where the Japanese were expected to land their troops. Failing to find any sign of the Japanese landing, they continued sailing north. When the flotilla was discovered by Japanese reconnaissance aircraft, Admiral Phillips on the *Prince of Wales* decided to cancel the operation and return to Singapore.

Around 11am on 10 December, the Japanese launched a series of aerial attacks on the two capital ships. The *Prince of Wales* was hit by a series of four torpedoes causing her to lose power and begin to list. *Repulse* had been hit by a bomb but managed to dodge nineteen torpedoes before she was finally struck, causing her to heave over. This was followed by a succession of three torpedoes hitting home and fatally wounding her.

Brown kept a diary and described the sinking:

'11.15; and here they come! The guns of the Prince of Wales just let go. At the same instant I see the flame belching from the guns of the Wales, ours break into a chattering, ear-splitting roar. The nine Japanese aircraft are stretched out across the bright blue, cloudless sky like star sapphires of a necklace.

I instinctively hunch over, sort of a semi-crouch, and at the same instant there is a dull thud. The whole ship shudders. Pieces of paint fall from the deck over the flag deck.

Fire on the boat deck. Fire below! That just came over the loudspeakers. There are fountains of water all around the ship. Some are near misses. I've never been so close to so many guns firing at once. The roar of the pom-poms and the hard, sharp crack of the 4-inch high altitude guns are deafening. The flashes are blinding and suddenly the smell of cordite is strong. I am standing on the port side of the flag deck, in the lee of an air funnel, eight feet from a battery of pom-poms. Most of the bombs are hitting the water ten or thirty yards off the port side. Beautiful fountains of thick white at the base and then tapering into a fine spray.

The first bomb was a direct hit. Someone on the flag deck says: "Fire in Marine's mess and hanger."

I gape open-mouthed at those aircraft coming directly over us, flying so that they will pass from bow to stern over the Repulse. The sky is filled with black puffs from our ack-ack. They seem a discordant profanation of that beautiful sky. But the formation of Japanese planes, coming over one behind the other, is undisturbed. . .

We got one of the bombers! It is coming down fast, in black smoke. All our guns are still going. I am now near one of the multiple Vickers guns. It is firing 2,000 half-inch shells a minute. God, what a racket! That bomber smacked into the water about a half a mile away. . .

Distant specks appear. Now they are identifiable. Nine torpedo-carrying bombers, circling four or five thousand yards away at about a half-mile altitude. Circling in a huge sweep, they are swooping lower. Now they are like moths around our flaming guns. . .

The Repulse is twisting and snaking violently to avoid torpedoes. . .The torpedoes seem small, dropping flat into the water, sending up splashes, then streaking toward us. Those bombers are so close you can almost see the colour of the pilot's eyes. The bombers are machine-gunning our decks as they come in. . .We are putting up a beautiful barrage, a wall of fire. But the bombers come on, in a long glide, from all angles, not simultaneously but alternately. . . About 300 yards distant from the ship and 100 yards about the water, they drop their torpedoes. But this is deadly business, too. Three gunners ten feet from me slump over with Japanese machine-gun bullets in them. It's difficult to comprehend sudden death. But they are not the only casualties in this terrible moment. A torpedo bomber has just dropped a tin fish and banked without gaining altitude. It glides beautifully, parallel with the Repulse at a ten-degree angle, and still tracers are ploughing into it. . . It strikes the water and immediately bursts into flames. . .

93

There follows a fifteen minute pause during which the gunners inflate their life-jackets, something Brown would later regret not doing. The decks were littered with the debris of battle. The dead and wounded are removed and ammunition distributed as the crews wait for the next attack.

> '*I see ten bombers approaching. . . It's definitely a torpedo attack. A plane is diving straight for the middle of the ship off the port side, 500 yards away, and tracers are rushing to meet it. . . The torpedo strikes the ship about twenty yards astern of my position. It feels as though the ship has crashed into dock. I am thrown four feet across the deck but I keep my feet. Almost immediately, it seems, the ship lists. From the loudspeaker comes: "Prepare to abandon ship. God be with you".*

There was no panic or pushing as Brown and Gallagher joined the crew making their way to the quarter deck. Suddenly, there was another enormous explosion to starboard and the list got steeper.

> '*The ship is heeled over at a nasty angle. Gallagher says; "You all right, Cec?"*
> *"Yeh, I guess so. No air in my belt though. The hell with it."*
> *"Better blow it. This is it, Cec."*
> *"Yes, Gal. I guess it is. Good going, kid."*
> *"We'll stick together."*
> *We grin at each other, a weak grin."*'

The two reporters dropped into the sea and were soon picked up by a destroyer. Both Brown and Gallagher had survived and were able to send their sensational reports when they reached Singapore. Ian Morrison of *The Times* saw them the next morning:

> '*Brown and Gallagher were even now hammering out their stories in the Press office attached to the Combined Services Public Relations Unit. Both looked worn and unshaven, Gallagher suffering still from giddiness caused by getting oil into his system as he was floundering about in the water.*'

When Brown's report was received, he was showered with compliments and, even better, a $1,000 bonus from a grateful CBS. Unfortunately, the

British authorities did not join in the universal praise heaped on Brown. He disliked the attitude of the local British hierarchy, declaring: '*Singapore society goes dancing almost every night, making money out of huge shipments of rubber and tin, and counting on the United States Navy to keep them from harm.*'

By early 1942, the British officials had had enough and revoked his credentials. Brown was on his way back to America to take up a prime spot on CBS's daily news program. This was not to everyone's liking. William Shirer and other colleagues found the bombastic Brown even more unbearable and resented his elevation.

Among the many correspondents left at Singapore was 24-year-old Ian Morrison, the Australian-born correspondent for *The Times*. Educated at Winchester and Cambridge, he taught English at a university in Japan from 1935-37. From there he was taken on as private secretary to the British Ambassador in Tokyo before working in Shanghai. He initially worked as assistant to *The Times*'s China correspondent before becoming the representative of the British and Chinese Corporation. He managed to escape as the Japanese entered the International Settlement in the city. Moving to Singapore, he was made deputy director of the Far Eastern Bureau of the Ministry of Information.

'The Times, *finding themselves without a war correspondent in Malaya, cabled asking if they could nominate me immediately to the post of war correspondent in Malaya. Their string man was David Waite, the able young editor of the* Singapore Free Press, *but David Waite was tied to Singapore and was not able to make trips up-country.*'

With the imminent prospect of war with Japan, he was re-appointed special correspondent (Far East) by *The Times* on 9 December 1941. Morrison's intimate knowledge of the region meant he spent the rest of the war covering South-East Asia. As a consequence, he contracted the diseases prevalent in that area: dengue fever, topical ulcers, amoebic dysentery and recurrent malaria. He also survived two plane crashes and was twice wounded.

He was also more measured in his opinions than Cecil Brown, who knew little of the Far East. Morrison wrote after the fall of Singapore that:

'*Alone of cities in the Far East* [Singapore] *gave its inhabitants the illusion of security. Aeroplanes droned overhead during the day. . . there was hardly an hour in the day when one looked up into the sky*

*and failed to see an aeroplane of some description. There were
frequent fire practices, when the big naval guns that protected the
island would hurl their shells many miles out to sea. After nightfall
powerful search-lights played over the water or shone upwards into
the sky.'*

The arrival of the *Prince of Wales* and *Repulse* completed the illusion that
the island was impregnable:

*'Singapore was not a fortress. It was a naval base... . Huge naval
guns pointed out to sea. It is very possible, indeed probable, that
Singapore was impregnable against direct assault from the sea. In
the same way the Maginot Line was certainly impregnable against
direct assault launched from the east. But unfortunately the Maginot
Line was never assaulted from the east, nor was Singapore attacked
from the sea.'*

At the beginning of the war there were some twenty correspondents in
Singapore, including a large corps of Australian newsmen, intent in reporting
from this northern outpost of Australia's defence. Morrison was one of a
small group of correspondents who travelled north into Malaya to try and
interpret the confusing and constantly shifting fronts. For the correspondents
it was an arduous but not a particularly illuminating assignment.

The almost total absence of the RAF meant that transport on the roads,
including the staff cars used by the correspondents, were sitting targets for
the ever-present Japanese aircraft.[33] Rarely did the correspondents reach the
firing line as there was a constant danger of being cut off. There was no front
line, only outposts, which the Japanese were able to surround and overrun.
The correspondents learned of small pockets of survivors trapped behind
Japanese lines, enduring days in the jungle as they attempted to find their
way back to their own lines.

Despite some determined opposition, the disastrous Malaya Campaign
lasted from 8 December 1941 to 31 January 1942 and was one of constant
retreat. By the time the British had crossed the Johor Causeway back onto
Singapore, their casualties had amounted to 60,500. The Japanese, who were
outnumbered two to one, had suffered lightly, losing 5,171 killed and 3,378
wounded.

Ian Morrison sent his newly-wed bride away to Batavia and remained to
report on the inexorable Japanese occupation of Singapore and the

crumbling morale of its citizens and defenders. Even with the enemy so close, the censors were still causing frustration amongst the correspondents. Morrison wrote:

> *'It is the misfortune of correspondents in wartime that most of the officers appointed to deal with them are men who are physically or intellectually unfit for active service... . The question arose that evening whether we might use the word 'siege' in our messages. The spokesman, however, would not permit us to use this word, because, he said, it would have a depressing effect on local morale... . It was eventually agreed that the horrid word 'investment' should be substituted. But something went wrong in the censorship and when I looked at my messages in the morning to see how they had been treated by the censor I found that the word 'siege' had been excised and the incredible word 'besiegement' substituted. It is a word that is not even to be found in the English dictionary. Sub-editors at* The Times *office must have thought that their Singapore correspondent was suffering from shell-shock when they received a message beginning: 'The besiegement of Singapore began officially at 8.00 this morning.'*

It took the Japanese six days from 8 February to overcome the poorly organised defence of Singapore. With the writing on the wall, Morrison went to the docks and hired a sampan to see if there were any boats available to escape the ever-tightening grip on the city. He found one that was about to leave and, without any luggage, immediately boarded her. She was a Dutch boat carrying crates of aircraft that were no longer of use and so the captain was returning with his cargo to Batavia. The ship made for the safety of the numerous small islands to the south of Singapore, taking cover during the day and travelling at night before reaching the temporary safety of Batavia.

Morrison's fellow *Times* correspondent, David Waite, was not so fortunate. He left Singapore harbour on 12 Feb 1942 under a heavy aerial attack on the overcrowded HMS *Giang Bee*, a Chinese-owned coastal steamer commandeered as a patrol vessel. She carried some 350 refugees, mostly women and children. It did not take long before the ship was overtaken by a squadron of Japanese destroyers. The *Giang Bee* had been repeatedly bombed, which had destroyed most of the lifeboats. Nevertheless, the Japanese ordered the ship to be abandoned and sank it with gunfire leaving the helpless passengers floundering in the sea. Most were drowned, including David Waite. Those who survived and reached land were soon captured to endure years of harsh captivity.

Another newsman on the *Giang Bee* was Eric Davis of the British Malaya Broadcasting Corporation, an offshoot of the BBC. He managed to reach land and met up with another escapee from Singapore, Kenneth Selby-Walker, the Far Eastern manager of Reuters. They were joined by Hedley Metcalf, an Australian photographer for the *Singapore Straits Times* and *Melbourne Herald*, and Bill Findon of the London *Daily Express*, who had just flown in from India. All three men were misled by the Dutch chief censor that Java could withstand any attack by the Japanese and that they would miss out on a story of a lifetime if they left. By early March it was obvious that the Japanese were overrunning the whole of the Dutch East Indies.

On 6 March, Selby-Walker sent his last telegram saying: '*I am afraid it's too late for a safe departure. I have only myself to blame.*' It would appear all the journalists boarded a Dutch fishing vessel at Surabaya in an effort to escape capture. The next day the Japanese caught up with them and the vessel was sunk without any survivors.

In the words of Winston Churchill: '*the ignominious fall of Singapore to the Japanese was the worst disaster and largest capitulation in British history.*'

Chapter 9

Italy

Once Sicily had been secured on 17 August 1943, the Allies prepared to invade Italy. After the expulsion of the Axis from North Africa, there was some disagreement about extending the fight to Sicily and Italy. Winston Churchill particularly wanted to invade in order to remove Italy as an enemy and to open the Mediterranean to Allied shipping. A coup on 24 July ousted Mussolini and he was replaced by Marshal Pietro Badoglio. Although Badoglio kept the appearance of loyalty to the Axis, he was secretly negotiating an Armistice with the Allies which was signed on 3 September.

It was on this day that Montgomery's Eighth Army crossed the straits of Messina and landed in Calabria, the 'toe' of Italy.

As Montgomery had predicted, there was light opposition as the Germans had withdrawn further north to where Field Marshal Albert Kesselring anticipated the main thrust of the Allies' attack would fall. This proved to be a prescient decision as the main amphibious invading force landed at Salerno, 35 miles south of Naples.[34] On 9 September, the US Fifth Army, under the command of General Mark Clark, distrusted by subordinates and superiors alike, waded ashore.[35] Clark had decided that to achieve maximum surprise the assault would not be supported by naval or aerial bombardment. In fact, the Germans were waiting for them and on one beach a loudspeaker proclaimed: 'Come on in and give up. We have you covered'.

Minefields, established strongpoints and many 88mm guns confined the Fifth Army to a narrow beachhead. It took until 15 September before the beaches were secure largely thanks to naval gunfire and massive aerial bombing. It was on this day that Eric Lloyd Williams, a South African correspondent with Reuters, appeared with two colleagues in a Jeep from an area that was believed to be in enemy hands. Initially arrested as enemy spies, they were soon able to prove their identities and tell their story.

They had been with the Eighth Army as it advanced to link up with the US Fifth Army. Frustrated with Montgomery's cautious advance, Williams, Daniel De Luce of AP and another unidentified correspondent drove their borrowed Jeep from Eighth Army HQ at Nicastro in central Calabria about 160kms from Salerno. At first they thought that there were elements of the Eighth Army ahead of them in the wild hilly country. When they realised that this was not so, they considered turning back. Williams recalled: '*But no – curiosity prevails and we decide to keep together and to push ahead and see around a few corners.*'

It took two days and two nights to complete the journey. On the way, they were feted as liberators as they drove through the few remote villages they came across. Reaching the Fifth Army lines, they provided information that enabled the two armies to link up. Not only were the trio able to send off their scoops, but they were also personally congratulated by Field Marshal Harold Alexander, commander of the Fifteenth Army Group. They were, however, severely reprimanded for taking a Jeep and not informing their accompanying officer of their intentions. As they had reconnoitred such a swath of territory and found it free of the enemy, they were forgiven.

Daniel De Luce decided to leave Italy and cross the Adriatic to the Balkans, becoming the first Allied correspondent to report first-hand the strength of resistance by the partisans to the Nazis in Yugoslavia. His reports resulted in the award of a Pulitzer Prize.

A fellow AP correspondent, Joseph Morton, ran into trouble. He was covering an OSS operation in Slovakia when the cabin which contained fifteen Allied intelligence officers and several Slovak resistance fighters was stormed by a Nazi counter-partisan unit. Although the Allied officers and Morton were in uniform with correct documents, the SS chose not to treat them as prisoners of war and ordered they should be killed immediately. They were taken to the Mauthausen-Gusen concentration camp and shot. Morton was the only Allied correspondent to be executed during the Second World War.

Part of the Fifth Army included British X Corps, which was positioned nearer to Naples. As the perimeter grew deeper, the British began to advance up the coast. On 28 September, the press corps suffered three fatalities.

Stewart Sale was a protégé of Edgar Wallace and had worked for the *Buckingham Mail*, the *Sunday News* and *The Daily Telegraph* before joining Reuters. He had flown on a bombing raid over Berlin and covered the Salerno landing. Along with Alexander Austin of the *Daily Herald*, who was the lone Fleet Street witness of the Dieppe Raid, and William Munday of the *News Chronicle* and *Sydney Morning Herald*, he had followed the infantry to the town of Scafati, about 15 miles from Naples, and waited while the troops cleared the Germans from the back streets.

When the church bells began to ring and the townsfolk emerged from their shelters, the three correspondents entered the town. Sale and his companions began interviewing some of the soldiers. Frank Gillard of the BBC was on hand to report the great welcome the British troops received:

'Things looked absolutely safe. Suddenly, gunfire broke out again. A German half-track with a big gun mounted had returned to do battle. It was early afternoon. Reporters scattered, seeking cover. But for Sale, standing at a street corner with two other correspondents, it was too late. A German shell landed among them and they were killed outright.'

Basil Gingell, the *Exchange Telegraph* correspondent, had accompanied the three men and recalled:

'I had left my Jeep and had walked down the road with my friends. We stood in a knot by a street corner watching the assembly of armour when there was a blinding flash and a terrific explosion shook the ground. I was flung a great distance and was buried in falling debris. When I was able to look around I saw my companions were dead.'

The Salerno landings had been a costly failure. In four months, the Allies had slogged just 70 miles from Salerno and were still 80 miles from Rome. Field Marshal Alexander quipped: 'All roads lead to Rome, but all the roads are mined.'

The fine autumn weather deteriorated into Italy's winter face: rain, sleet, floods and mud. Wooden bridges hastily erected to replace those destroyed by the Germans were swept away by the fast-flowing swollen rivers. The Allies were now confronted by the seemingly endless mountain ranges that the Germans had skilfully turned into formidable defensive positions. Italy definitely was not 'the soft under-belly of Europe'.

That first winter, the Germans held the appropriately named 'Winter Line', which stretched across the width of Italy. In fact the primary defence line was the Gustav Line with two subsidiary lines to the west. About fifteen German divisions were employed in its defence, manning gun pits, machine-gun posts and their lofty positions protected by mines and barbed wire. It was to take the Allies from mid-November 1943 to late May 1944 to push the enemy from this first defensive position to his next prepared line.

One of the most graphic descriptions of what it felt like to be wounded was written by a skinny 27-year-old from New Jersey. Newly transferred from the Pacific was war correspondent Richard Tregaskis of the International News Service (INS). He had come ashore at Salerno with the 82nd Airborne Division and followed them to the Volturno Valley where they were confronted by the twin peaks of Monte Santa Croce and Monte Corno. The November weather was bitter as the reporter accompanied two Ranger officers up Corno. The attack had stalled because the Germans held a cave near the crest and had resisted all attempts to shift them. The Rangers were about to employ an old but effective weapon, the Bangalore torpedo.[36] The climb was steep and the two miles took two hours. Tregaskis recalled:

'I kept my eyes on the rocks underfoot – and soon realised that we were following a literal trail of blood. Some of the stones were spattered with dark-red spots. The trail was the only negotiable route up the precipitous slope... .

Gradually we progressed along the flank of the ridge running between the peaks of Corno and Croce.'

His companions told him that he could get a good view of the fighting from the top of the ridge, and moved off to check other positions.

'While I watched, a squirt of black smoke dabbed the skyline. Then another, and another. They were German hand grenades, probably tossed from the base of the great white boulder. Somewhere at the foot of that boulder, I knew, the Germans were hiding in their cave. Presumably...the squad which had the job of lowering the Bangalore torpedoes over the rock and down into positions where they might blast the German strongpoint... Finally, I saw a great explosion blossoming from the white rock itself – perhaps the detonation of the Bangalore torpedoes or a charge of dynamite.

Yarborough and Tomasik [the Ranger officers] came back from their inspection tour, and we started down the tedious trail towards home. I felt a healthy fatigue. For the first time in several weeks, I had a bang-up eyewitness story of an action at a crucial sector of the front.'

Tregaskis paused to talk to some of the Rangers while his companions went on. Writing some notes, he started to hurry to catch up:

'I was making my way along a relatively straight stretch where German mortar shells had been falling on the previous day. Then I got it.

I heard the scream of something coming, and I must have dived to the rocks instinctively... . Then a smothering explosion descended around me. It seemed to flood over me from above. In a fraction of a second of consciousness, I sensed that I had been hit. A curtain of fire rose, hesitated, hovered for an infinite second. In that measureless interval, an orange mist came up quickly over the horizon, like a tropical sunrise, and set again, leaving me in the dark. Then the curtain descended gently.

I must have been unconscious for a few seconds. When a rudimentary awareness came back, I knew everything was all wrong. I realised that I had been badly hit. I was still stretched on the rocks. A couple of feet from me lay my helmet which had been gashed in a least two places, one hole at the front and another ripping through the side.

There was no pain. Everything seemed finished, quiet, as if time had stopped. My mind formulated frantic questions. What's wrong? Why can't I talk? What am I going to do? And then I felt a slight easing of tension, a slight relaxation. I knew, then, that even though I could not utter the words, I could still think. I had lost my power of speech, not my power to understand or generate thought. It was clear to me what I wanted to say, but I couldn't say it.

A shell was coming. I knew that because I heard the sound of the approaching projectile. But the sound was just a tinny little echo of something which had once been terrifying and all powerful. And the explosion, while it seemed to rattle my skull, was certainly not terrifying.'

His attempt to communicate with a fear-stricken soldier who scrambled by came out in gibberish. Finally a medic found him, bandaged his head, gave him a shot of morphine and disappeared to find other wounded. Tregaskis realised that he had to try to take himself to a field station and began descending the trail. He found that his right arm was hanging limply and everything appeared as if in a dream:

'Then a shell came. I heard the same ragged, distant whistling and the rattling explosion, as I automatically fell to the rocks for protection. I waited for the rest of the group of shells to arrive, and they were close. I looked up and saw tall spouts of smoke and high explosive all around me – but it was all unreal, like a movie with a feeble sound track. Probably the concussion of the shell burst which had hit me. I was amazed, but not frightened, as one huge shell burst suddenly sprang into being, towered over me like a genie. It was so close that I could have reached out and touched it. Yet none of the flying fragments had brushed me.'

With blood running down his face and glasses, he continued on his painful way only to be mortared once again. Finally he caught up with Colonel Yarborough who half carried him down the mountain to the first of many field hospitals he was to see in the next few weeks.

He was operated on in one of these. The delicate and long operation in which fragments of bone had to be removed from his brain and a tantalum plate fitted to his skull. It was the left side of his brain that had been damaged causing him to lose control of speech. With the help of a book of poetry, he gradually recovered his power of speech and six months later was discharged.

When he was sufficiently recovered, he joined the Allies as they began the breakout from the Normandy beachhead. Tregaskis became the first correspondent to fly in a fighter during a dogfight with enemy planes and, in 1945, returned to the Pacific to fly five bombing missions. He transferred to USS *Ticonderoga* carrier where he flew with a torpedo bomber squadron in an attack on the Japanese battleship *Ise*. By the time the war ended he had flown thirty-two combat missions. He was also on board USS *Missouri* for the surrender of the Japanese. Ironically having survived all the dangers of war, Tregaskis died in a swimming accident off Hawaii at the age of 56.

Christopher Buckley of *The Daily Telegraph* was accompanying the Eighth Army up the Adriatic side of Italy and had not met with the same fierce opposition as those of the Fifth Army to the west. This changed in one extremely ferocious battle that was dubbed 'Little Stalingrad' for the deadliness of its close quarter fighting. Between 20 and 28 December it was fought between a battalion of German paratroopers of the 1st Parachute Division and the Canadian 2nd Infantry Brigade's Loyal Edmonton Regiment at Ortona, the strategically important deep water port on the east coast. The Germans had constructed a series of skilfully designed defensive positions and were ordered to fight for every last house and tree. The house-to-house fighting was vicious, with the Canadians losing 1,375 dead and 964 wounded, a quarter of all Canadians lost during the entire Italian Campaign. The German casualties were unknown but heavy. Tragically, over 1,300 civilians died during the fighting.

Buckley, along with CBC correspondents Ross Munro and Matthew Halton, witnessed the plight of the citizens when they took shelter in a cellar. Buckley wrote:

'What a strange clutter of humanity it was. There were some five or six Canadian soldiers, there were old women and there were children innumerable. A painter of genius – Goya perhaps – might have done justice to the scene. I felt no verbal description could do so. In the half-darkened room, the pasta for the midday meal was simmering over the fire in the corner. Haggard, prematurely aged women kept emerging shyly one after another from some inner chamber where an old man, the grandfather of one of the numerous children was dying... . Another old man was uttering maledictions against Mussolini. Then his wife surprisingly produced a jeroboam of Marsala and a half dozen glasses and moved among the soldiers, filling and re-filling glasses... . The children clambered around the Canadian soldiers and clutched them convulsively every time one of our anti-tank guns, located only half a dozen paces from the door of the house, fired down the street in the direction of one of the remaining German machine-gun posts. Soon each one of us had a squirming, terrified child in his arms. And the old lady went on distributing Marsala.'

Another British correspondent, the BBC commentator Cyril Ray, was even more closely involved. He was mentioned in despatches for grabbing a rifle and leading a platoon of Canadians that had lost all its officers and NCOs. As a pacifist who perversely enjoyed his role, Ray later recalled that he was relieved that he did not have to kill any Germans.

Ray spent Christmas in a house with German parachutists living next door, typical of the close fighting in Ortona. No one fought in the streets as it was instant suicide. Instead, the Canadians used the tactic of 'mouse-holing', employing the PIAT and other anti-tank guns to breach the walls as the houses in Ortona shared adjoining walls. The Canadians would then lob in hand grenades and storm though the 'mouse holes'. Every house had to be taken room by room and Canadian tanks were invaluable in blasting upper rooms and taking out troublesome snipers. As one senior officer remarked: 'Everything before Ortona was a nursery tale.'

A similar situation was about to unfold at the town of Cassino, which stood astride Route 6, the main central highway to Rome. As an alternative there was Route 7 which ran about 12 miles inland from the west coast. This, however, was not an appetising choice for it followed a narrow coastal plain dominated by mountains on either side, causing bottlenecks to the advance.

The Allied leaders had completely misjudged the Italian terrain and weather. The photographer, Robert Capa, summed it up nicely: '*Between Naples and Rome, Mr Winston Churchill's "soft underbelly of Europe" was pregnant with hard mountains and well-placed German machine-guns. The valleys between the mountains were soon filled with hospitals and cemeteries.*'

Christopher Buckley compared it with fighting in the First World War: '*It seemed so terribly reminiscent of 1916, of a war fought in terms of advance of a few hundred yards over shell-torn ground, every yard purchased with a man's life.*'

In an effort to outflank the Gustav Line and enable an attack on Rome, Churchill sanctioned an amphibious landing further up the coast at Anzio. The operation depended completely on surprise and the occupation of the surrounding Alban Hills, not least to cut the German supply line to Cassino. Just three British correspondents were allowed to accompany the invasion: Wynford Vaughan-Thomas of the BBC, Basil Gingell, the Press Agencies representative, and Norman Maynard Clark of the *News Chronicle* representing the newspapers.

Clark later recalled the landing: '*We embarked at Salerno. The force was too small for the job mainly because many of the landing craft used at Salerno had been withdrawn and sent for the Second Front* [the Normandy landings].'

The amphibious invasion was accomplished without any opposition on the dark, moonless early morning of 22 January 1944. Clark in his full kit, including a greatcoat, was soaked through when his landing craft made contact with the beach. The ramp went down and Clark and the brigade commander were the first out, expecting a short wade to the beach. Instead they plunged into about 20 feet of water – the craft had beached on a sandbank well short of the beach – the obligatory life belt saved their lives.

The narrow beach was secured without a shot being fired and the troops moved forward. Clark saw a car's headlights approach and an ambush was set. The five German occupants gave up without a fight as they were too drunk to offer any resistance. As the troops crossed a field towards a nearby farmhouse, they suddenly came under fire from an armoured car that emerged from behind a barn, killing one of the British officers. The armoured car turned sharply to avoid the returning fire and overturned in a ditch. Clark said that the two Germans they captured were wearing pyjamas. The burst of firing alerted the Germans and their artillery went into action. With the American General, John P. Lucas, preferring to remain at the beachhead in order to consolidate and dig in against any counter-attack, the moment was lost.[37] Robert Capa, who had waded ashore with the Rangers, observed: '*The fifth day at Anzio, we knew we were not going to be in Rome for a long time, that we would be lucky to hold the small piece of land we had taken on the first day. The Germans outnumbered us, and there was not a square yard of the bridgehead that they couldn't observe or fill with shells.*'

The surrounding hills were soon occupied by German troops and the long siege of Anzio began. Churchill must have had a sense of déjà vu as his bold plan was reminiscent of his ill-fated Gallipoli campaign. Unlike Gallipoli, Churchill would not countenance a withdrawal from Anzio.

Clark complained about the crippling censorship, for the correspondents were not allowed to radio their reports to Naples but had to send them already censored by sea, which took two days. These arrived too late as the newspapers had already printed the official military communiqués. Clark also took issue with Churchill, who accused the war correspondents of forewarning the Germans of the Anzio landings. Churchill did have the good grace to apologise in Parliament and absolved the journalists of all blame.

Ernie Pyle, the GI's friend, arrived at Anzio two months after the Allies were put ashore. What he found was a beachhead under constant German artillery fire. Fellow correspondent, Eric Sevareid, described it as: '*living in a bull's-eye*'. Alan Whicker, who was an officer in the British Army's Film and Photo Unit, recalled that the US Army Public Relations had taken over a villa next to his unit for their war correspondents. One morning, the Luftwaffe dropped several bombs in the area:

'*In a panic the Press – including Ernie Pyle, a famous American Correspondent – took-off for the cellars, scrambling downstairs so fast that some tumbled and hurt themselves. As they left hospital after treatment for various bruises and sprains they were handed Purple Heart medals. Then they wore them. Now that did call for courage.'*

On 5 April, Ernie Pyle first made reference to 'the thousand-yard stare'; the unfocused gaze of a battle-weary soldier.[38] When driving with an officer friend, he saw lines of soldiers returning to the rear:

'Their clothes were muddy and they were heavily laden. They looked rough, and any parade ground officer would have been shocked by their appearance.'

Pyle's friend said that they had not been on the frontline but in reserve.

'How can you tell things like that? Well, I made my deduction on the fact that their beards weren't very long, and although they were tired and dirty, they didn't look tired and dirty enough. My friend based his on that, too, but more so on the look in their eyes.
"They don't have that stare," he said.
A soldier who has been a long time in the line does have a "look" in his eyes that any one with practice can discern.
It's a look of dullness, eyes that look without seeing, eyes that see without transferring any response to the mind. It's a look that is the display room for thoughts that lie behind it – exhaustion, lack of sleep, tension for too long, weariness that is, too great, fear, misery to the point of numbness, a look of surpassing indifference to anything anybody can do to you. It's a look I dread to see on men.'

On a lighter note, Norman Clark was asked by his friend Wynford Vaughan-Thomas to help him with a new piece of recording equipment. Thomas learned that a nightingale had been heard on the frontline and he was anxious to record it. The two men struggled with the unwieldy set until they came to the tree where the nightingale was alleged to sing. Setting up the equipment, they lay in their foxhole waiting for the bird to oblige. After an hour or so of silence, one of the officers offered some drastic advice. Apparently the bird only sang to the accompaniment of firing. Ordering his men to start firing, they provoked a fire-fight. Suddenly, the nightingale began to sing.

The Allies had spent a miserable and dangerous winter fighting amongst the ruins of Cassino overlooked by the mass of Monte Cassino. Perched on top of the mountain was the Benedictine Abbey of Monte Cassino, one of Europe's oldest monasteries. Convinced that lack of progress was due to the Germans using the abbey as a lookout point, the Allies decided to launch a bombing raid. On 15 March 1944, about 500 bombers dropped more than 1,000 tons of bombs in just over three hours. A recently-arrived Martha Gellhorn remembered thirty years later:

'I watched it sitting on a stone wall and saw the monastery turning into a muddle of dust and heard the big bangs and was absolutely delighted like all the other fools.'

She had probably learned of the terrible error that had set this pointless destruction in motion. A British intelligence officer intercepted a German message and made a translation slip which indicated that the enemy was using the abbey as a command post. In fact, the Germans were bound by an agreement with the neutral Vatican not to occupy the building. Another Intelligence officer checked the intercept, saw the error, but by that time the bombers were on their way. Ironically, the ruins created an excellent defensive position for the Germans and it was many months before the Allies were able to take the mountain.

Another American correspondent, Homer Bigart of the *New York Times*, described Cassino the day the fighting stopped:

'Cassino is a bleak, gray, smoking ruin, which, with a little sulphur added, would be more grim than a Calvanist conception of hell.

The city, when we entered it at 12.30pm, was silent. For the first time since January no shells crumped down amid the skeleton walls of the few score buildings still erect... . Fewer than 150 prisoners were taken in Cassino. Many came down from the abbey when the Poles approached, preferring to surrender to the British. Thus ended the bitterest battle of the Italian campaign.'

Bigart also mentioned that during the previous day two British reporters approaching the abandoned defences along Route 6 were killed by mines when they stepped off the road to avoid a sudden outbreak of enemy mortaring. These unfortunate correspondents were Cyril Bewley of Kemsley Newspapers and Roderick MacDonald of the *Sydney Morning Herald*, who had been sent to replace William Munday killed on 28 September 1943.

With the Gustav Line breached, Kesselring began to pull back to the next well-prepared position north of Rome, the Gothic Line. Now with an opportunity to cut off the German retreat, General Clark refused to obey Alexander's order and instead headed for Rome, where he intended to be acknowledged as the city's liberator. There were many senior officers who thought he should have been court-martialled for allowing the Tenth German Army to escape to the formidable Gothic Line.

General Clark had his personal photographer and nearly fifty public relations officers under his command all dedicated to producing the most favourable publicity. Eric Sevareid of CBS wrote that he and other correspondents were told to refer to the troops as 'General Mark Clark's Fifth Army', and photographers told to take pictures only of the 'good side' of Clark's face. Robert Capa, who had already left for England, remembered that General Clark's 'good side' was the one that displayed the three shiny stars on his cap.

On 5 June 1944, Rome was declared an open city and US forces marched in with no opposition. General Clark basked in the adulation and publicity as the general who liberated Rome. Sadly for him it was to be a short-lived hollow victory.

Sevareid was present next day when General Clark called a press conference on the steps of the Campidoglio (City Hall) and then feigned surprise saying: 'Well, gentlemen, I didn't really expect to have a press conference here. I just called a little meeting with my corps commanders to discuss the situation.' As the cameramen took Clark's picture, he spread his map on the balustrade and posed as if he was pointing something of interest. Homer Bigart muttered to Sevareid: 'On this historic occasion I feel like vomiting.'

While the assembled correspondents were tapping out their reports on the fall of Rome, a BBC correspondent burst into the Allied press HQ: 'Boys, we're on the back page now. They've landed in Normandy'

Eric Sevareid later recalled that:

'every typewriter stopped. We looked at one another. Most of us sat back, pulled out cigarettes and dropped our half-written stories about Rome on the floor. We had, in a trice, become performers without an audience...a troupe of actors who, at the climax of their play, realise that the spectators have all fled out of the door to watch a more spectacular performance across the street.'

When the news reached Mark Clark, deflated he remarked: 'How do you like that? They didn't even let us have the newspaper headlines for the fall of Rome for one day.'

From this day, the Italian Campaign was increasingly of secondary importance, with Field Marshal Kesselring fighting a slow rearguard series of battles.

One of the many correspondents who felt deflated by the invasion of Normandy trumping his story was the *Toronto Star*'s correspondent Paul Morton. Although he had spent a year in Italy, he had been confined to interviewing soldiers and Italian civilians. In fact he spoke fluent Italian, which was probably the reason he was approached by the British Special Operations Executive (SOE) to undertake a dangerous assignment by parachuting behind Nazi lines and covering the partisan war in Northern Italy. The prospect of covering this largely unreported subject created the prospect of a major scoop. This was too much for Morton to resist and he accepted the assignment.

He spent two weeks intensive training, including parachuting. A friend cautioned him: 'The SOE don't play by the "Marquis of Queensbury rules". Don't cry if you are let down by the SOE. These people have a very bad reputation for doing that if it suits them.'

After his training, he was armed as a precaution in case he had to fight. The plight of his namesake, Joseph Morton of AP, who had been executed while reporting the OSS activities in Slovakia, was still fresh in the mind. The night before his drop behind German lines, he met a few of his commando instructors in the Rome officers' mess. After several drinks and egged on by his friends, he produced his Beretta .45 fired a couple of rounds at the bottles behind the bar. He was immediately thrown out of the bar, an episode that would come back to haunt him.

A few hours later, he was onboard a Halifax bomber heading 200 miles behind enemy lines. They were looking for a signal fire set by the partisans but instead of one they spotted two in the darkness below. Picking the one with a flashing light, Morton dropped through the floor hatch at 1,000 feet. When he landed, he found that the group was not the British-backed Monarchist partisans, but a rival group of communists. They had hoped that their second signal fire would trick the British into dropping weapons to them.

With little option, Morton and his companions went on the run with this group calling themselves Garibaldini. He experienced several close encounters with the Germans including one he later related:

'The first German bullets to scythe into the hillside on which we lay started skirting our hidden positions at about seven o'clock in the morning. The undergrowth hid us effectively. Except for the random fusillades of the enemy, we were not uncomfortable as we lay in the shade of the rising Italian sun... and waited for death.

Young Captain Mike Lees, always a responsible British officer, looked shocked. Then a wide grin blanketed Captain Mike's handsome face. He tightened his gun belt, shot a nervous glance at Geoff Long and me, then shouted, "Avanti! Let's pay the bastards back". And with that, the whole crowd of us took off down the valley side.

Running where? We were off to attack the German patrol. It was more like a rumble than a skirmish. Had I been a German I would have been scared silly.'

Morton and his colleagues finally met up with the Monarchist partisans, which included escaped British prisoners of war and Allied air crews shot down over Italy. After two months of adventure, Morton and his comrades managed to reach the coast, buy a sturdy boat and row it to France. From there they returned to Rome.

Morton was taken aback by the cool and rather hostile reception he received. Although he was allowed to send off his despatches to the *Toronto Star*, he was chided by a couple of senior Canadian public relations officers for his inappropriate behaviour in discharging his Beretta in the officers' mess. They also took away his accreditation and he was ordered home by his editor. Although his first despatch had been published praising the contribution and bravery of the Italian partisans, the rest had been discarded. The editor accused Morton of fabricating his reports and he was sacked. He never found another reporting job.

There has only recently emerged an explanation for Morton's unfair treatment. While he was behind Nazi lines a directive from the Psychological War Bureau (PWB) stated that: 'Allied propaganda should now play down partisan services.

'Publicity given the Patriots has grown to a point where it is out of proportion to the war effort in Italy. There is evidence certain elements are making political capital out of the activities of the Patriots. It is incorrect to speak of the Patriots as liberating any particular area, if they are in control of any place it is because the Germans have withdrawn and are not taking action.

'We should remember it is the Allies who are liberating Italy with the help of the Patriots. The Patriots are unable to liberate of their own accord. Play down very gradually the activities of Patriots to liberate Italy and to the rest of the world.'

By inadvertently teaming up with the communist Garibaldini, Morton fell foul of a shift in ideological positions. As Morton reflected wistfully:

'I went behind enemy lines and emerged as a kind of agent. I went in as a reporter and came out as a kind of soldier. I sometimes wish I had never gone in at all.' [39]

By the end of April 1945, the fighting had reached the Lombardy Plain and the final chapter was in sight.

Christopher Lumby, *The Times* veteran correspondent was there to see the end. In the Great War he was one of the last correspondents to leave France during the confused days of 1914 when Lord Kitchener expelled all war reporters.[40] On his return to England he quit Fleet Street and was commissioned into the Manchester Regiment. Having survived the war, he returned to reporting for *The Times* and, from 1940, covered the North African and Italian Campaigns. In the confusion of the final days before the surrender, Lumby and a fellow press colleague entered Milan two days ahead of the Allied troops and were greeted at liberators by the Italian partisans. Lumby learned that Mussolini, his mistress, Clara Petacci and twelve members of his cabinet had been captured and executed near Lake Como. Their bodies were brought back to Milan's working class district of Loreto and displayed in the square. Lumby was able to identify the Fascist leader and was first with the news of his death. The mutilated bodies of Mussolini and Petacci and five others were hung upside down outside the forecourt of an Esso garage in the square.

This grisly display heralded the end of the Italian Campaign and two days later the surrender was signed.

Chapter 10

Fight Back in the East

The Japanese army, having swept through Malaya, taken Singapore and overrun the Dutch East Indies, now turned their attention to Burma, then part of the British Empire. In what became Britain's longest continuous campaign of the war, it was fought by a combination of British Commonwealth, American and Chinese forces against the Japanese determination to invade India and advance into China and occupy Chongqing, the Nationalists' headquarters. The campaign was fought in dense mountainous jungle with few roads but many rivers, with a climate that took more lives than any fighting. Another limiting factor for both sides was the heavy and continuous monsoon rain, which effectively allowed campaigning for only six months each year.

For the British in Burma, 1942 was a bad year. The Japanese occupied Rangoon in March and, in a retreat that resembled the events in Malaya, fell back to north-east India. With the Middle East being Britain's immediate priority, the forces in the Far East were starved of men and resources. There were additional crises to attend to, not least the disastrous famine that struck Bengal which left three million dead. Another drain on the British was the violent protests to 'Quit India', which took large numbers of British troops to suppress.

In this state of unpreparedness, the British launched a small offensive into the Arakan in west Burma. Unable to penetrate very far, the attack was repulsed and the beaten army retreated back to India.

To illustrate the remoteness and poor communications of the border that separated eastern India from Burma, it took the correspondent Alaric Jacob of the *Daily Express* five and half days to travel from Calcutta to the front at Imphal. He and two reporter colleagues, Stuart Emeny of the *News Chronicle* and Martin Moore of *The Daily Telegraph*, with Tony Beauchamp, the official photographer, were sent there for a crash-course in jungle survival. The object of this experience was to enable them to march with the newly-formed 77th Indian Infantry Brigade. This Long Range Penetration group, otherwise known as the Chindits, was the brainchild of Brigadier Orde Wingate, one of the war's original thinkers.[41] He had already operated a similar group in the East Africa Campaign of 1940-41 known as Gideon Force. His commander-in-chief then was General Wavell, who was now in command of the Far East Force, and was eager for some display of retaliation against the Japanese. The Chindits were trained to target enemy lines of communication and generally create havoc many miles behind Japanese lines.

In early February 1943, General Sir Geoffrey Scoones, the commander of IV Corps which defended the trackless frontier, summoned Jacob and told him that the following day he and his companions would be marching into Burma with the Chindits. He stipulated that they could go as far as the Chindwin River, but from where they had to find their own back. 'You must promise me not to go further, for you are not a fighting man and could not pull your weight. Besides, they might be in there half a year and I dare say you have other things to do.'

Operation Longcloth was the first expedition by the Chindits, which was made up of a force of 3,000 men and numerous pack animals. As Wingate explained to Jacob: 'This expedition will live off the country and for the rest be supplied entirely by air. The animals are very important. Should my pack-train become diseased and die we would be scuppered.' He added that a mule could also, at a pinch, provide meat should supplies become short.

The three correspondents and photographer joined the long serpentine column as it crossed the border into the thick jungle. During the midday heat they rested and set off again as evening approached. Jacob describes how the going became increasingly difficult:

> *'Now the track narrows till it is not more than eighteen inches wide. The mules with their load panniers keep crashing against the trees; loads are displaced and it requires infinite patience to tighten girths and prevent things from falling off and getting lost... . Up mountain sides which have a gradient of one in two. The path winds over flat slippery rocks, through streams rushing down from the mountains....*
>
> *A mule misses its footing and crashes over a precipice, screaming in a horrible human way as it goes over. There is a gun on its back which must be retrieved, so the column halts while muleteers lower*

themselves over the tree-spattered 'kud', as they call the mountain sides, with ropes and crowbars. It seems one of the elephants had gone over the kud too, but he scrambles back under his own power. I believe those creatures could carry a load across a tight rope.

Now we stumble down into a valley where a few campfires are. We are told to halt and fall out. We obey, literally. Take a step out of line, spread a blanket, lie down, nibble biscuits, drink water and fall asleep. Soon we wake up when the sweat on our bodies turns icy cold. The night seems interminable.

Three days and three nights we spend marching to the Chindwin. The track is one upon which thousands of refugees left Burma last year. Skeletons are still lying in the undergrowth... We find human bones along the path where poor wretches, worn out with disease and fatigue, had laid down to die... .

And now we get our first sight of the Chindwin, a broad stream down there fifteen hundred feet below, its channel hung with mist. Reconnaissance parties have already swum across and report the opposite bank is momentarily clear of Japanese, but there is always a chance that an enemy launch may come up the river, so anti-tank guns are mounted along the bank to guard the crossing.

I wade some way over and park on a sandbank to watch the crossing. The thunder ceases and the moon reappears. A long line of men and animals stretches behind us from the margin of the jungle to the water's edge. In a sky now clear, the sinister sound of aircraft is heard. We stand stock still, trying to escape observation and try to get the animals to do likewise. The plane circles around as though observing. I see it pass across the moon's aura. "O.K. boys, it's one of ours getting a bearing to drop supplies." And sure enough, the pilot switches on his lights. A flare goes up from the opposite bank and the machine makes its run, releasing its load of food and ammunition. The first aerial reinforcement has succeeded.'

The column once again disappeared into the jungle, leaving the four newsmen with their military minder standing somewhat isolated on the bank of the Chindwin and facing a 120-mile slog back to the border. Both Jacob and Emeny suffered from stomach problems which slowed their journey. Despite this, they made better progress going back than on the way out: '*we were all a little Jap-conscious: that gave wings to our feet, too.*'

The correspondents had to sit on their observations for three months until May 1943, when the public learned of this morale boosting raiding behind Japanese lines. Wingate's brigade had penetrated more that 1,000 miles, cutting the Myitkyina railway in eighty places, setting ambushes, destroying bridges and causing much disruption. Wingate regarded this expedition as one of fact-finding and was better prepared the following year, when a much larger force with greater air support created havoc behind enemy lines. Despite its seeming success, the expedition took a heavy toll on the troops with many returning suffering from long-term sicknesses.

The second expedition was launched on 5 March 1944. Nine days later, on the 14th, Orde Wingate was killed when his Mitchell B-25 airplane crashed into a hillside near Imphal during a storm. Among the nine others who perished was Alaric Jacob's colleague, Stuart Emeny, and Stanley Wills of the *Daily Herald*, who had arrived a few weeks earlier. They had accompanied Wingate when he visited 'Broadway', one of the Chindit landing sites behind Japanese lines.

Warfare in such a high and remote region brought more than its fair share of air crashes with its hazardous mixture of bad weather, over-burdened and over-worked transport aircraft. Vern Haugland of AP disappeared on 12 August 1942, when the plane he was on crashed in a storm between Australia and New Guinea, not a rare occurrence.

Another correspondent who did manage to survive a crash was CBS's Eric Sevareid. He had been sent to investigate the turmoil that was America's relationship with Generalissimo Chiang Kai-shek and his Chinese Nationalist Army, who was still embroiled in the Sino-Japanese War, which started in 1937. The American government supported Chiang and sent as their military advisor, General Joe Stilwell, who became highly critical of the incompetence and corruption of the Chinese army.[42]

The journey facing Sevareid was particularly perilous as it involved flying the 'Hump' over Japanese-held Burma, the towering Himalayas and into China, and was used to deliver Lend-Lease supplies to Chiang. Sevareid joined sixteen military personnel boarding a Curtiss-Wright C-46 cargo plane, bleakly known by the aircrews as the 'Flying Coffin'.

Successfully taking off on the morning of 2 August 1943, the C-46 was about an hour into its journey when an American soldier leaned over and shouted above the engine noise at Sevareid: 'Know what? Left engine's gone out.' Praying that the plane could fly on one engine, Sevareid was further alarmed when one of the crew rushed back to the main door, removed it from its hinges and started throwing out the cargo. Then he called out that all passenger baggage had to be jettisoned. The roar of the one engine and the wind rushing past the open doorway was deafening. Sevareid reluctantly tossed his newly-purchased luggage out of the door.

Then the overworked right engine caught fire and the terrifying scene was completed when the door of the cockpit burst open and the crew grabbed parachutes from a pile. Sevareid was already wearing a parachute but had never made a jump. There was no warning or order to jump but the other passengers seemed to know what to do and began hurling themselves out of the aircraft. Sevareid hesitated at the door frozen with fear and unable to join the others hurtling through space. Suddenly the plane lurched into a dive and Sevareid overcame his fear and jumped. He yanked the parachute ring and the chute opened above him. As he descended he saw the plane erupt in a fire-ball on a nearby mountainside.

Landing heavily but without injury, he made his way towards the wreckage and was overjoyed to be joined by all who had been onboard except the co-pilot whose body was later found in the wreckage. Fortunately, the radio operator had transmitted a distress call and an hour or so later they heard the sound of an aircraft and were relieved to see another American transport. It dipped its wings to signal that they had been seen and dropped a bundle containing knives, blankets, C-rations, a couple of rifles and a note instructing them to remain near the wreckage.

Unbeknown to the survivors, they had landed in Nagaland, an even more remote part of the border area and home to tribes who went in for head-hunting. It was also well behind Japanese lines. As the passengers gathered around the supplies, they heard a rhythmic chanting and watched as about twenty tattooed tribesmen dressed in breechcloths and armed with spears and knives formed a semi-circle around them. Both parties stared at each other in silence. Then Sevareid, recalling all the Westerns he had seen, stepped forward, raised his palm and said: 'How!' This seemed to break the spell and there were smiles all round as the Americans were escorted to the Naga village. As they arrived, another plane circled overhead. Sevareid ran back to the clearing to retrieve the additional supplies and found another note with the warning: 'Do not go to the native village as they are probably not friendly.'

The plane also dropped three parachutes attached to which were a senior medical officer and his assistants. They had plenty of broken bones, sprains, cuts and bruises to treat. The party moved from the village to the clearing where the Nagas erected three huts for them. It took two tense weeks of waiting for the rescue party, expecting at any moment that the Japanese might discover them or the Nagas might decide that they wanted some new trophies to adorn their pikes.

When the rescue party arrived it consisted of several dozen Nagas, two American soldiers and led by the local British representative, Philip Adams, a tall, fair-haired young man sporting a cigarette holder. As Sevareid later wrote, Adams was regarded by the Nagas as something akin to a king of those dark and savage hills.

The exhausting 120-mile trek back to civilisation took a week. When Sevareid recovered, he sent a dispatch in which he concluded:

'There was hardship, but I couldn't report that we suffered terribly. The truth is that many of us enjoyed the whole affair.'

When Japan entered the war, Chester Wilmot returned to Australia with his reputation enhanced for his outstanding broadcasting from North Africa. He was recognised as one of the best correspondents in the Middle East having spent several months under siege at Tobruk and, on 25 November 1941, had been slightly wounded while covering Operation Crusader in Libya. Back home, he was welcomed by the Australian Broadcasting Corporation (ABC) and appointed principal war correspondent in the Pacific.

As Britain's influence in the Far East declined with her attention focused on Nazi Germany, Australia turned to America as her principal defender. The Americans planned to use Australia and New Zealand as bases from which they could launch attacks on the Japanese in the Pacific. Despite the fact that not all Australians were happy about accepting American military assistance, the Australian Prime Minister, John Curtin, appointed General Douglas MacArthur as Supreme Commander of the South West Pacific Area (SWPA) which gave him direct command of the Australian military.

Another returning Australian from the Middle East was General Thomas Blamey, who was appointed commander-in-chief of the Australian military forces. He was a man who attracted praise and adverse comment in equal measure. A veteran of the First World War, he had a distinguished service record. In 1925 he resigned from the regular Army and took up the position of Chief Commissioner of the Victoria State Police. In 1936 he was forced to resign after a series of scandals including the discovery of his police badge in a brothel and an attempt to cover up the shooting of a police officer. Despite additional suspicions of corruption, he rejoined the Australian Army in 1939 and commanded I Corps in the Middle East.

On 19 February 1942 the Japanese launched a 242-plane attack on Darwin. The port area was damaged and the effect on Australia was considerable. It was the largest of almost 100 raids against Australia during 1942-43 and provoked a response from the ill-prepared Australian Army.

Attention focused on Port Moresby, the capital of New Guinea, about 500 miles north-east of Queensland. The Japanese had made Port Moresby an essential objective as it would give them a base from which they could strike north and eastern Australia, including the cities of Brisbane, Sydney and Melbourne. They had already invaded the north and eastern part of New Guinea and were ready to advance across the Owen Stanley Mountain Range, via the Kokoda Track, to take Port Moresby. General Blamey ordered that the area be secured and an inexperienced militia force was sent to the village of Kokoda, which was situated midway along the Track.

Chester Wilmot, Osmar White of the *Melbourne Sun* and photographer Damien Parer were sent to cover the fighting and soon became aware of the terrible conditions in which the soldiers had to fight. The campaign lasted four months and was fought in thick jungle and appalling terrain. The Kokoda Track soon turned into a hilly morass churned up by many feet. The correspondents struggled along with 21 Brigade as it was forced back by a stronger Japanese force. The Japanese managed to get within 30 miles of Port Moresby but exhaustion and lack of ammunition forced them to retreat. It had been a close run thing, but the ill-equipped Australians had managed to prevent the all-important capital from being captured. Wilmot and White, full of admiration for the troops, were highly critical of the failings of the Australian military. White exposed the Australian's inadequate jungle training, the failure to provide the soldiers with proper equipment and campaigned to have the army adopt green camouflaged campaign uniforms. When Wilmot tried to broadcast their views, they were heavily censored. Later, many of their suggestions were implemented.

When Wilmot and his companions reached Port Moresby they found that General Blamey had taken over and dismissed the commander of the New Guinea Force, the popular General Sydney Rowell, for protesting too vehemently. Wilmot, who disliked Blamey, immediately took Rowell's side, even appealing to Prime Minister Curtin about what he saw as an unjustified sacking. When his representations failed, Blamey had Wilmot's accreditation removed and there were even rumours that Blamey tried to have Wilmot conscripted into the army. There was a history between Wilmot and Blamey. In October 1939, Wilmot reported the rumour that Blamey was taking bribes

Gerda Taro and Robert Capa
in pre-Spanish Civil War days.

Louis Delaprée, killed when
his plane was shot down.

Gerda Taro under fire at Cordoba.

Ernest Hemingway and Martha Gellhorn – the new glamour couple in Spain.

George Steer, *The Times,* who reported the bombing of Guernica

The destruction of Guernica.

Virginia Cowles and Martha Gellhorn (seated) in London, 1940.

Clare Hollingworth in pre-war correspondent days.

William Shirer (right) at the French surrender at Compiègne. 1940

Edward Murrow, CBS, a good friend of Britain.

Sefton 'Tom' Delmer.

Guy Romilly in captivity at Colditz Castle.

Leland Stowe – dismissed as being too old at 39.

Mel Jacoby, *Time-Life* – escaped from the Philippines only to be killed in a freak accident.

Robert Bowman (left) CBC with colleague at Dieppe Raid.

Alan Moorhead and Alex Clifford in North Africa 1942.

Alan Moorhead in Europe, 1944.

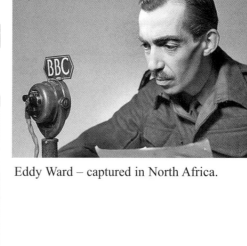

Eddy Ward – captured in North Africa.

Margaret Bourke-White – only female photographer to film a bombing raid.

Chester Wilmot reporting from Tobruk.

Bernard Gray – managed to
get aboard a submarine but
was lost at sea.

HMS *Urge* lost with
all hands.

US female reporters. From left to right:
Mary Welsh, Dixie Tighe, Kathleen
Harriman, Helen Kirkpatrick, Lee Miller
and Tania Long.

Martha Gellhorn at
Monte Cassino
interviews Gurkhas.

Alexander Anderson, Reuters, whose account of the bombing of HMS *Illustrious* sealed his reputation.

Richard Dimbleby, BBC, 1945.

Ernie Pyle – Anzio 1944.

Ernie Pyle – the Soldiers' Reporter.

Ian Morrison, Far East correspondent.

Edgar Rice Burroughs – witnessed the attack on Pearl Harbor 1941.

Cecil Brown, CBS. On board HMS *Repulse* when it was sunk.

Noel Monks (left) and Ian Morrison (third left) at the funeral of fellow correspondent Byron Darnton, Papua New Guinea 1942.

Godfrey Talbot, BBC – replaced Richard Dimbleby in North Africa.

Eric Sevareid, CBS. Crashed behind enemy lines in Burma.

Alaric Jacob, *Daily Express* and Reuters.

Chindit correspondents – S. Enemy, M. Moore, T. Beauchamp and Aleric Jacob.

Richard Tregaskis, International News Service – severely wounded in Italy.

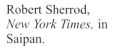

Robert Sherrod, *New York Times,* in Saipan.

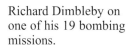

William Chickering, *Time-Life*, killed in kamikaze attack.

Richard Dimbleby on one of his 19 bombing missions.

'The Writing 69th'
– Gladwin Hill,
William Wade,
Robert Post,
Walter Cronkite,
Homer Bigart,
Paul Manning.

Walter Cronkite with
crew of a Marauder
before an attack on a
rocket site.

Guy Byam, BBC – disappeared during a
bombing raid.

William Lawrence, known as
'Atomic Bill' after witnessing the
atom bomb attack on Nagasaki.

Richard Hottelet's crashed B-17.

Richard Hottelet, CBS.

Grave of Kent Stevenson, BBC.

Wynford Vaughan-Thomas, BBC 1944

Robert Capa – the most celebrated
Second World War photographer.

Bill Walton, *Time-Life,* parachuted behind
enemy lines on D-Day.

One of Robert Capa's iconic D-Day photographs.

Ian Fyfe, *Daily Mirror,*
killed on D-Day.

Tom Treanor, NBC, killed in 1944.

Bill Downs, CBS reporter from D-Day to Surrender.

Ernest Hemingway with his close friend, Colonel 'Buck' Lanham, 1944

Osmar White in Berlin.

Canadian Paul Morton, who accompanied the Italian partisans and whose reputation was destroyed.

Alan Wood, *Daily Express,* at Arnhem.

Stanley Maxted and Guy Byam after their escape from Arnhem.

Edward Kennedy – disgraced war correspondent.

Virginia Irwin and Sergeant Wilson pose before unofficially entering Berlin.

from a laundry contractor at Puckapunyal Army Base in Victoria and temporarily had his accreditation terminated.

Unable to report the war from the front, Wilmot broadcast regularly for the ABC in Sydney as well as publishing his experiences in Tobruk. Later he accepted a job reporting for the BBC and made a permanent move to England.

General Blamey further fuelled his controversial reputation amongst his soldiers when he delivered an infamous speech to the men of 21 Brigade, who had fought a valiant fighting retreat down the Kokoda Track. Taking a lead from General MacArthur, who was not impressed by the fighting capabilities of the Australian soldier, he told his men that their retreat back along the Track was a defeat, that they had been licked by an inferior enemy in inferior numbers, adding: 'it is not the man with the gun that gets shot; it's the rabbit that is running away'.

Osmar White was transferred to cover the American attacks in the Solomon Islands. While he was observing the amphibious assault on Rendova Island, the tank-landing ship he was on was attacked by a Japanese bomber. A 500-pound bomb struck the craft killing the four men standing beside him in the wheel-house and severely wounding him in the legs. It took eighteen months of remedial surgery before he was able to return to the field in time for the final push into Germany.

The third member of the trio, Damien Parer, regarded as one of the finest combat cameramen in the war, was fated to die while filming the US Marines in their assault on the small coral island of Peleliu. The two-month long battle for the island, which was expected to take just four days to secure, was controversial because of its minor strategic value and for the highest casualty rate of all Pacific amphibious operations. Parer was killed by Japanese machine-gun fire on 17 September 1944. He was reported to have been walking backwards behind a tank to capture the expression in soldiers' eyes as they went into action.

Ian Morrison of *The Times*, having escaped from Singapore, reported from Java until that too was overrun by the Japanese. He then took his wife and young children to Australia, which he used as his base for the remainder of the war. He reported on the US–Australian campaign against the Japanese in New Guinea and accompanied the Americans on an eight-day long march over the Owen-Stanley Mountains to acclimatise the 126th Combat Team. At the end of this gruelling experience, Morrison was reported to be the least exhausted of the force.

Morrison was visiting an Australian field ambulance clearing station at Soputa on the north coast of New Guinea when it was attacked by Japanese fighters and bombers. Despite the tented hospital displaying prominent Red Crosses, the enemy inflicted forty killed and fifty wounded. Among the casualties was Ian Morrison who received shrapnel wounds.

The terrain of New Guinea precluded large-scale overland movements which forced MacArthur to use amphibious assault and parachute troops in the Huon Peninsula and Markham Valley. When approaching one of the airfields in the Markham Valley, the plane in which Morrison was travelling experienced engine failure and had to force land. Fortunately the passengers escaped with minor injuries.

Not long after, in December 1943, he was on an aircraft that took four correspondents to observe the amphibious landing on Cape Gloucester in western New Britain. This time the landing was not so controlled. Two correspondents, Pendril Raynor of the *Brisbane Telegraph*, Brydon Taves of UP and two members of crew were killed. Morrison and Hayden Lennard of ABC survived, although Morrison suffered fractured vertebrae. December 1943 was a bad month for war correspondents with five losing their lives in the South West Pacific Area.

Morrison wrote in critical terms to Ralph Deakin, his manager in London, about other newspaper correspondents in the Far East:

'*The opposition is not so far very impressive. I suppose the first eleven is batting in Europe. The best of them is Stuart Gelder of* News-Chronicle. *Reuters have a poor team. Not, I suppose, that we should complain.*'[43]

Morrison moved to India and the Burma front. After the Kohima battle when the Japanese were repulsed, the Fourteenth Army under General Slim steadily advanced into Burma until there were just small pockets of enemy resistance. In the six-week Battle for Ramree Island off the coast of Burma in January to February 1945, the British managed to drive nearly 1,000 Japanese into a dense mangrove swamp. Calls to surrender were ignored as the defenders tried to withdraw across ten miles of swamp. Without food or water, the blood of the many wounded attracted hundreds of giant saltwater crocodiles which tore into the tattered remnants of the Japanese garrison. Reports appeared in the newspapers of nights filled with screams, gunfire and sounds of animal attacks. Some claims exaggerated the number of victims as 1,000, but it is likely that at least

500 Japanese met a grisly end in what was the world's worst recorded crocodile attack

Another example of the Japanese refusal to surrender was told by Ian Morrison. Using a report given to him by Captain Ian Colquhoun, a former leader-writer for the *Manchester Guardian*, Morrison submitted the following in March 1945:

'I was sitting this afternoon in a quiet spot on the banks of the Myitinge River. The water was cool and inviting. Men were diving from improvised springboards and revelling in the cool water. I was talking to the adjutant of a battalion of The Royal Berkshire Regiment, one of the units of the 2nd British Division. I remarked on the contrast between the recent arduous adventures of the battalion and the peacefulness of the scene before us.

"Peaceful, hell!" said the adjutant, "Listen to that." There had all the time been the sound of aircraft in the background, but as he spoke the rattle of their cannon shattered the quiet of the afternoon. I asked what it was all about.

"About six hundred yards away," said the adjutant, "there are some mad Japanese. They have a gun, and they insist on firing it, although they know we are going to get them any moment now. They're a bloody nuisance, but they won't go away."

It appeared that all the Japanese who fought round Mandalay these few were left. They were on an island, in a marsh, dug in, and quite resigned to their inevitable fate. They had a gun and ammunition and a job to do. Although we blitzed them with guns and mortars and rocket-firing aircraft, they were still there, fewer in number but still firing. One of their two guns had been knocked out. As we were destroying it they shelled us with the other. We could see them picking up the shells and ramming them home.

These men are typical of the best that the enemy has brought against us. They are a real problem for the men of the 14th Army – not "the green hell of the jungle" so beloved of head-quarters-keeping correspondent, not the diseases which we have learned to conquer. These are the men we have to beat. They are not fanatics, for their courage is cold and calm and calculated. The courage of soldiers who have been trained and trained to do their duty until each single one of them is killed.

'There are fewer of them that there were, for we are reducing the Japanese forces in north Burma to a rabble, hopeless and aimless. But still a few remain who have to be sought out in their isolated positions and killed each one of them.'

He concludes with the sentiments echoed by all those fighting in the Far East that they are, indeed, the 'Forgotten Army':

'We shall kill these gunners. We shall kill their successors and all who strive to emulate them. But the process will be dangerous and hard – another phase of the strange fighting in the East which is sometimes so little appreciated by those who are dazzled by the sound and fury and the epic scale of the European fronts.'

The Pacific War is most associated with the steaming jungles of New Guinea and Guadalcanal, coral islands like Tarawa and the volcanic ash of Iwo Jima, but one of the most hellish battles was fought on the bleak and forbidding Attu, the westernmost island in the Aleutians. This 1,000 mile-long island chain extended west from the Territory of Alaska and was, therefore, part of the United States.[44]

Although it took nearly a year for the Americans to react, it was politically important to expel the Japanese from this remote island. Described as the loneliest spot on earth, Attu had a vicious climate and forbidding terrain. If it had not been part of America it would probably have been bypassed.

Samuel Eliot Morison, author of the US Navy's official history of the Second World War, described the dread the military felt for Attu and the rest of the Aleutians:

'Sailors, soldiers and aviators alike regarded the assignments to this region of almost perpetual mist and snow as little better than penal servitude.

To the soldiers who had to fight not only the Japanese but the weather and terrain of the island, it must have seemed that the Creator of the universe was an unskilled apprentice when He brought Attu into existence.'

The celebrated crime writer Dashiell Hammett who spent eighteen miserable months on the Aleutians as a corporal in the US Army wrote:

'Modern armies had never fought before on any field that was like the Aleutians. We could borrow no knowledge from the past. We would have to learn as we went along, how to live and fight and win this land, the least known part of our America.'

A jumble of sheer snow-capped peaks, barren valleys of brown tundra, narrow beaches and perpetually shrouded in a freezing mist, Attu measured roughly 35 miles in length and 15 miles in width. The Japanese garrison of 2,900 was outnumbered by the 15,000 Americans who took part in the battle. That numerically superior figure does not explain the reality for the attackers. Harold Baldwin of the *New York Times* wrote:

'Sudden squalls around Attu; the holding ground for ships is dangerous, in fact impossible; fog is almost always prevalent, and the clinging white mist is so thick that soldiers advancing in skirmish line across the rocky hills lose sight of each other; the supporting fire of naval vessels cannot be observed; planes cannot bomb.'

The battle for Attu began on 11 May 1943. The Japanese had skilfully prepared strong defensive positions which, along with the Arctic conditions, made life for the American infantrymen extremely tough. Russell Annabel of UP wrote in the *Saturday Evening Post* about the suffering of the troops:

'Your outfit would move into a position under cover of fog and darkness, and you would dig a foxhole and put up a breastwork of sod and rocks. You were already wet from fording streams and falling into sinkholes in the dark, and now seepage began trickling into the foxhole, so that presently you were standing in a foot or more of bitterly cold water. You couldn't search for a drier place, because by that time the Jap snipers and mortar crews would have spotted you. So you crouched there, returning their fire, and after a while, strangely, your feet and legs no longer ached.'

Bob Sherrod of *Time* wrote of the 17th Infantry:

'They were gaunt and haggard. Not one of them had shaved in 16 days they had been fighting. Red beards and black beards and dirty blond beards covered their faces. Each wore two pairs of long wool drawers, two or three pairs of heavy socks under their soaked

leather boots, a wool shirt or two, a sweater and a parka. But no amount of clothing seemed enough on this Attu mountainside. Most of the men were shivering as the icy wind pierced their bones. Their feet were wet and probably black with cold, as are most feet on Attu.'

Finally the Japanese defences were breached. If any offer of surrender was extended to the Japanese, the Americans soon had their answer. Throughout the rest of the war, the Japanese chose death over surrender. On 29 May, the Japanese commander, Colonel Yasuyo Yamasaki, led his surviving men in the war's largest banzai charge.

The shock of the sudden attack broke through the American front line and men in the rear were soon fighting hand-to-hand. The fighting continued until nearly all the Japanese had been killed. Those that survived chose to commit suicide with hand grenades.

Robert Sherrod counted 800 enemy corpses. He wrote:

'The results of Jap fanaticism stagger the imagination. The very violence of the scene is incomprehensible to the Western mind. Here groups of men had met their self-imposed obligations to die rather than accept capture by blowing themselves to bits. I saw one Jap sitting impaled on a bayonet which was stuck through his back – evidently by a friend. All other suicides had chosen a grenade. Most of them simply held grenades against their stomachs or chests. The explosive charge blasted away their vital organs. Probably one in four held a grenade against his head.'

There were more ghoulish details of this mass suicide and the editorial of the *New York Times* echoed the theme:

'The Japanese are aboriginal savages who will fight to the death and to the last man, and in that respect are even tougher than the Germans.'

This is why the Pacific War particularly resonates with the Americans who could not rely on capturing an enemy bent on killing as many US soldiers and then committing suicide.

Attu represented one of the worst casualty exchange rates of the entire Pacific Theatre. The Army's official history rated the campaign:

FIGHT BACK IN THE EAST

'In terms of numbers engaged, Attu ranks as one of the most costly assaults in the Pacific. In terms of Japanese destroyed, the cost of taking Attu was second only to Iwo Jima. For every hundred of the enemy on the island, about seventy-one Americans were killed or wounded.'

Bob Sherrod's next assignment was with the US Marines and a series of battles that are forever associated with this corps. Sent to cover the landings at the Tarawa Atoll in the Gilbert Islands, Sherrod and a fellow correspondent, Bill Hippie of AP, accompanied the attack on the island of Betio. This small, flat island was approximately two miles long and only 800 yards wide at its widest point. A long pier was constructed from the north shore from which ships could unload clear of the shallows but remain inside the lagoon. More importantly, an airfield was cut straight down the centre of the island and the taking of this strategically important island would enable the Americans to capture the Marianas Islands which brought the Philippines and Japan in range.

The Japanese had worked intensely for nearly a year to fortify Betio with 500 reinforced pillboxes, numerous firing pits and fourteen coastal defence guns in concrete bunkers. These were manned by approximately 4,800 highly trained and fanatical marines of the Imperial Japanese Navy. The American force, the largest yet assembled for a single operation in the Pacific, consisted of seventeen aircraft carriers, twelve battleships, twelve cruisers and sixty-six destroyers. The thirty-six transports carried about 35,000 troops.

The attack started on 20 November 1943 with a massive naval bombardment that seemed to engulf the whole of this small island. This was augmented by waves of carrier-born dive-bombers until it seemed that nothing could survive such a heavy and prolonged bombardment. Then the order was given for the Marines to board the landing craft and head for the tree-lined beach. As the craft approached they were met by increasingly heavy fire from the hidden strongpoints that appeared to be untouched by the shelling.

Bob Sherrod accompanied the fifth wave and as they neared the lagoon he looked around the ramp to see what was happening on the beach:

'For the first time I felt something was wrong. The first waves were not hitting the beach as they should. There were very few boats on the beach, and these were all amphibious tractors which the first wave

used. There were no Higgins boats on the beach, as there should have been by now.[45]

Almost before we could guess at what bad news was being foretold, the command boat came alongside. The naval officer shouted, "You'll have to go in straight away, as soon as I can get an amphtrack for you. The shelf around the island is too shallow to take the Higgins boats." This was indeed chilling news. It meant something had been dimly foreseen but hardly expected: the only way the Marines were going to land was in the amphtracks which could crawl over the shallow reef that surrounds Betio.'[46]

This meant that the landings would be slow as there were not enough amphtracks to carry all the Marines ashore but they would act as a shuttle to get the men to where they could wade the rest of the way to the beach.

'There we were already getting the hell shot out of us, with a thousand yards to go. I peered over the side of the amphtrack and saw another amphtrack three hundred yards to the left get a direct hit from what looked like a mortar shell.'

The amphtrack took Sherrod and the remaining fifteen Marines over the reef and dropped them by a sunken hulk of a Japanese freighter.

'I looked. The rusty old ship was about 200 yards beyond the pier. That meant some 700 yards of wading through the fire of machine guns whose bullets already were whistling over our heads.

The fifteen of us scurried over the side of the amphtrack into the water that was neck-deep. We started wading. No sooner had we hit the water than the Jap machine guns really opened up on us. There must have been five or six of these machine guns concentrating their fire on us – there was no nearer target in the water at that time – which meant several hundred bullets per man. . . It was painfully slow, wading in such deep water. And 700 yards to walk slowly into that machine-gun fire, looming into larger targets as we rose onto higher ground. I was scared, as I had never been scared before.'

Sherrod spotted that they had passed the end of the pier and called to the Marines on his right to make for the shelter under the pier. The other seven carried onto the beach, losing three killed in the water. Sherrod noticed, as he waded to comparative safety, that thousands of fish had been washed ashore, killed by the shellfire and bombing.

The Marines that had made it to the shore were sheltering behind the coconut log shelf at the head of the beach. Now the problem was the snipers hiding in the fronds of the many coconut trees overlooking the beach. Any movement was greeted by a bullet and one unlucky Marine was killed a few feet from Sherrod. The crack of the rifle indicated that the sniper was close by. Sherrod recalled:

'A Marine jumped over the seawall and began throwing blocks of TNT into a coconut-log pillbox about fifteen feet back of the seawall against which we sat. Two more Marines scaled the seawall, one of them carrying a twin-cylindered tank strapped to his shoulders, the other holding the nozzle of the flame-thrower. As another charge of TNT boomed inside the pillbox, causing smoke and dust to billow out, a khaki-clad figure ran out the side entrance. The flame thrower, waiting for him, caught him in its withering stream of intense fire. As soon as it touched him, the Jap flared up like a piece of celluloid. He was dead instantly but the bullets in his cartridge belt exploded for a full sixty seconds after he had been charred almost to nothingness. It was the first Jap I had seen killed on Betio – the first of four thousand. Zing, zing, zing, the cartridge belt bullets sang. We all ducked low. Nobody wanted to be killed by a dead Jap.'

Nearby, Sherrod watched a team set up an 81mm mortar. One of the Marines got up to a kneeling position and was shot, falling into a hole. His companion went to his aid and was shot through the heart. Once again the combination of TNT and flamethrower attacked the pillbox, throwing dirt and gun 50 feet into the air, and once again, the ammunition was ignited and dozens of bullets zipped around inside the pillbox.

Instead of an anticipated victory within hours of landing, the Marines now faced a night on the beach having suffered about forty per cent casualties. Reinforcements were being landed at the pier but, under cover of darkness, some Japanese had swum to the disabled landing craft and the sunken freighter and started firing at the beach and newly-arrived reinforcements.

By dawn on the second day, three Marine battalions held precarious footholds that were barely off the beach. Sherrod later learned that:

'During the night the Japs, apparently because their communications had been disrupted and many of their men undoubtedly had been stunned, had not counter-attacked. Probably as many as 300 Japs, we learned later, had committed suicide under the fierce pounding of our naval guns and bombs.'

The Japanese had used the darkness to replace the snipers killed the previous day and their fire was more frequent than ever. Sherrod wrote:

'Somebody brings in the story of a Jap sniper whose palm tree roost was sprayed repeatedly. But he kept on firing, somehow. Finally, in disgust, a sergeant took a machine gun and fired it until he had cut the tree in two, near the top. The fall is supposed to have killed the Jap.'

By the end of the second day, the Marines managed to push back the enemy towards the east end of the island. Sherrod noted that at 6.03, the first American Jeeps rolled down the pier:

'If a sign of certain victory were needed, this is it. The Jeeps have arrived.'

By the end of the third day after staging a final banzai attack in which 300 Japanese were killed, the island of Betio was finally taken.

Sherrod stayed with the Marines and accompanied them in the taking of Saipan and the epic battle of Iwo Jima. He came through the Pacific campaign unscathed but a fellow correspondent was not so fortunate.

During the taking of Okinawa, in what was the largest amphibious assault in the Pacific war, the 77th Infantry Division was tasked with capturing the small island of Ie Shima just off the north-west coast of Iwo Jima. It was expected to be a small scale operation, and most of the correspondents decided not to accompany the attack. One who did was the famous Ernie Pyle, recently transferred from Europe. The soldiers all knew him for his championing their cause and some were taken aback by his appearance: a short, white-haired man in fatigue clothes that were too big for him. He had declared that he was tired of the war and had been hospitalised in France in 1944 with war neurosis saying he had, 'lost track of the point of war'. Nevertheless, the men of the 77th were rather flattered that he was reporting on the sideshow that was Ie Shima.

The operation went well with few casualties. On the second day, Pyle accompanied the colonel and two other officers in a Jeep heading for the front. A witness said:

> *'As they reached a crossroads, still some distance from the front lines, the Jap machine gun, hidden in a patch of woods, suddenly opened up on them. The gun was a sleeper. Our troops had been moving up and down the road all morning and most of the day before. This was the first time it had revealed itself.*
>
> *Pyle and the others jumped from the Jeep and took cover in a ditch beside the road. The machine gun fired another long burst, and Pyle was dead. The rest withdrew. Several groups attempted to recover the body, once with support tanks, but each time they were driven back.'*

Ernie Pyle had died instantly when a bullet hit him in the left temple. He was buried on the island along with others soldiers of his beloved infantry. His body was later reinterred and buried in Honolulu.

Another deadly threat manifested itself as the Allies drew closer to Japan – the aerial kamikaze suicide attacks. Despite war correspondents reporting from many of the Allied ships closing in on the Philippines and outlying Japanese islands, only one was killed by a kamikaze attack. On 6 January 1945, William Chickering of *Time Life* was watching the landings at Lingayan Gulf in the Philippines from the bridge of the battleship USS *New Mexico*, when it came under an attack by a kamikaze plane. The suicide aircraft hit the bridge killing thirty-one, including the captain, several officers, Lieutenant General Herbert Lumsden, Winston Churchill's personal representative to General MacArthur, and William Chickering.[47]

The fanatical no-surrender attitude of the Japanese decided the fate of the cities of Hiroshima and Nagasaki, when America dropped her atom bombs rather than attempt a landing in Japan. The combined shock of this terrible bomb caused Emperor Hirohito to intervene and accept the terms of unconditional surrender. The formal surrender ceremony was held on 2 September 1945 aboard the US battleship *Missouri* anchored in Tokyo Bay.

Chapter 11

Bombing Correspondents

In 1942, when America began flying bombing missions from England and North Africa, war correspondents were invited along as observers. By early 1943, the RAF had followed suit, following the successful live broadcast of a raid by Richard Dimbleby for the BBC. There was, however, a much earlier participation by a couple of war reporters who were invited to fly with the RAF on the remotest border of the war.

On 4 July 1940, the Italians launched an attack across the Eritrean border and captured the important Sudanese railway junction at Kassala. One of the war correspondents covering the African campaigns was the Australian journalist, Alan Moorehead, reporting for the *Daily Express*. Moorehead applied for permission to take part in a bombing raid and to his surprise it was granted. Such requests had always been turned down in France and England. It was probably the first time journalists had been granted permission to fly on a bombing mission and Moorehead, together with Ronald Matthews of the *Daily Herald*, travelled from Khartoum to RAF Erkowit in eastern Sudan.

They learned that the purpose of the raid was to divert enemy attention away from an important convoy sailing up the Red Sea. Unlike future bombing raids involving correspondents, this was to be a low level dive bombing with all the exhilaration and danger that entails:

'So then Watson [the leading pilot] and Matthews and the other pilots and I climbed into three separate Blenheims and squeezed down among the instruments. We carried no observer, so there was a spare seat for both Matthews and me with a good view.

Matthews was in the left-hand machine, Watson in the centre and myself in the right being piloted by a laconic young Canadian who handed me a stick of chewing-gum – a welcome thing at that moment.

BOMBING CORRESPONDENTS

I wanted now only to get in the air...

There was a flight of an hour and a half to target – ninety minutes of pondering what it would be like. I hated that ride. It was slightly bumpy, and the other machines, so close that one felt their wings would touch, kept rising and sinking out of sight. I watched the other rear gunners spinning their glassed-in turrets in search of enemy aircraft. I traced the path of the Gash River and the thin ribbon of railway that led us to Kassala. I tried to work out the meanings of the dials before me. But it was no good. There was nothing to do, nothing to arrest the mind and lift it up and away from the dread and senseless apprehension.

In despair I fingered my wristwatch again and again, believing it must have stopped. Then, unexpectedly, my Canadian bumped me on the arm and pointed ahead. There was Kassala breaking through the ground mist. There the jebels [hills], there the town, there the railway yards. And in a few seconds we were going down to bomb. It wasn't necessary to wait any more. With huge overwhelming relief I leaned over for a fuller view. As I moved, the three aircraft dipped in a long easy dive. There was no drawing back nor any desire for anything but to rush on, the faster the better. Now the roar of the power-dive drowned even these sensations, and with exhilaration of one long high-pitched schoolboy's yell we held the concrete huts in the bomb sights and let them have the first salvo. I saw nothing, heard no sound of explosion, as the machine with a great sickening lurch came out of its dive and all the earth – jebels, townships, clouds and desert – spun round and sideways through the glass of the cockpit. Then, craning backward, I glimpsed for a second the bomb smoke billowing up from the centre of the compound. It all looked so marvellously easy then – not a human being in sight on the brown earth below; all those ten thousand men huddled in fear of us on the ground. A burst of tracer shell skidded past the slanting windows of the cockpit. So they were firing from the ground then, and it meant nothing. Nothing now could interrupt the attack.

Already Watson was shaping for his second run and closer in this time. We followed him in a dive, skidding first left and then right at over 300mph to throw off the aim of the gunners below. Then the straightening at last for a final swoop dead on the target. This time I heard the machine-gun spouting from the leading edge of our

*machine, felt the lift as the load of bombs were released and heard
again the rear gunner blasting from his turret as the aircraft nosed
upward into the sky again... .*

*We turned at length, all three of us, for the last attack, flying back
over a forest to the west of the town. Coming now at this new angle
we found new points to bomb, and faintly Watson's salvo sounded
through the motors as we came down for the last time. Looking across
as we dived, I saw where his starboard wing was ripped in two places
and the fuselage was peeling back under the force of the wind.*

*Then again the earth was turning and pitching as we came out of
it and I felt sick. Sick, and nursing a roaring headache. Like that I
was borne up and out of it into the pure air beyond the ground-fire,
beyond harm's way.'*

In late 1942, for the first time, seven American correspondents were invited
to accompany a US bomber raid. On 2 October 1942, they boarded the large
ungainly Consolidated Liberator B-24s as part of a large force of heavy
bombers sent to attack shipping and harbour installations at Navarino Bay
in Greece.

After long hours of droning monotony, they reached their target. Edward
Kennedy of AP recalled:

*'We all look a little like Mickey Mouse in the black snouts which are
oxygen masks. It is cold up here and I see that a fly which came with
us has expired for lack of air. It won't be long now.'*

Winston Burdett of CBS stood huddled between the two pilots in his plane
watching the approaching Navarino Bay with its targets of two large supply
ships. In the one of the lead planes, Grant Parr of the *New York Times*
crouched just behind the forward cabin and stared down through the open
bomb-bay:

*'It was deathly cold, but I was too excited to notice... With a jar, the
bombs fell away, seemingly too wide of their mark. Then momentum
and wind drift whipped them in toward the transports like a fast
curve breaking over the plate.'*

In a following B-24, George Lait of INS huddled beside the bombardier in
the plexi-glass nose and watched the flak explode around them. He saw:

'gun flashes from three enemy cruisers and gun flashes from shore batteries. Just as our plane was directly over the target, bombs from preceding planes hit the ships. Our plane was tossed like a cockershell. The target was ablaze.'

Henry Gorrell of UP was in the last plane to drop its bomb-load and was the most vulnerable to air attack. Looking out of a window:

'I saw earth, sky, planes above, planes below, all mixed with ack-ack puffs as our pilot twisted, turned, side-slipped... Someone shouted, "There he is, for God's sake, open fire." A machine gun started clicking and shell cases flew all over the place. I looked at Jorgensen [the pilot] and thought he was hit, but it was only muscular contraction as bullets whizzed past. One of the gunners shouted that he had knocked down a Messerschmitt and Frost [the waist gunner] got a second one... The German pilot attempting a suicidal collision, came straight in toward our plane. Frost gave him another burst and the Messerschmitt crumbled apart in the air. "That got him for sure, sir," said Frost. Then he added, 'I've been shot, sir.'"

Gorrell volunteered to go and attend to the gunner. He found that he had been shot in the knee and was bleeding badly. The reporter applied a tourniquet to stem the flow. Taking off his gloves to reach the first aid kit, he found that it was covered in frost and the iodine swabs were frozen. His hands went numb but he managed to patch up the gunner. The other gunner was also wounded in the leg but not seriously, which was more than could be said for the plane. She had been riddled with gunfire which had shot away the superchargers, ruined the automatic steering device, damaged the hydraulics and one of the ailerons had been shot off.

The plane managed to return safely to base and land without further damage. Not only had Gorrell secured an exciting story but he also received the Air Medal for his part in treating the wounded crewmen, the first of only two war reporters to be honoured.

One of the correspondents who turned down the opportunity to take part in a bombing mission was Ernie Pyle, whose comments appeared in *Editor and Publisher*:

'We got a real kick out of Ernie Pyle's dispatch Wednesday from the Central Tunisian Front telling how he turned down a bid to go on a bombing mission. Scripp-Howard's grey-haired roving reporter, now

a war correspondent, showed as much courage in declining to risk his neck unnecessarily, to our mind, as dozens of reporters did when they went on such missions.

Pyle said it was a tough decision to make and we heartily agree. "I knew the day of that invitation would come," he wrote, "and I dreaded it. Not to go brands you as a coward. To go might make you a slight hero or a dead duck... My sole purpose in going would be to perpetuate my vanity, and I've decided to hell with vanity.'

One of only two female correspondents to fly on a bombing mission was the redoubtable Margaret Bourke-White. In 1942 she began covering US bomber crews stationed in England during their day-time raids on Nazi Germany but she knew that there was little chance of actually flying mission. Then the Americans became involved in the North African campaign and she made her way to Algeria by sea. En route, the troop-ship, SS *Strathallan*, was torpedoed and Margaret spent a night in a life boat until rescued by an escort destroyer.

When she arrived in Algiers, she ran into an old friend, General Jimmy Doolittle, who asked if she still wanted to fly a bombing mission, adding: '*Well, you've been torpedoed. You might as well do everything.*'[48]

The raid was to destroy a German airfield of El Aouina near Tunis. On 22 January 1942, she took off in a B-17 Fortress, taking as many shots as she could before she was forced to don mittens as they climbed to 15,000 feet. Joining the bombardier in the nose, she recalled:

'Far below our fleet of planes, things were happening which I could see but not interpret. A white plume rose one mile high into the sky, and next to it grew a twin plume of black, tipped with spasmodic flashes of red. The fiery flashes darted higher. What could it be, I wondered? I'd better take a picture of it, just in case. And suddenly it dawned on me. These are our bombs bursting on the airfield. This is our target we came to demolish.

Then I saw another spectacle. In the air quite close to us were black spreading spiders, with legs that grew and grew. I couldn't imagine what they were. Suddenly I realised. They were shooting at us! We were hit twice in the wing, but only lightly damaged. Later I learned that two of our airplanes had been shot down.

Next day we got the reconnaissance report of our raid. Timing had been perfect. We caught the airfield when it was filled with German

planes. We had destroyed by bomb blast and fire more than 100 of
them. Our mission was effective and successful.'

The other female correspondent to take part in a flying mission was Martha
Gellhorn. This occurred towards the end of the war after her many requests
to fly had been turned down. Ever persuasive and without her accreditation
papers which she had lost, Gellhorn talked her way on board a three-man
Northrop P-61 Black Widow fighter on a flight over Germany. She wrote in
her notebook, as she was wedged on a cushion behind the pilot's seat
clutching an ill-fitting oxygen mask over her mouth:

'Terrified beyond belief. The plane was very beautiful, like a delicate
deadly dragonfly. The bombed factories and houses, the pitted
ground... Burning smoke and the Rhine ugly and flat here and like a
sewer river... In this immensity of sky, C-47s like plough horses...
This land is a desert and these people who loved order and finally
insanely wished to impose their order, are now given chaos as a
place to live in.'

The inaccuracy of bombing raids was well-known amongst the Allies,
except, perhaps, aircrews. In Naples during the Italian Campaign, Eric
Sevareid reported the showing of a recruiting film extolling the pinpoint
accuracy of American bombers that was shown to GIs fresh from the front
which was greeted with derision: 'Recruiting films should never be sent
where they can be seen by combat soldiers.' Especially not soldiers who had
witnessed the destruction of US-controlled bridges, Allied lines and the
sixteen bombs that hit the Fifth Army's HQ compound 17 miles away from
the target of the great abbey of Monte Cassino.

As it dawned on the authorities that good publicity might be an effective
way of getting the public firmly behind the war effort, a daring experiment
was put into action. Richard Dimbleby, who four months before had returned
from North Africa in apparent disgrace, was invited to be the first BBC war
correspondent to go on an RAF bombing raid. For the first time a live
commentary on what an aircrew experienced in the night attacks over
German cities would be heard by millions of people.

Dimbleby himself viewed the project with some trepidation as he did not
enjoy flying. Nevertheless, he and his sound engineer Stanley Richardson
reported to 106 Squadron based at Syerston in Nottinghamshire where they
attended the briefing. The target was Berlin, which had not been attacked

for over a year. Now the RAF was equipped with the new heavy bomber, the Avro Lancaster, and able to deliver a far deadlier bomb load. Dimbleby was allocated the flight leader's aircraft flown by a 25-year-old Squadron Leader named Guy Gibson.[49]

At 4.30pm on 6 January 1943, they took off towards the approaching darkness. Dimbleby counted between thirty and forty bombers around him 'seemingly suspended in the evening air'. As they gained altitude, a kink in the tube of his oxygen supply caused him to pass out until the flight engineer untwisted the tube. As they crossed the enemy coast, Dimbleby saw his first flak:

> *'It was bursting away from us and much lower. I didn't see any long streams of soaring into the air as the pictures suggest: it burst in little yellow winking flashes and you couldn't hear it above the roar of the engines. Sometimes it closes in on you, and the mid or tail gunner will call calmly and report its position to the Captain so he can dodge it.'*

The 'thirty and forty' aircraft were joined by other squadrons until there were 200 aircraft heading for the German capital. Approaching Berlin, Dimbleby was amazed at the criss-cross pattern of searchlights which seemed impossible to evade: '*a tracery of sparkling silver spread across the face of Berlin.*' The flak increased, although half of the flak personnel were absent that evening and was lighter than usual.

> *'As we turned in for our first run across the city, it closed right around us. For a moment it seemed impossible that we could miss it, and one burst lifted us in the air as though a giant hand had pushed up the belly of the machine.'*

For Dimbleby, the experience was terrifying, with death only a moment away. To his dismay, the bomb aimer could not see the target, so Gibson flew around again. Dimbleby was struck by the contrast between the bright flashing of the target area and the sudden peace of the surrounding darkness. Once more they entered the turmoil of searchlights, flares and flak only for the second run to be aborted. A third effort brought success and the bomb load released to Dimbleby's immense relief. Gibson then threw the aircraft into a series of violent corkscrew manoeuvres to escape the searchlights. This was more than Dimbleby could stand and he vomited down the ladder into the bomb-aimer's compartment.

Despite his air-sickness, Richard Dimbleby delivered a memorable report that was broadcast two days later. It says something for his fortitude in overcoming his dislike of flying that Dimbleby went on to report a further nineteen missions.

A colleague of Dimbleby was not so lucky. Canadian-born Kent Stevenson flew from Fiskerton, Lincolnshire with 49 Squadron on 22 June 1944. They were part of a 130 Lancaster raid on the synthetic oil plant at Wesseling, 15 miles south of Cologne. The raid turned into a disaster for the squadron as six of their aircraft were shot down with the loss of forty-six crew, including Stevenson.

The public relations department of the 8th US Air Force came up with the title 'The Writing 69th' for the eight American correspondents who were selected and trained to fly bombing missions. The group also considered the name, 'The Flying Typewriters' and 'The Legion of the Doomed'. The eight members of this short-lived group were Walter Cronkite of UP, Paul Manning for CBS, Robert Post of the *New York Times*, Andy Rooney of *Stars and Stripes*, Denton Scott for *Yank* magazine, Homer Bigart of the *New York Herald Tribune*, William Wade of International News Service and Gladwin Hill for AP. In addition, five newsreel cameramen took part in the training as well as the film director William Wyler.

The week-long training course was crammed with a multitude of tasks including how to fire the aircraft's weapons, despite rules barring non-combatants from taking up arms, adjusting to flying at high altitudes, enemy identification and parachute training.

The first and last mission of 'The Writing 69th' was the raid on the Focke-Wulf aircraft factory in Bremen.

For this mission only five of the correspondents took part – the absentees were Scott and Manning, while William Wade's aircraft turned back with mechanical problems early in the flight. When the group of Flying Fortresses and Liberators reached their target, they found Bremen was too overcast and the raid was diverted to the submarine pens at Wilhelmshaven.

Reporting a bombing mission is at best a hodgepodge of disconnected scenes. William Cronkite wrote that it was like a poorly edited home movie with:'*bombs falling past you from the formation above you, a crippled bomber with smoke pouring from one motor limping along thousands of feet below, a tiny speck in the sky that grows closer and finally becomes an enemy fighter, a Focke-Wulf peeling off above you somewhere and plummeting down, shooting its way through the formation; your bombardier pushing a button as calmly as if he were turning on a hall light, to send our bombs on their way.'*

Homer Bigart's impression was much the same as Cronkite's. They were too high to see where their bombs landed and much of their attention was taken up with worrying about the amount of flak and the fighters that appeared from nowhere giving their gunners little chance of hitting them.

It was the B-24s, the Liberators that sustained the most punishment. Flying in one of these was Robert Post. As the group flew over Oldenburg, it was intercepted by German fighters. Post's B-24 was shot at by a Focke-Wulf and exploded in mid-air. Only two members of the crew managed to parachute to safety, while the rest of the crew including Post were killed. This effectively ended 'The Writing 69th', not one of public relation's conspicuous successes.[50]

Ed Murrow described the raid on Berlin on the night of 2 December 1943 when he accompanied RAF Lancaster D-Dog, part of a 440 bomber mission. On the journey out he saw the bursts of yellow flame as several Lancasters fell victim to the German night-fighters. The navigator announced that the attack ought to begin in exactly two minutes. Murrow noticed:

'We were still over the clouds. But suddenly those dirty gray clouds turned white. We were over the outer searchlight defences. The clouds below us were white, and we were black. D-Dog seemed like a black bug on a white sheet... "Target indicators going down". The same moment the sky ahead was lit up by bright yellow flares. Off to starboard, another kite went down in flames. The flares were sprouting all over the sky – reds and greens and yellows – and we were flying straight for the centre of the fireworks. D-Dog seemed to be standing still, the four propellers thrashing the air. The clouds had cleared, and off to starboard a Lanc was caught by at least fourteen searchlight beams. We could see him twist and turn and finally break out. But still the whole thing had a quality of unreality about it... Another Lanc was coned on our starboard beam. The lights seemed to be supporting it. Again we could see those little bubbles of coloured lead driving at it from two sides. The German fighters were at him.

And then, without warning at all, D-Dog filled with an unhealthy white light.'

Murrow's aircraft had been caught by the searchlights and the pilot immediately reacted with a series of dives, turns and corkscrewing.

140

BOMBING CORRESPONDENTS

'And then I was on my knees, flat on the deck for he had whipped the Dog back into a climbing turn. The knees should have been strong enough to support me, but they weren't, and the stomach seemed to be in some danger of letting me down, too… It seemed that one big searchlight, instead of being twenty thousand feet below, was mounted on our wing tip. D-Dog was corkscrewing. As we rolled down on the other side, I began to see what was happening to Berlin.

The clouds were gone, and the sticks of incendiaries from preceding waves made the place look like a badly laid out city with the street lights on. The small incendiaries were going down like a fistful of white rice thrown on a piece of black velvet.'

After being flung around the sky, D-Dog escaped the searchlights, levelled off and dropped its bomb load. Even escaping from the Berlin area was not easy and the German fighters were still downing the Lancasters. Finally D-Dog reached the safety of her home station. The raid had not been a success as strong cross-winds made high-level bombing inaccurate. Also, the German fighters had shot down forty aircraft and among those killed were two fellow reporters, Norman Stockton of Australian Associated Newspapers and Lowell Bennett of International News Service.

Murrow flew twenty-five Allied combat missions in Europe despite opposition from CBS who regarded him as too valuable to be regularly risked. Richard Hottelet was startled at the way that Murrow went out of his way to court danger and death in the air: *'If I went up in B-26s it wasn't because I was driven, but because it was, unhappily, part of my job. Ed went up because he was driven.'* Murrow's motive for taking the risk was in part due to feeling he had become desk-bound in London and done little in the way of frontline war reporting.

Wynford Vaughan-Thomas describes the bombing raid he went on *'as the most terrifying eight hours of my life'.* He described a burning Berlin in a similar way to Ed Murrow: *'like watching someone throwing jewellery on black velvet – winking rubies, sparkling diamonds all coming at you.'*

Robert Clapper was an outstanding Washington columnist who supported Britain from the start of the war, and received threats on his life from isolationists. He later volunteered as a war correspondent and took part in a bombing raid on the marshalling yards at Rome. On his fourth tour, he reported from the Pacific and was on board the aircraft carrier USS *Bunker Hill*, as the naval task force approached Eniwetok in the Marshall Islands.

On 29 January 1944, he chose to fly with a Navy bomber which was softening up the Japanese-held islands prior to invasion. As they reached Eniwetok, the squadron commander flew in close to the rest of the flight so Clapper could get a better view of the operation and collided in mid-air with another aircraft and both plunged into an Eniwetok lagoon. He was the sixteenth American war correspondent to be killed since Pearl Harbor. As Clapper had been invited to fly by the Secretary of the Navy, it was felt only fitting that he receive a posthumous Purple Heart.

The ultimate bombing missions of the Second World War were the most terrifying. On 6 August 1945, an American Superfortress B-29 named *Enola Gay* dropped the first atomic bomb on the city of Hiroshima. The devastation was enormous, flattening the city and causing 70,000 instant deaths.

Despite the use of this awesome new weapon, Japan made no moves to react to the Allies' Potsdam Declaration of 'unconditional surrender'. With no sign of a Japanese surrender, the United States sent a second Superfortress loaded with a heavier atomic bomb code-named Fat Man. The target was the industrial port of Nagasaki on Japan's southernmost island of Kyusha.

Three specially designed Superfortresses took part in the attack, two of which carried scientific measuring equipment. In one was the *New York Times* science correspondent, William L. Lawrence, who had been chosen as the sole reporter from the inception of the Manhatten Project.[51]

The three aircraft took off from the island of Tinian in the Marianas at 3.50am on 9 August 1945. An hour into the flight they flew into an electrical storm. Lawrence noted:

> *'a strange eerie light coming through the window... and as I peered through the dark all around us I saw a startling phenomenon. The whirling giant propellers had somehow become great luminous discs of blue flame. The same blue flame appeared on the plexi-glass windows in the nose of the ship, and on the tips of the giant wings it looked as if we were riding the whirlwind through space on a chariot of blue fire.'*

Captain Bock assured Lawrence that there was no danger as the phenomenon was St Elmo's fire.[52]

Lawrence wrote probably the most vividly descriptive report of the detonation of the atomic bomb and was later awarded a Pulitzer Prize.

'It was 12.01 and the goal of our mission had arrived. We had heard the prearranged signal on our radio, put on our arc-welder's glasses and watched tensely the manoeuvrings of the strike ship about half a mile in front of us.

"There she goes," someone said.

Out of the belly of the Great Artiste *what looked like a black object went downward.*

Captain Bock swung around to get out of range; but even though we were turning away in the opposite direction, and despite the fact that it was broad daylight in our cabin, all of us became aware of a giant flash that broke through the dark barrier of our arc-welder's lenses and flooded our cabin with intense light.[53]

We removed our glasses after the first flash, but the light still lingered on, a bluish-green light that illuminated the entire sky all around. A tremendous blast wave struck our ship and made it tremble from nose to tail. This was followed by four more blasts in rapid succession, each resounding like the boom of cannon fire hitting our plane from all directions. Observers in the tail of our ship saw a giant ball of fire rise as though from the bowels of the earth, belching forth enormous white smoke rings. Next they saw a giant pillar of purple fire, 10,000 feet high, shooting skyward with enormous speed.

By the time our ship had made another turn in the direction of the atomic explosion the pillar of purple fire had reached the level of our altitude. Only about forty-five seconds had passed. Awestruck, we watched it shoot upward like a meteor coming from the earth instead of from outer space, becoming ever more alive as it climbed skyward through the white clouds. It was no longer smoke, or dust, or even a cloud of fire. It was a living thing, a new species of being, born right before our incredulous eyes...

Then, when it appeared as though the thing had settled down into a state of permanence, there came shooting out of the top, a giant mushroom that increased the height of the pillar to a total of 45,000 feet. The mushroom top was even more alive than the pillar, seething and boiling in a white fury of creamy foam, sizzling upward and then descending earthward, a thousand Old Faithful geysers rolled into one.

It kept struggling in an elemental fury, like a creature in the act of breaking the bonds that held it down. In a few seconds it had freed itself from its gigantic stem and floated upward with tremendous speed, its momentum carrying into the stratosphere to a height of about 60,000 feet.

But no sooner did this happen when another mushroom, smaller in size than the first one, began emerging out of the pillar. It was as though the decapitated monster was growing a new head.

As the first mushroom floated off into the blue it changed its shape into a flowerlike form, its giant petal curving downward, creamy white outside, rose-coloured inside. It still retained that shape when we last gazed at it from a distance of about 200 miles.'

Lawrence came in for much criticism when he disputed the notion that radiation sickness was killing survivors of Hiroshima and Nagasaki. He was accused of being on the payroll of the War Department and faithfully parroting the government line which led to half a century of silence about the lingering effects of the bomb.[54]

Chapter 12

D-Day

T he invasion of Europe, two years in the planning, was recognised in
the words of General George C. Marshall, General Eisenhower's
Army Chief of Staff: 'The greatest news story of modern times.' But
how much should the media be involved in D-Day? The problem for the
Allied commanders was how to keep secret the details of this 'greatest news
story'. The Supreme Headquarters of the Allied Expeditionary Force
(SHAEF) even sought to ban press speculation about the time and place of
the anticipated invasion. Eisenhower confided to Churchill in February that
he was devoting considerable time every day trying 'to discover the best
means of keeping the press securely in the dark, while at the same time not
appearing to treat them as complete outsiders.'

In fact, Eisenhower chose the right strategy in co-opting the media and
declared that he would consider every journalist 'a quasi-staff officer of
mine'. Only accredited journalists could gain access to SHAEF and
eventually the battlefront. To be accredited, the journalists had to submit to
a rigorous background check, sign a pledge to abide by military regulations
and submit all copy to military censorship.

The journalists, of course, could not be prevented from speculating about
the expected invasion, and used bits of information to make predictions
about when and where it would take place. Churchill was alarmed when a
British journalist showed him privately the main outlines of the invasion
plan which he had put together from fragments of information unwittingly
given him by a number of officers. Even more disconcerting were the rather
accurate surmises as to Allied plans which correspondents made in the
absence of official statements. The situation became worse as the number
of correspondents rapidly increased in anticipation of D-Day.

By 6 June 1944 there were a total of 530 newsmen, photographers and
radio correspondents accredited by SHAEF.[55]

Months earlier, correspondents who were to accompany the invading force underwent an intensive course of special training in front-line conditions. These included instructions in gunnery, signals, reconnaissance, aircraft and tank recognition and map-reading. Those accompanying the airborne groups had to learn and practise jumping with paratroopers from transport aircraft. They all went on assault courses, ran cross-country, learned how to live rough and cook in the field. There was probably never a fitter corps of pressmen. In the end, they were no longer regarded as civilians in khaki fancy-dress but fellow participants but with an unusual and specialised non-combatant job.

On 5 June 1944, 6,939 vessels, including 1,213 warships and 4,126 landing craft gathered south of the Isle of Wight in the largest seaborne invasion in history. In the early hours of 6 June, the RAF dropped hundreds of dummy paratroopers designed to distract German anti-paratrooper units. At the same time, in less than fifteen minutes, six gliders landed and captured two important bridges over the Caen Canal. As much as the capture of the bridges had been a textbook operation, the rest of the drops had been a near disaster, with units landing miles from their objectives.

One of three correspondents selected to fly with the airborne troops, David Woodward of the *Manchester Guardian* described the first hours of the invasion:

> *'It was nearly dark when they formed up to enter the planes, and by torchlight the officers read to their men the messages of good wishes from General Eisenhower and General Montgomery. Then from this aerodrome and from aerodromes all over the country an armada of troop-carrying planes protected by fighters and followed by more troops aboard gliders took to the air. The weather was not ideal for an airborne operation, but it was decided to carry it out. The Germans would be less likely to be on their guard on a night when the weather was unfavourable for an attack. First came parachutists whose duty it was to destroy as far as possible the enemy's defences against an air landing. Then came the gliders to seize various points, and finally more gliders carrying equipment and weapons of all kinds. Out of the entire force of planes which took the unit into action, only one tug and one glider were shot down.'*

Woodward's participation in the invasion was brief as he was injured when the glider made a less than soft landing and was returned to England later that day.

Approaching midnight on 5 June, Richard Dimbleby recorded the departure of the 6th Airborne Division from an airfield in southern England. They were bound for the drop zones behind Ouistreham and Sword Beach. One of the aircraft carried his fellow BBC correspondent, Guy Byam, who had joined the Corporation in April.

The 26-year-old Guy Byam had crammed more than enough action into his short life. At the outbreak of the war, he volunteered and was commissioned with the Royal Navy Volunteer Reserve and took part in Combined Services operations in Norway. He then served on HMS *Jervis Bay*, a 14,000-ton liner converted into an armed merchant cruiser. On 5 November 1940, she was the sole escort of a convoy of thirty-seven ships homeward bound from Canada when the commerce-raiding pocket battleship, *Admiral Scheer*, was spotted. Heavily armed, the 10,000-ton German raider closed on the convoy. The *Jervis Bay*'s captain, Edward Fogarty Fegen, sailed for the *Admiral Scheer* in order to get his own guns in range. Meanwhile, the convoy managed to scatter. Although she was outranged, the *Jervis Bay* was repeatedly hit but managed to fire off a few shots of her own. Badly damaged, she finally sank and Guy Byam was one of the sixty-five survivors. For his action, Captain Fegen was awarded a posthumous Victoria Cross.

Byam survived the Battle for France but, on 3 February 1945, he was flying with the crew of a US 8th Air Force Flying Fortress in a raid over Berlin when it sustained serious damage from anti-aircraft fire and crashed into the North Sea, killing all onboard.

The 6th Airborne Division departed at 23.30 hours and reached their drop zone an hour later. Byam, the first correspondent to land in France, reported:

> '*And you fly out over the Channel and the minutes go by, and the stick commander says that the pilot has told him we are over a great armada of naval ships. And then it is something else he says – something that gives you a dry feeling in your mouth – flak – and the word is passed from man to man. The machine starts to rock and jump. Ahead of us a comforting thought. Lancasters are going for the flak and a coastal battery is one of their objectives.*
>
> *We're near the coast now and the run in has started – one minute, thirty seconds. Red light – green and out – get on, out, out, out fast*

into the cool night air, out, out, out over France – and we know the drop zone is obstructed. We're jumping into fields covered with poles! And I hit my parachute and lower my kitbag which is suspended on the end of a 40-foot rope from my harness. And then the ground comes up to hit me. And I find myself in the middle of a cornfield. I look around and even with a compass I can't be sure where I am – and overhead hundreds of parachutes and containers are coming down.

The whole sky is a fantastic chimera of lights and flak, and one plane gets hit and disintegrates wholesale... sprinkling a myriad of burning pieces all over the sky.

The job of the unit with which I jumped was to occupy the area and prepare the way for gliders – we were to rendezvous near a copse, but I can't find it, so I go to a farmhouse and ask the way of a farmer and his wife standing on the porch of their house. It's a tricky business this moving about in enemy countryside at night. But we are well, in hand and at the most I shall meet my own patrols. I find the unit after having been sniped at once and challenged a number of times. They are assembling under a hedge.

Like a tentacle into the air was the radio-set aerial, and the major was signalling.

Allied soldiers talking to each other through the night.'

Guy Byam's may not have been the most insightful of reports but it was significant as being the first from France. It did, however, demonstrate the contrast of a live off-the-cuff commentary with that of a reporter with a pencil and a pad who had time to give thought to the situation and produce a more detailed and considered analysis.

A more experienced commentator, Chester Wilmot, made his landing by glider with the 9th Parachute Regiment and Canadian Brigade just to the west of Varaville. He described the lottery of landing in the dark in craft which had little control once they began their descent:

'With grinding brakes and creaking timbers we jolted, lurched, and crashed our way to a landing in northern France early this morning. The glider in which I travelled came off better than most. The bottom of the nose was battered in... the wings and tail assembly were slashed here and there, but she came to rest on her three wheels, even though she had mown down five stout posts that came in her path, and

virtually crash-landed in a ploughed field. No one was even scratched.

We shouted with joy…and relief…and bundled out into the field. All around us we could see silhouettes of other gliders, twisted and wrecked – making grotesque patterns against the sky. Some had buried their noses in the soil; others had lost a wheel or a wing; one had crashed into a house, two had crashed into each other. And yet, as we marched off past these twisted wrecks – thanking heaven for our good fortune – troops were clambering out almost casually as they might leave a bus. Some had to slash away the wooden fuselage before they could get out their Jeeps and trailers; but almost without exception they soon had them on the road.

But as we moved off the landing zone we were promptly reminded that we were still in the middle of enemy territory. We could hear Germans shouting excitedly at a church nearby, starting a car and driving furiously off. A quarter of a mile away a German battery was firing out to sea…from positions all around us German ack-ack batteries sent up streams of tracer. The airborne forces had gained their first foothold in France by a daring night landing…but we all of us knew that it'd be harder to hold the ground than it had been to take it.'

Another glider-borne correspondent became the first newsman casualty of the invasion. Ian Fyfe, a young reporter with the *Daily Mirror*, had enthusiastically answered his editor's call for a volunteer to join British troops on a top-secret mission. After a spell of intensive training, Fyfe took his place with men of the 9th Parachute Battalion in a glider bound for France in the early hours of 6 June. Sadly, Fyfe never made the landing for his glider was one of the many lost, probably shot down as they crossed the Normandy coast. No wreckage or bodies were ever discovered and Fyfe was described as 'missing'.

On the western flank of the invasion *Time* correspondent, William Walton, joined the 82nd Airborne Division as they parachuted behind Utah, the US-designated beach. Walton, a qualified parachutist cabled:

'I plunged out of the plane door happy to be leaving a ship that was heading toward flak and more Germans. The jump was from such low altitude that there was only a moment to look around in the moonlight after my chute opened. The fields looked so small that one couldn't miss a tree or hedge. Anyway, I couldn't.

I landed in a pear tree, a rather good shock absorber. But the trouble was I didn't filter through to the ground; instead I dangled about three feet above the ground unable to swing far enough to touch anything.

My chute harness slipped up around my neck in a strangle hold, covering the knife in my breast pocket. I was helpless, a perfect target for snipers and I could hear some of them not far away.

In a hoarse, frightened voice I kept whispering the password, hoping someone would hear and help. From a nearby hedge I heard voices. I hung still for a moment, breathless.

Friends! Then I heard them more clearly. Never has a Middle Western accent sounded better. I called a little louder. Quietly, Sergeant Auge, a fellow I knew, crept out of the hedge, tugged at the branches and with his pigsticker cut my suspension cords. I dropped like an overripe pear.

It took me two seconds flat to struggle out of my harness and drag my type-writer-laden frame into the hedge. There were three of us there, moving through the shadows one by one.

We picked up five more men in the next hour and a half. It was four in the morning before we joined the brigadier general, who headed our jump. He did a wonderful job of assembling the men, forming patrols to guard our perimeter and feel out German strength.

Soon after dawn, he decided our position was not only untenable, it was tough. The only escape was across three-quarters of a mile of swamp to a railway track.

At 7:30, we plunged into the chest-deep swamp, holding our guns overhead and wading. Sometimes you'd step into a pothole up to your neck. When machine-gun bullets started pinging around us the sweat began to trickle. Water filled our pockets and every ounce became a pound. A few men were killed in that crossing, but most of us got across to the railway. By then our last ounce of energy seemed gone. But we went on two miles, panting and puffing up the track to dry land. Snipers were still taking a wham at us every now and then. Half our equipment was gone, but my typewriter was waterproofed, and I have it still.'

With the airborne troops scattered about the flanks and the combined RAF/USAAF bombers hitting gun-emplacements, bridges and roads, the

Germans were now alerted to the anticipated invasion. The American 8th Air Force dropped a vast weight of bombs on the beaches to detonate the extensive minefields as the Allied landing craft began their approach. The Allied warships contributed a huge bombardment on targets further inland.

The Germans had sown the beach area and approaches with a large array of mines and these occupied the minesweepers and engineers in their efforts to clear a path to the beach. One craft that hit a beach-defence mine carried former BBC cricket commentator, Howard Marshall:

'As we drove in we could see shell-bursts in the water along the beach, and just behind the beach, we could see craft in a certain amount of difficulty because the wind was driving the sea in with long rollers and the enemy had prepared anti-invasion, anti-barge obstacles sticking out of from the water – formidable prongs, many of them tipped with mines, so that your landing barge swung and swayed in the rollers; and they're not particularly manageable craft, it would come in contact with one of the mines and be sunk. That was the prospect which faced us on this very lowering and difficult morning as we drove into the beach.

And suddenly, as we tried to get between two of these tri-part defence systems of the Germans, our craft swung, we touched a mine, there was a very loud explosion, a thundering shudder of the whole craft, and water began pouring in.

We were some way out from the beach at that point. The ramp was lowered at once, and out of the barge drove the Bren gun carrier into about five feet of water, with the barge settling heavily in the meanwhile. Well, the Bren gun carrier somehow managed to get through it, and we followed wading ashore. That was one quite typical instance of how people got ashore, and when they got ashore seemed to be in perfectly good order, because the troops out of that barge immediately assembled and went to their appointed places, and there was no semblance of any kind of confusion...

The troops were moving all along the roads, and the tanks were out already and going up the hills, that in fact we dominated the situation; and that our main enemy was the weather and that we were beating the weather; that we had our troops and our tanks ashore, and that the Germans weren't really putting up a great deal of resistance.'

Howard Marshall had been fortunate in landing on one of the few lightly defended beaches. Elsewhere, things were not so easy.

The Americans were having a particularly torrid time at Omaha Beach due, in main, to being blown off course by a mile and landing at heavily defended sections.

The photographer, Robert Capa, was ruminating on his decision to accompany E Company, 16th Infantry Division in the first wave to land on Omaha, and trying to convince himself that the invasion would be a pushover. As the sun slowly rose, the first waves of invasion craft were launched into the choppy sea with predictable results:

'In no time, the men began to puke. But this was a polite as well as a carefully prepared invasion, and little paper bags had been provided for the purpose. Soon the puking hit a new low. I had no idea this would develop into the father and mother of all D-Days.'

The landing craft had been launched miles from the shore and the approach seemed to take hours with the sound of gunfire increasing.

'It was now light enough to start taking pictures, and I brought my first Contax camera out of its waterproof oilskin. The flat bottom of our barge hit the earth of France. The boatswain lowered the steel-covered barge front, and there between the grotesque designs of steel obstacles sticking out of the water, was a thin line of land covered with smoke – our Europe, the "Easy Red" beach.

My beautiful France looked sordid and uninviting, and a German machine gun, spitting bullets around the barge, fully spoiled my return. The men from my barge waded in the water. Waist-deep, with rifles ready to shoot, with the invasion obstacles and smoking beach in the background – this was good enough for the photographer. I paused for a moment on the gangplank to take my first real picture of the invasion. The boatswain, who was in an understandable hurry to get the hell out of there, mistook my picture-taking attitude for inexplicable hesitation, and helped me make up my mind with a well-aimed kick in the rear.

The water was cold and the beach still more than a hundred yards away. The bullets tore holes in the water around me, and I made for the nearest steel obstacle. A soldier got there at the same time, and for a few minutes we shared its cover. He took the waterproofing off his rifle and began to shoot without much aiming at the smoke-hidden beach. The sound of his rifle gave him enough courage to move forward and he left the obstacle to me. It was a foot larger now, and I felt safe enough to take pictures of the other guys hiding just like I was.

I finished my pictures, and the sea was cold in my trousers. Reluctantly I tried to move away from my steel pole, but the bullets chased me back every time. Fifty yards ahead of me, one of our half-burnt amphibious tanks stuck out of the water and offered me my next cover. I sized up the situation...and made for the tank. Between floating bodies I reached it, paused for a few more pictures, and gathered my guts for the last jump to the beach.

The tide was coming in and now the water reached my farewell letter to my family in my breast pocket...I reached the beach and threw myself flat and my lips touched the earth of France. I had no desire to kiss it.'

The Americans had managed to land on Omaha but found themselves unable to advance beyond the low bank which gave them some protection. Capa continued shooting until his roll was finished. When he came to reload his camera, he found that his hands were shaking so much that he could not perform this routine task. The nightmare, for which he had volunteered, was not over.

'The men around me lay motionless. Only the dead on the waterline rolled with the waves. An LCI braved the fire and medics with red crosses painted on their helmets poured from it. I did not think and I didn't decide it. I just stood up and ran toward the boat. I stepped between two bodies and the water reached my neck. The rip tide hit my body and every wave slapped my face under my helmet... I reached the boat. The last medics were just getting out. I climbed aboard. As I reached the deck I felt a shock, and suddenly was all covered with feathers. I thought, "What is this? Is somebody killing chickens?" Then I saw the superstructure had been shot away and that the feathers were the stuffing from the kapok jackets of the men who had been blown away.'

Capa had used three rolls of film and exposed 106 frames, which he delivered for developing. Unfortunately, the darkroom technician was as anxious as Capa to see the invasion images and, in his haste, dried the film too quickly. The excess heat melted the emulsion on all but 10 frames, but these survivors became photographic classics.

Robert Capa had managed to escape uninjured but a fellow American had the unenviable claim of being D-Day's first wounded correspondent. Henry 'Hank' Jameson of AP was accompanying the 9th Air Force Engineers as they landed at Omaha. An 88mm shell hit their landing craft and the force of the explosion threw Jameson against an armoured car, dislocating his shoulder and injuring his leg. He was returned to England and was able to give America its first eye-witness account of the invasion.

The only female war correspondent to land on the first day of the invasion was Martha Gellhorn. She had been relegated by her magazine, *Collier's*, to the position junior to her estranged husband, Ernest Hemingway, and as such, not included amongst the correspondents to accompany the first wave of troops into France.

With little to do but wait, Gellhorn decided to travel to one of the south coast ports where the great armada was setting off for Normandy. Reaching the docks, she saw a white hospital ship and, when challenged by a military-policeman, she explained that she was going to interview the nurses. When he waved her through she climbed aboard the ship, found a toilet and locked herself in. As the ship weighed anchor and began to steam out into the English Channel, she went on deck and, unchallenged by the crew, scribbled down her observations:

> *'The weather gets rainier and colder every minute... a seascape filled with ships, the greatest naval traffic jam in history... so enormous, so awesome, that it felt more like an act of nature than anything man made.'*

As they approached the French coast she heard:

> *'Double and triple clap of gunfire. Barrage balloons looking like comic toy elephants, bouncing in the high wind above the massed ships, and you could hear invisible planes flying behind the gray ceiling of cloud. Troops were unloading from big ships to heavy barges or to light craft, and on the shore, moving up brown roads that scarred the hillside, our tanks clanked slowly and steadily forward.'*

The hospital ship had anchored in the American sector off Omaha Red. Soon LCTs arrived packed with wounded, both American and German, from the beach. Gellhorn found she could be of help by translating and doing non-medical tasks:

'When night came, the water ambulances were still churning in to the beach looking for wounded. Someone on an LCT had shouted that there were maybe a hundred scattered along there somewhere. It was essential to try and get them aboard before the nightly air raid and before the dangerous dark cold could get into their hurt bodies.

Going into shore, unable to see, and not knowing this tricky strip of water, was slow work... We finally got onto a barge near the beach and waded ashore, in water to our waists. Everyone was violently busy on that crowded, dangerous shore. The pebbles were the size of apples and feet deep, and we stumbled up a road that a huge road shovel was scooping out. We walked with the utmost care between the narrowly placed white tape lines that marked the mine-cleared path, and headed for a tent marked with a red cross.

The wounded were being brought here by trucks but the staff from the hospital ship diverted the trucks to the shore-line where the LST was ready to accept the casualties, despite waiting for the tide to change. With nightfall came the threat of enemy aircraft bombing the beach and shallows.

Suddenly our flak and tracers started going up at the far end of the beach. "We've had it now," said the stretcher-bearer. "There isn't any place we can put those wounded." The stretcher-bearer and I said to each other gloomily that, as an air-raid shelter, far better things than the hold of an LST had been devised, and we went inside, not liking any of it, and feeling miserably worried about our wounded...

The ack ack lifted a bit... I clambered like a very awkward monkey up a ladder to get some coffee and so missed the spectacle of two German planes, falling like fiery comets from the sky. They hit the beach to the right and left of us and burned in huge bonfires which lighted up the shore.'

Finally the tide turned and the LST was able to bring the uncomplaining wounded to the hospital ship. Once filled, the ship sailed back to England. Martha Gellhorn filed her story and as a result was punished for crossing to France without permission. She was sent to an American nurses' training camp and told that she could cross to Normandy only when the nurses were ready to go.

Ernest Hemingway was not in the best of shape having been involved in a drunken car crash in London. He had sustained a gash on his head that required fifty-seven stitches and damage to both knees. Nevertheless, he recovered enough to board an attack transport and sail towards Omaha Beach in the seventh wave. Unbeknown to him, his estranged wife was in the same area, the difference being that Hemingway had been designated 'precious cargo' and was forbidden to land with the troops. The American battleship *Texas* was firing over Hemingway's landing craft as they made for the beach. Typically, he captured the sense of men heading for enemy fire:

> *'Those of our troops who were not wax-gray with seasickness, were watching the* Texas *with looks of surprise and happiness. Under steel helmets they looked like pike-men of the Middle Ages to whose aid in battle had suddenly come some strange and unbelievable monster... The big guns sounded though they were throwing whole railway trains across the sky.'*

Hemingway could see infantry advancing up the rising land beyond the beach.

> *'Slowly, laboriously, as though they were Atlas carrying the world on their shoulders, men were climbing. They were not firing. They were just moving slowly... like a tired pack train at the end of the day, going the other way from home.*

Unable to resist a gratuitous result of an explosion, Hemingway wrote:

> *'Meantime, the destroyers had run in almost to the beach and were blowing every pillbox out of the ground with their five-inch guns. I saw a piece of German about three feet long with an arm on it sail high up into the air in the fountaining of one shellburst. It reminded me of a scene in Petroushka.'*

He concluded:

> *'It had been a frontal assault in broad daylight against a mined beach defended by all the obstacles military ingenuity could devise.*

D-DAY

The beach had been defended as stubbornly and as intelligently as any troops could defend it. But every boat from the Dix [Hemingway's transport Dorothea M. Dix*] had landed troops and cargo. No boat was lost through bad seamanship. All that were, were lost by enemy action. And we had taken the beach.'*

In his article published by *Collier's* on 22 July, Hemingway betrays his barely concealed wish to be in command of an assault unit. This time he implied that, without his calm advice and guidance to the young naval lieutenant in command, the landing craft would probably never have reached the beach. He did, however, obey orders and remained on board while the craft disgorged the seasick soldiers. To his annoyance, however, he learned that Martha had landed on the same beach a few hours earlier.

During his enforced stay in England, Hemingway flew with the RAF on several flying missions without mishap. He did, however, narrowly miss injury when a V1 rocket landed nearby in London.

It was not until 18 July that Hemingway managed to return to France. He accompanied one of Patton's armoured divisions as the colourful general returned to what he did best: fighting. Dressed in a new neatly pressed uniform, topped with a shiny black ceremonial helmet, Patton stood on the bonnet of his Jeep and delivered one of his inimitable rallying speeches: *'Men, I'm here to fight beside you. I am going personally to shoot that paper-hanging goddamned son-of-a-bitch just like I would a snake.'*

Another American correspondent, the antithesis of Ernest Hemingway, was Reuter's Marshall Yarrow. Selected to accompany the American airborne troops, he wrote:

'I landed in Normandy with the first glider forces in the invasion, before dawn on D-Day. The aerial procession was a sight I shall never forget. The sky looked like a giant Christmas tree, aglow with heaving clusters of red and green lights.

Great balls of fire started to stream through our glider as we circled to land. I loosened my safety belt to remove my Mae West and could not get it fastened in the excitement. I was thrown to the floor as our glider smashed and jarred on the earth, slid across the field, and crashed into a ditch. For a moment I lay half stunned but the red-hot zip of machine-gun bullets an inch or two above my head revived me in a hurry. I took a wild dive out of the emergency door and fell into a ditch, waist-deep in stinking water overlaid with scum. We had landed in a strongly defended zone several miles from our designated point. Lights still glowed in the glider. There was a deafening crash: a mortar shell had split it in half.

I don't know why, but I looked at my watch. It was 4.15 am. Mortars and machine-guns chattered. I was – and I admit it – in a panic. My one desire was to get home. I must have got out of the glider on the wrong side because I was all alone. For a moment I thought of all my friends and wondered what the office would think if I failed to get any dispatches from me. I wrote myself off as a dead loss – literally and figuratively. I clung to the mud and prayed... '

Later in the day, the airborne troops had managed to organise themselves and drove the Germans from a nearby village. To Yarrow's dismay:

'Ten minutes later, the Germans counter-attacked and the war started all over again. Eager to keep out of trouble, I hiked for the woods and spent a miserable night with an American colonel and a very dolorous sow in a clump of super-sharp raspberry bushes. Then I proceeded to the HQ establishment. It was a hike along the hedges of about three miles, and I know I shall be permanently humpbacked from keeping my head down. A sergeant who watched me from a distance introduced me to his friends as the "best in the hedge-crawling business". It is an honour I am proud to accept. Whatever else, correspondents do make some contribution to the war effort. I calculate the Germans used about 5,000 rounds of ammunition on me that first day.'

Marshall Yarrow was later quoted by UFO experts for spotting some unusual phenomena in the skies over German-held territory. Published on 13 December 1944, he wrote:

'The Germans have produced a "secret" weapon in keeping with the Christmas season. The new device, which is apparently an air defence system, and resembles the glass balls that adorn Christmas trees. They have been seen hanging in the air over German territory, sometimes singly, sometime in clusters. They are coloured silver and are apparently transparent.'

On one of the British beaches, Richard Dimbleby was amazed to see that the tremendous battle that was raging all about did not interrupt the routine of one civilian:

> *'Long stretches of empty roads shining with rain, deserted, dripping woods, and damp fields – static, quiet – perhaps uncannily quiet – and possibly not to remain quiet. But here and there a movement catches the eye, as our aircraft on reconnaissance roar over a large and suspicious wood – three German soldiers running like mad across the main road to fling themselves into cover.*
>
> *And nearer the battle area, much nearer the battle area than they, a solitary peasant harrowing his field, up and down behind the horses, looking nowhere but before him and at the soil.'*

On the night of 8/9 June, the Royal Navy destroyer, HMS *Beagle*, was involved in a dramatic rescue. She was accompanying a small convoy of American LSTs (Landing Ships Tanks) bound for Utah Beach on the Cotentin Peninsula, when they were attacked by a couple of German E-boats in enemy waters, about 18 miles north-east of Barfleur. The Reuter's correspondent, Desmond Tighe was on board and reported in the *Evening News* of: *'The most courageous and cold-bloodied rescue venture I have ever seen.'*

With *Beagle* leading the convoy, the E-boats managed to get amongst the lumbering craft and torpedo two of the LSTs, which began to blaze furiously. *Beagle* immediately turned towards the stricken craft and attempted a rescue in a sea lit up like a bonfire. She lowered scrambling nets, threw lines and launched a whaler in an attempt to pluck as many as she could from the freezing water. The survivors were hauled aboard, covered in oil and shivering with cold. One of the LSTs had sunk but the fire on the other had gone out. She was still carrying her precious supply of tanks, Jeeps and other equipment, but had drifted into a known minefield. Tighe wrote:

> *'Steaming inside the minefield off the peninsula of Cherbourg, a British destroyer, HMS* Beagle, *...saved the lives of some American soldiers from a blazing tank landing craft... It was 2am. With rain falling, when the craft was struck, and as we began rescue work the destroyer's searchlights were deliberately turned on, illuminating the grey waters and the struggling figures. The blazing hulk of the landing craft made us stand out as an easy target. The bravery of the*

Beagle's *officers and ship's company was something I shall never forget.'*

The *Beagle* managed to rescue over 250 American servicemen. The ship's captain fretted that he would probably be court martialled for endangering his ship but, in the event, the American command heaped enough praise upon him that no charges were brought.

The E-boats operating out of Cherbourg and Le Havre were considered such a potential menace that Admiral Ramsay, the Allied naval commander-in-chief, requested Bomber Command to attack these bases. He also ordered his own fast craft, the Motor Gun Boats, to carry out an anti-E-boat sweep in the Cherbourg area. It was during one of these exercises was that another British correspondent was killed. On 11 June, Arthur Alfred Thorpe of the *Exchange Telegraph*, died from machine-gunfire while standing next to the captain of a MGB during an attack on an E-boat flotilla.

Bill Downs, the boisterous and hard-working CBS correspondent, reporting from the British sector found the relative German and Allied positions difficult to identify:

'There is no definite front line in this Battle of France. I found that out the other day when I made a trip to within a mile of the town of Tilly, directly south of Bayeux. The countryside is very close, with high, thick hedges along the roads. Patches of woodland dot the countryside. The wheat and oats and rye are high, about ready for a good harvest. It is a sort of concentrated Iowa. It is perfect country for snipers.

We were driving down one road when we came to a clear patch. We heard the crack of a Spandau machine gun – and before we realised what it was, there was another burst of fire. The dust alongside our Jeep spurted as if it had come alive. A sniper had taken a crack at us. Luckily his aim was bad. We got out of there in a hurry.

Further down the road, we came upon some very fresh Germans. They were lying in the road, killed a few hours before. But we saw tank tracks and decided to follow up. Then we came to a group of Tommies crouching behind a group of farm buildings next to an orchard. We joined them and discovered to our surprise that they were men of the Reconnaissance Corps. They were looking for German tank infiltration... needless to say, we were not. It was no place to be armed only with a pencil.'

160

With the Allies established on the 60 miles of beaches from the Orne River in the east to the Cotentin Peninsula in the west, they set about breaking out of Normandy. They were aided by the Franco-American-led invasion of southern France, code named Operation Dragoon, which had the effect of diverting some enemy resources and securing the undamaged dock facilities at Marseille. The FFI (Forces Françaises de Intérieur) made their presence felt by disrupting the railway system thus delaying German reinforcements arriving in enough numbers to withstand the Allied advance.

Probably the most important reason for the Germans being starved of reinforcements was the launch of a huge Russian offensive, code named Operation Bagration, along the entire Eastern Front during June to September. By October the Russians had reached the outskirts of Warsaw, taken Romania and entered East Prussia.

Despite these obstructions, diversions and desperate news from the east, the Germans put up a stiff resistance, especially at Caen, where the British and Canadians were unable to penetrate the town's defences. In the west, the Americans had become bogged down in the advance towards St Lô. Finally, both these tough-nuts were taken by mid to late July.

The *News Chronicle* correspondent, Norman Maynard Clark and Cornelius Ryan of *The Daily Telegraph* had arrived with General George Patton's Third Army in July.[56]

Clark later recalled that he found Patton: '*an able and witty man. Highly intelligent.*' Asked why the Allies had not closed the Falaise Gap and encircled the Germans, Patton explained: '*When you get rats in a sack you leave the neck open to allow them to escape and then hit them hard there.*'

Both correspondents had witnessed the final fall of St Lô and had reached the west coast of the Cherbourg Peninsula at the small village of Genets. Across the estuary stood the tidal island commune of Mont St Michel, connected to the mainland by a causeway.[57] Word came to them that the German garrison wished to surrender. Until a few days ago the garrison was 200 strong, but had been withdrawn leaving just four Germans to man an observation post at the top of the town.

Clark and Ryan composed a note inviting the Germans to surrender:

'German Soldiers – Our armoured forces are actually beyond Pontorson. You are cut off and cannot escape. The war is over for you, but you can save yourselves by surrendering.

To surrender you must come to Genets without weapons and accompanied by a guide and carrying a white flag which is clearly visible.

A local fisherman took the note across the estuary but returned in the early hours with the news that the four prisoners were waiting to be captured. Clark and another unnamed correspondent volunteered to wade across the 2-3 miles of estuary guided by the fisherman. The way was littered with mines referred to as 'Rommel's Asparagus', but the guide was able to bring them through safely.

Ryan chose to drive across at low tide with his driver and two members of the village resistance group, where they joined their companions. He recalled:

'All the inhabitants of Mont St Michel came out to greet us. They threw flowers and gifts. To one side, standing complete with their equipment, stood our four prisoners waiting to be transported back. They certainly were a sorry spectacle, and the people here were not slow in showing what they thought of them.

Our driver, the only member of our party with a gun, searched them and locked them up in a gaol and pocketed the key. Then the Mayor gave a long speech, thanking us for coming and invited us to lunch.

Speech after speech was made by the resistance group, while in the narrow cobbled roadway, people sang songs. Flags mysteriously appeared and everyone wore tricolour rosettes.

This continued for hours, but we were in an awkward situation. We had not seen any American soldiers for some hours – except for a small patrol which came into the town after we arrived. We gave them two prisoners and they left. We did not know how far our troops had reached, and whether we now commanded the countryside.

A little after midnight the coastline erupted with AA fire as German planes began bombing the Pontorson road. One crashed in flames less than a mile away. Another fell just behind the Mount and burned fiercely on the sands.

In the morning a German pilot surrendered to us outside the town. Then, with the cheers of the townsfolk ringing in our ears, we set off in triumph with our prisoners.'

Norman Clark recalled that after the celebratory lunch, the correspondents were presented with the bill for the champagne: 'very Norman!' Also he remembered that Ernest Hemingway arrived the following day, obnoxiously drunk and insulting, boasting how he had been involved in the nearby fighting. It would appear that legends rarely seem all that legendary to their contemporaries and peers.

Hemingway liked Mont St Michel and, for a few weeks, it became a rest and recreation target for his drinking cronies like Robert Capa, William Walton, Charles Collingwood and the *New Yorker* writer, A.J. Liebling. The lunches were long with Hemingway at the head of the table dominating any discussion. This remained their bolt-hole until the breakout was achieved and Paris became the next news story.

Chapter 13

Paris and the Race for the German Border

Both Generals Eisenhower and Bradley had no plans for an immediate liberation of the French capital. Their intention was to bypass Paris, which had little strategic importance, and head at all speed for the German border. These plans were thwarted by the appearance of Roger Gallois, a French Resistance leader, who pleaded the case for taking the city.

He said that the Parisian Maquis had risen against the German occupiers but were under intense pressure and in danger of being defeated. Paradoxically, the German commander in Paris, General Dietrich von Choltitz, had been ordered by Hitler to destroy the city before surrendering it to the Allies. Von Choltitz was loath to carry out such an outrageous instruction but the Führer's order had to be obeyed. The only way he could get around the problem was to send word to Gallois to urge the Allies to hurry and occupy the city.

While Montgomery's army headed north to Belgium and the Netherlands, the main American force, together with General Leclerc's French 2nd Armoured Division approached Paris from the south-west. Word soon got out of this change of plan and dozens of correspondents clamoured for the opportunity to cover this story as well take the opportunity of a break from living rough. Having left the Cotentin Peninsula, there was still fighting to do to clear Brittany of the enemy and the towns of Le Mans and Rennes soon fell. The apparently unstoppable advance reached the cathedral city of Chartres, south-west of Paris. It was from here that the last report by the *Los Angeles Times* and NBC correspondent, Thomas Treanor, was published on 18 August 1944 the day before he died from injuries sustained when an American tank swerved and crushed his Jeep.

'We came to a bridge which had just been blown up by a German paratrooper... who had landed behind our lines just before the fight. He had gone to the bridge, hung his explosive, attached a wire to it and then had run the wire to a fox hole alongside the road... where he waited for a good opportunity to throw the switch and blow some truck or tank to kingdom come.

But he seems to have lost his nerve because he blew the bridge when there was nothing on it. At the moment of explosion, thirty-two Germans who stationed themselves in the area, opened up on the bridge with machine-guns, driving some nearby combat engineers to cover.

One engineer, Corporal John O'Brien of West New York, NJ, dived into the hole where the German paratrooper had hid and landed on top of him. The German surrendered to O'Brien and his commanding officer.'

Treanor went on to describe the sniping from the cathedral towers and the treatment of collaborators: *'I remarked to one woman in the crowd that I could not understand why nearly all the collaboratists (sic) were women. She looked at me as though I were a simpleton and laughed heartedly.'*

Another incident he witnessed was the discovery of an unnamed war correspondent:

'We visited a hospital where a wounded British correspondent had been found. He had been ambushed and shot in the stomach. The Germans had picked him up and laid him on the hood of their car and taken him to a military hospital.

While engaged in this Good Samaritan act they incidentally stole his wallet, stole 150 pounds in American traveller's cheques which they can never cash, stripped off all his clothes and finally took his wrist watch. The medic who took his watch explained, "We are your kamerads and have been very good to you".'[58]

The British correspondent he mentions was undoubtedly Bill Makin of Kemsley Newspapers. He had been severely wounded when a group of war correspondents, including Alexander MacGowan of the *New York World-Telegram and Sun*, ran into an ambush by two machine-gun firing German light tanks. Captured by the Germans, Makin was taken 50 miles on the bonnet of a military vehicle to a hospital near Chartres and operated on by a German surgeon. When the Germans evacuated the area, he was treated by the Americans but succumbed to his wounds on 26 August 1944.[59]

MacGowan's capture was reported around the world and the *New York Times* headline read: 'MACGOWAN OF SUN CAPTURED IN FRANCE. NAZIS REPORT COMPANION HURT IN SCRAPE.' A couple of days later, the 60-year-old MacGowan managed to elude his captors by leaping from a prisoner-of-war train in the middle of the night and making his way back to Allied lines.[60]

Ernest Hemingway, tiring of travelling in the dust of Patton's tanks, attached himself to the Paris-bound 4th Division and the 22nd Infantry in particular. The 22nd's commander was Colonel Charles 'Buck' Lanham. Both men formed a strong bond, and Hemingway used Lanham as the model for the hero, Robert Cantwell, in his novel, *Across the River and into the Trees*.[61]

Norman Clark joined the Free French 2nd Division commanded by General Leclerc as they entered Paris through the Quai de Lyon in the south of the city. The population were ecstatic in their welcome and Clark, as the only man in British uniform, came in for particularly enthusiastic mobbing from the women. Later he found that the correspondents were billeted in the Hôtel Scribe, which seemed appropriate for the journalists.

Clark recalled that as they were in the hotel's reception, one of his fellow correspondents, Paul Bewsher of the *Daily Mail*, received a mixed surprise. In 1940 Bewsher was staying at the Hôtel Scribe but was forced to leave Paris in a hurry when the Germans gained entry. As Bewsher registered he was handed his clean laundry, which he had left behind, together with his unpaid bill.

Norman Clark described the scenes in Paris over the next few days, with collaborators being beaten and sometimes shot. One day he met a Belgian dentist and his wife and was invited to their penthouse suite at the Hôtel de Crillon overlooking the Place de la Concorde. The pleasant little party was interrupted by gunfire and Clark wandered over to the balustrade to investigate. He found that a Vichy Milice gunman had opened up with a machine gun on the crowds below and was firing from a position by a water tower just above where he was standing. The French troops below were returning fire and Clark had to endure the exchange with bits of the hotel falling on his prone form.

Coincidentally, this incident was being broadcast live from below by the BBC's Richard Dunnett and was heard by Norman Clark's wife. To the accompaniment of gunfire, an excitable Dunnett reported:

'Somebody had fired out on the crowd from the Hôtel Crillon and the tanks are firing back – the tanks massed in the square are firing back at the hotel, and I'm standing looking just straight across at it – smoke – smoke rising... the tanks were all lined up facing the hotel, and they gave it a tremendous salvo. But the crowds are keeping remarkably calm really. They've managed to get behind the tanks and they're just pushing their way back. There's no disorder, no rioting – pushing their way back as the tanks open up again, and blast a hole in the building. I can see smoke coming out. The tanks have shot at the left-hand corner of the building and just under where the flag of France is flying – it's a remarkable thing, because a lot of people were standing on the roof.'

One of course was Norman Clark. When the firing died down, he went down to reception where the manager spotted his British uniform and sent him with a half a dozen armed resistance fighters to search for the snipers. Somewhat reluctantly Clark helped search all the rooms and finally came to the sniper's nest by the water tower. He found the petrified figure of a hotel porter in his green baize apron lying with a machine gun resting on his stomach which the sniper had left as he made his escape.

Ernest Hemingway, now happily attached to General Barton's 4th Division, was having the time of his life. In what could hardly be described as a love note, he wrote to Mary Welsh: *'Life was jolly, full of shooting and fighting over small hills, along dusty roads, in and out of wheat fields, with burned-out enemy tanks, wrecked Kraftwagons, captured 88s, and the dead from both sides.'*

Hemingway invited his photographer friend Robert Capa, to join him as there was plenty of opportunities to take pictures of fighting. Capa found Hemingway had been made an honorary member of the 4th Division and General Barton had assigned him his own staff: a public relations officer, a cook, a driver, a photographer and a former motorbike champion called Red Pelkey.

Learning of a small village which supposedly had been taken by part of the 4th Division, Hemingway decided to take his entourage to investigate. Taking the lead, with Pelkey driving the motorbike, Hemingway roared ahead, with Capa and the others following more discreetly in a Jeep. As the motor-cycle combination rounded a bend, a shell landed close to Hemingway's bike and he was thrown into a ditch. Pelkey ran and joined Capa's Jeep protected by the curve. A barely concealed Hemingway came under fire from tracer bullets fired by a German tank standing at the entrance to the village.

When he finally made it to safety, Hemingway was furious with Capa for standing by in the hopes of taking a picture of the writer's dead body. This spat decided Capa that service with Hemingway was too unpredictable and he voted to rejoin the proper army.

Undeterred Hemingway formed what he described as a reconnaissance group of FFI fighters he found in Villedieu-les-Poêles, a village near Paris. Deciding that they were in need of leadership and were not adequately armed, Hemingway managed to persuade a quartermaster to release a supply of guns and grenades.[62]

Word of this soon reached the authorities and an investigation took place at a hotel in Rambouillet. The charges against him were serious and he was in danger of losing his correspondent's credentials. In the event, he managed to persuade the senior officers that he did not carry arms and that his little scouting group had supplied useful information. Cautioned about his status as a war correspondent, Hemingway realised that he had pushed his luck and in future he did stick to the rules.

Another correspondent who overstepped the mark was the independently wealthy and charming Charles Collingwood of CBS. Not for him the tedium and discomfort of living under canvas with the rest of the war correspondents, for he was always able to find a handy chateau or hotel to host lavish parties and dinners. Naturally his guest list included high-ranking officers and he built up an enviable information network. In his quest to be first with the news, he wrote a detailed and emotional account of the entry into Paris – an event that had not yet happened. When he finished typing, he recorded the story on his tape recorder and sent it off to the London office with instructions not to send it to America until he gave the word. Through a combination of administrative errors, the tape was sent and broadcast in America. When the public heard the news, there was great jubilation with dancing in the streets, car horns blaring and the name of Charles Collingwood printed on the front-page of every newspaper.

As if to reinforce Collingwood's story, the BBC broadcast a bulletin in support. This, however, came from a different source: namely Captain André Vernon, head of the Resistance information office in London. Vernon had shamelessly written a false news bulletin that: *'Paris had liberated itself.'* He admitted he had done it to put pressure on the Allies to enter Paris as soon as possible.

Back at Rambouillet, the news was greeted with astonishment and anger by the dozens of correspondents waiting for Leclerc's 2nd Division to march on the city. In Collingwood's case, he managed to blame military press officers and censors for the error, which few believed. When other stories replaced the Paris liberation, Collingwood's unethical attempt at a scoop was soon forgotten, if not forgiven, by most of his peers. It would appear that as long as you had fame and good contacts, as in the case of Ernest Hemingway and Charles Collingwood, you could get away with a mild rebuke.

On 29 August, after General De Gaulle had laid flowers at the tomb of the Unknown Soldier at the Arc de Triomphe, he drove to Notre Dame Cathedral for a thanksgiving service. Helen Kirkpatrick was on hand to describe the scene:

'The general's car arrived on the dot at 4.15. As they stepped from the car, we stood at salute and at that moment a revolver shot rang out. It seemed to come from behind one of Notre Dame's gargoyles. Within a split second a machine gun opened up from behind the Hotel de Ville. It sprayed the pavement at my feet. The generals entered the church with people pressing from behind to find shelter.

Suddenly an automatic opened up behind us – it came from behind the pipes of Notre Dame's organ. Other shots rang out and I saw a man ducking behind a pillar above. Beside me FFI men and police were shooting. For one flashing instant it seemed a great massacre was about to take place as the cathedral reverberated with the sound of guns. There was a sudden blaze and a machine gun sprayed the centre aisle, flecking the tiles and chipping the pillars to my left. Time seemed to have no meaning. Spontaneously, a crowd of widows and bereaved burst forth into the Te Deum as the general stood bareheaded before the altar.'

Bill Reid of the BBC took up the description:

'It was a most extraordinary scene, as the snipers were spotted around the gallery by the police and by the soldiers, and there was a smell of cordite right throughout the cathedral. But Paris had come to celebrate the solemn Te Deum with General de Gaulle at the head of them. And then, when it was all over, the general marched right down the aisle; heaven knows how they missed him, for they

were firing the whole time; there were blinding flashes inside the cathedral, there were pieces of stone ricocheting around the place.'

The Notre Dame outbreak appeared to be the signal for similar desperate acts to start throughout the city. Douglas Williams of *The Daily Telegraph* witnessed some of these:

'As we drove back to the Ritz Hotel shots rang out in several streets. The Rue de Rivoli was deserted as we drove rapidly down it. The Place Vendôme was equally empty. Passers by were crouching in doorways watching a group of Maquis exchanging shots with snipers on the top floor of a house next to the Ministry of Finance.'

Very quickly these desperate last ditch acts were soon mopped up and the correspondents, somewhat reluctantly, rejoined the advance on the German border.

The British and the Canadians had not been involved in the Paris liberation. Instead, they were heading north towards Belgium and the Netherlands in an effort to overrun the V-weapon sites that were terrorising the population of London and the south of England. The Germans had launched their first attack with these retaliatory weapons on 13 June 1944 in response to the D-Day landings. After this initial launch of ten V-1s, the attacks became sustained at a rate of about 100 a day.[63]

Having crossed the Seine, taken Rouen and made Le Havre untenable for the E-boats based there, the 2nd Canadian Division had the satisfaction of capturing Dieppe and avenging the memory of their losses two years earlier.

Frank Gillard of the BBC was with the Canadians as they entered the town on 1 September:

'Many of these troops were the same men who'd made that gallant attack just over two years ago. What a memorable return this was. At one point in the town the people had crowded out into the road, leaving only a very narrow lane for the traffic to pass through. We wondered why until we reached the spot, and then we saw. A Nazi flag was spread out on the ground, and you were simply obliged to drive right over the swastika and trample it in the dust...

It was about the flying-bombs that the people wanted to talk to British people like myself. They reeled off a great list of bomb sites just around Dieppe which are lost to the enemy. Most of them, they told us, had been blown up by the Germans a few days ago. They described how these robots used to come over the town just after they were launched – how any amount of them crashed into the sea – how some exploded within a few seconds of being sent off. They were anxious to know how the people of Britain are standing up to these attacks and how much damage is being done.'

Now the 'bomb-coast' and the road to Belgium were wide open and the Germans were in full retreat. Chester Wilmot reported:

'The British Second Army is going hell for leather to the buzz-bomb bases. Our troops know that the task is to get the flying-bomb sites and there's no holding them. Already British columns have overrun five sites which the Germans had prepared for the launching of flying-bombs and one that was to be used for the V-2. . .

For twenty-four hours the survivors of the German Seventh Army and the fifth Panzer Army have been virtually without orders. Their Commander – General der Panzertruppen Heinrich Hans Eberbach – was captured early yesterday morning. He was taken by surprise at his tactical headquarters in the woods just south of Amiens. As the British tanks came in one side of the wood about half-past six, the general and two officers of his personal staff jumped for their cars and tried to race out the other side, past the English tanks which were fast outflanking them. Machine gun bullets riddled the cars. The occupants dived to a ditch and the tank crews raced in to grab their prisoners.'

It was decided to bypass the northern French ports of Boulogne, Calais and Dunkirk and to leave the German garrisons to 'wither on the vine'. Unlike the Canadians with Dieppe, the British were denied the opportunity of taking Dunkirk, the site of their greatest defeat. Christopher Buckley of *The Daily Telegraph* wrote a piece about the efforts the German Command made to keep up the morale of these isolated garrisons which had no chance of being relieved. Fast E-boats were making the dash from the islands at the mouth of the Scheldt to deliver supplies and distribute and collect mail:

'The letters were written. An army lorry kept exclusively for the transport of this mail was despatched. As might have been expected,

this truck drove straight into our lines only a few miles from the city. Within a few hours, transcripts had been made of a number of these captured letters, which were subsequently printed and dropped as leaflets upon the German troops inside Calais – an appropriate way of blowing the gaff upon the claims made by the German Command.'

Matthew Halton of CBC interviewed General Brian Horrocks, commanding XXX Corps, who described this confusing period:

'And strange things are happening round about. The general said that the other day a Panther tank got loose in our rear and decided to shoot up one of our camps or laagers. The laager it chose to attack was an anti-tank regiment full of 17-pounder anti-tank guns. In less than a minute that tank was shot through with sixteen anti-tank shells. Sometimes we find German trucks driving along the road in one of our convoys. At that the general said: "My rear headquarters keep complaining that I have left them in the middle of the German Army."'

All the Allied liberators could count on being mobbed by a population ecstatically grateful. None more so than Belgium which produced the observation that the Allies 'coming into Belgium found their welcome more warm hearted than in France.'

Chester Wilmot described the approach to Brussels as he rode along with the Guards Armoured Division:

'Their main trouble was not dealing with the scattered German resistance but getting through the crowds who thronged the roadsides every mile from the frontier to Brussels... cheering, laughing, shouting people with wild delight in their voices and tears of joy in their eyes. They didn't wait for the Germans to go. As the news of our coming spread like wildfire from village to village, along main roads from Tournai to Brussels, Belgian women and children went down into cellars and cupboards to produce a mass of flags, streamers, rosettes, banners, placards and dresses that they'd been getting ready for months for this very day.

On the outskirts of Brussels we were halted again by a traffic block and suddenly machine-guns opened fire from a wood beside the road. Tanks swung their guns round and fired. Civilians threw themselves upon the ground, troops jumped from lorries and raced into the woods from one side while armed civilians went in from the other.. They collected twenty-five Germans from what had been a headquarters, and as the Germans left, Belgian civilians – men and women – swarmed in and came out with bottles of wine and beer, boxes of cigars and cigarettes, chocolates and sweets that had belonged to the Germans, and they pressed them into the hands of the British troops.

And so we went on until we came to Brussels itself, and there our welcome was wildest of all.'

It took just ten days to occupy Belgium, with the exception of the Scheldt estuary. The task of taking this waterlogged area fell to the Canadian Army who took a further month of hard fighting to overcome the well-established German defenders.[64]

Meanwhile, the American XX and XX11 Corps barely paused at Paris before continuing their advance towards the German border through Alsace-Lorraine. Norman Clark joined this advance and a little way outside Paris, he was with an armoured column that approached a small town. Here they found a train full of Germans and their Parisian girlfriends waiting at the station. A round or two from the tanks disabled the steam locomotive which persuaded the escaping Germans to surrender.

Clark recalled that their advance was so rapid with little opposition that he was with a patrol that crossed the German border on 3 September. Here they left their mark by setting fire to a village in the Moselle region before retiring. Because of the rapidity of the advance, the Americans had outstripped their supplies, so they pulled back to Nancy, which became their winter headquarters.

Chapter 14

Arnhem

With momentum favouring the Allies, they started to make miscalculations. Following their sweep through France and Belgium, the Allies were poised to enter the Netherlands from where they could attack the German industrial centre of the Ruhr. In order to do this, they needed to cross the Nederrijn or Lower Rhine in the north and thus avoid the formidable Siegfried Line. In between were three vital bridges which General Montgomery was confident could be taken before the Germans could destroy them and he obtained Eisenhower's agreement to mount this bold operation.

Codenamed Operation Market-Garden, the plan was to drop airborne troops at Eindhoven in the south, Nijmegen in the centre on the River Maas and Arnhem in the north. They were to hold the bridges and wait for the British armoured columns to race north up the only highway linking all three crossings. Out of necessity, these ground units had to advance on a very narrow front as the surrounding areas were unsuitable for armoured vehicles. The timetable was ambitious for they were expected to cover the 60 miles in two to four days. Despite these seemingly unlikely targets, the normally cautious Montgomery and his team thought the prize was worth the risk.

On the early afternoon of 17 September, the Market part of the operation began with the American 101st Airborne division landing by parachute and glider around the industrial city of Eindhoven. They managed to secure four of the five bridges assigned to them. A little earlier the Garden section of the advance began with the British XXX Corps moving across the Dutch frontier and dashing the 20 miles to join the 101st Airborne. Almost from the start, the Germans made life difficult for the vulnerable road-bound column. Chester Wilmot was with the advance:

'We attacked yesterday on a narrow front. Our tanks just had to batter their way down the main road, for the surrounding country is too sandy and swampy for the tanks to move over it. The tanks went forward behind an intense barrage from massed guns, which concentrated their fire down the sides of the road, over an area only five miles deep, and one and a half miles wide. Thousands of rounds came down along the side of the roads, but the gunners had orders to avoid the road itself, so that craters wouldn't impede our advance. I saw only five places today where shells had hit the road.

The barrage silenced the Germans at first: our leading squadron of tanks shot its way through the German roadblock, slipped through minefields that lined the road, and drove on with machine-guns and cannons firing into the trees on either side. But when the next squadron came up, with the infantry riding on the backs of the tanks, it came under a hail of fire as it reached the middle of a small clearing. There the Germans had laid an ambush with anti-tank guns and bazookas hidden only a hundred yards off the road. Within a couple of minutes, nine of our tanks were on fire. Fortunately nearly all the crews got out, and the infantry riding on top dived into roadside ditches and opened fire. By this time, other tanks farther back had spotted one German gun: they shot it up, and the crew surrendered. But the tanks had no means of sending the prisoners back, so they were ordered to ride on the backs of the tanks. The Germans were so scared that they immediately told our troops exactly where the other German guns were. The tanks called in the Typhoons, and they did the rest.'

Wilmot's BBC colleague, Cyril Ray, recalled:

'I was sour on it. For me, the whole of Market Garden was a dead flop. I had been due to go to Arnhem, but was taken out of that and sent with the Americans. I was the only Englishman there, except for Corps HQ. I felt sure that the British had had it, and before I was switched to Nijmegen, felt my goose was cooked... I felt this was a much safer option, and meanwhile all the chaps at Arnhem were dead ducks. Lots of people knew Arnhem was wrong, at the time. Browning [General Frederick 'Boy' Browning] told me that he had said to Montgomery that it was "one bridge too far".'

Ray was greatly impressed by the 82nd but had doubts about how he should report them:

> *'I thought it unlikely that the British public would appreciate that the best-trained and most professional airborne unit engaged in the operation of which Arnhem was a part was the United States 82nd Division.'*

He went on to say that: *'the 1st British Airborne Division was both insufficiently trained in street-fighting and under a commander it didn't know.'*

Ray's comments were echoed by some of the experienced members of the 1st Airborne Division. In Max Hastings' book *Armageddon* he quotes one veteran:

> *'The young recruits and officers seemed so innocent. In my platoon many blokes were fresh out of training. We had lost a lot of good chaps in Sicily and Italy. There wasn't the same spirit now. How could there be?'*

The 82nd did, however, have some advantages over the 1st British. They had gliders that could land heavy anti-tank guns and their radio sets worked. Also, they were commanded by the young and dashing General James Gavin, who had been in charge for much of their existence. Gavin endeared himself to his men by being the first man out on a parachute drop. It was Gavin who wisely decided to take the Groesbeek Heights between Nijmegen and the Reichswald Forest preventing any attack from across the German border.[65]

They had not, however, captured the main 600 yard-long bridge over the Waal. The Germans, alerted by the capture of Eindhoven and parachute drops, had rushed reinforcements to deny the Americans the southern end of the bridge. Even when the Armoured Division arrived, they could not penetrate the enemy's defences. With no other crossing within 25-miles either side of the bridge, the Americans had to improvise. Bill Downs of CBS reported that on the morning of the 20th:

> *'On Wednesday morning the infantry made their way westward through the town and got to the industrial outskirts along the river bank near the mouth of a big canal. Some British tanks went with*

*them to give them protection in the street fighting and to act as
artillery when the crossings were to be made. Accompanying them
were trucks carrying 26 assault boats in case of such an emergency.
Most of the men who were to make the crossing had never handled
an assault boat before.'*

The Germans got wind of this westward movement and rushed troops to
oppose the crossing:

*'The task force was under heavy shellfire, and several hundred
Germans with machine-guns were sitting on the opposite bank waiting
for the crossing. This was about noon. It was decided that the original
plan would proceed, but this time the men crossing the river would
have the help of heavy bombers – Lancasters and Stirlings flying in
daylight to drop their bombs on the opposite bank in tactical support
of the men from the assault boats.*

*At last everything was ready. The bombers went in, but didn't drop
their bombs close enough to knock out the machine-guns... The
shelling continued. Every man took a deep breath and climbed in...
and off across the river they started. At the same time, behind them,
the British tanks fired their heavy guns and our own heavy machine-
guns fired into the opposite bank giving the little fleet as much cover
as possible. A smoke-screen was laid, but it wasn't very effective
because of the wind.*

*And over on the other side of the river the enemy tracers shrieked
at the boats. The fire at first was erratic, but as the boats approached
the northern bank the tracers began to spread on to the boats. Men
slumped in their seats – other men could be seen shifting a body to
take over the paddling. One man rose up in his seat and fell
overboard. There was no thought of turning back. The paddling
continued clumsily and erratically, but it continued. One of the boats
had so many holes in it the men were baling out with their helmets –
it was also splintered when it reached the other side.*

*The fighting, though, had just begun. The 100 or so men who
arrived on the opposite bank fought their way forward with bayonet
and grenade, going from one machine-gun nest to another until they
had established a bridgehead only a few yards deep and several
hundred feet wide... The men on the opposite bank, seeing the
casualties suffered in the landing under fire, were not waiting for the*

boats. Some of them had stripped off their equipment and, taking a bandolier of ammunition, were swimming the river with their rifles on their backs… After an hour and a half of concentrated hell, the infantry was over.'

An attack on an old fort overlooking the northern end of the bridge silenced several 88mm guns that had covered the bridge. There was still heavy fighting to be done until the Americans finally captured the northern end of the bridge. After stubborn resistance, the Allies took the southern end with the vital bridge unblown by the Germans.

With the two objectives secured, albeit taking longer than anticipated, XXX Corps moved towards Arnhem and the relief of the 1st British Airborne Division just ten miles away. The narrow road, nicknamed 'Hell's Highway' by the Allied troops, was now heavily defended by the Germans and progress was disappointingly slow.

Frank Gillard described the problems on the BBC:

'Now the fighting became even more bitter. The position of our airborne troops beyond the Neder Rhine around Arnhem was becoming critical. On 21 September, Thursday, the Second Army battle on towards Arnhem. The enemy resisted fiercely. He fought his way back hedge to hedge and cottage to cottage. Our armour was moving in country where deployment was impossible. Each road ran along a high embankment. It was difficult to get off it and every vehicle moving along it made a perfect target silhouetted against the sky. Rain poured down interminably. The low-lying fields became swamps.'

By this time the men at Arnhem were into their fifth day of waiting for reinforcements. They had parachuted or landed by glider on the 17th along with the groups at Eindhoven and Nijmegen. Accompanying the 1st British Airborne Division was a Public Relations Team commanded by 31-year-old Major Roy Oliver.[66] Besides signallers, army photographers and censors, the group included two BBC correspondents, Stanley Maxted and Guy Byam, and two newspaper journalists, Alan Wood of the *Daily Express* and Jack Smyth of Reuters.

Stanley Maxted described the landing by glider:

'It gave some sickening bumps on landing, then braked quickly to a stop. At the same moment a yell came from the cockpit: "Out, out,

everybody out". The side-door slid up and I jumped blindly, landing on soft ground among young turnips. I started to run; looking up I saw another fleet of planes without gliders. Wisps of something started to stream from them: then suddenly the sky blossomed into many-coloured flowers that floated down with tiny dolls of men jerking and swinging below them…

Meantime machine-gun and rifle fire seemed to be all around.'

Later Maxted recorded:

'Just a few minutes ago the fighter cover showed up and right behind them came those lovely supply planes which you can hear up above us now. Yesterday and this morning our supplies came and were dropped in the wrong place. The enemy got them, but now these planes have come over and they've dropped them right dead over us.'

Instead of the light opposition that the paras expected, they were confronted by the 9th and 10th SS Panzer Divisions. Although British Intelligence was aware these crack troops were in the area, the information was dismissed by General Browning and not relayed to the British Airborne. With little more than machine-guns, rifles and mortars to keep at bay the tanks and 88mm guns of the SS, the paras managed to reach the northern end of the Arnhem Bridge from their dropping zone at Oosterbeek, some five kilometres away. Pockets of troops fought to keep the corridor open between Oosterbeek and the bridge against the superior numbers of well-equipped enemy. As the days passed, it was obvious that the troops on the bridge were fighting a losing battle against German armour and artillery. By Thursday 21st, the Germans had mopped up the last of the British troops holding out at the northern end of the bridge.

The radio sets carried by the Airborne Division all failed and the only one that could be used was the correspondents' set. Major Oliver, the PRO, had succeeded in getting his portable wireless set working soon after landing. This meant that the only news that Churchill, Montgomery and other senior officers could receive came through the despatches of Stanley Maxted, Guy Byam and Alan Wood.

The former Australian journalist, Alan Wood, reported on Friday 22nd:

'It's been a nasty morning so far, cold and misty and the German guns are plastering us plentifully with mortars, big guns and 88s. The 88s are worst because you don't hear them coming. Machine guns have just opened up on the right. In this patch of hell, our men are holding a few civilian houses which still stand. An old lady in black stumbled out of one of them a few minutes ago, and a British soldier ran out and put his arm around her. She collapsed and he carried her down to safety in a cellar.

It is now five days and five sleepless nights since we flew out from England. God knows what secret source of strength these fighting men have drawn from their guts which kept them going. Only one thing is certain. They will keep going until the Second Army gets here. More and more Second Army guns are firing in our support.'

The sound of friendly gunfire only made the agony of waiting more intense. By Monday 25th, shortage of food, water and ammunition added to the desperation felt by the defenders. Wood wrote in his diary:

'Only one battalion of the 2nd Army managed to get across the Rhine last night and we have not seen them yet. They are scattered, some being carried downstream before they got ashore, and they came under heavy fire.[67]

We had some critical moments yesterday, with the Germans attacking the whole time in different directions. Rather, they seemed critical, as the news came that we had had to give ground, first in one place and then in another. But the Germans never really broke through.

I don't think the Germans really have much strength here, otherwise they would have wiped us out long ago... The main trouble is cigarettes and food. Some of our men in the most forward positions have had nothing to eat for four days. Unfortunately, a sniper is covering the well, and we already lost one man shot there. And the bucket by now is riddled with bullet holes...'

Wood, Maxted and Byam make no mention of their fellow correspondent, Jack Smyth. He would appear to have covered the action away from the others for he was on the front line, possibly reaching Arnhem town. He had taken a short parachute course, but still asked advice from an officer before the drop and had to be helped on with his parachute. He recalled:

'On this fifth day (22nd) our force is still being heavily mortared, sniped, machine-gunned and shelled...When the Second Army arrives and relieves this crowd, then we may be told one of the epics of this war. In the meantime, they go on fighting their hearts out.'

Most of the men Smyth dropped with had been wiped out and he was wounded. Captured, he was tortured by the Gestapo to find out how many airborne troops the Allies had. Smyth, a native of Galway, pleaded that he was not only a non-combatant but also a neutral Irishman, but the Nazis would have none of it. Sent to a concentration camp, Smyth spent the final eight months with the threat of execution hanging over him until the camp was liberated by the Americans.[68]

Alan Wood wrote in his diary the events of Monday 25th, the eighth day of the battle:

'This is the end. We have been ordered to fight our way out tonight to join the Second Army on the south bank of the Rhine. The men have not been told yet. Everything is to proceed until the last minute, as if nothing was happening. Our radio operators will keep on sending out messages until the end, with occasional gaps at irregular intervals, so that the Germans will not get suspicious immediately we close down. By then, all the German prisoners will have been ordered into slit trenches. They are likely to stay there, because the shellings are getting heavier and heavier. They will wake up in the morning and find that we are gone. And we hope the Germans on each side of us will close in and start fighting each other before they realise we are no longer in the middle.

The withdrawal, called Operation Berlin, is to be made by small group. Our major, Roy Oliver, has the job of getting out our little Public Relations bunch, a mixed bag, consisting of three unarmed war-correspondents, two censors, armed with blue pencils, three cameramen, four radio operators and a RAF radar expert, who joined in with us when his radar equipment was destroyed. A rather scratch lot to lead through the German positions and across a broad river under fire. If Roy gets us through it will be the greatest military miracle since Moses led the children of Israel across the Red Sea. Fortunately, he is an old soldier. He tells us to muffle our boots with extra socks and strips of blankets.

There is no need to bother about destroying equipment: nearly everything we had was smashed long ago by shelling. But I had broken up my typewriter with a pickaxe so that the Voelkischer Beobachter *war correspondent never uses it.'[69]*

The withdrawal was orderly. Major Oliver's PRO group was to depart at 10.02pm on Tuesday, 26 September. Alan Wood wrote:

'The river crossing lay due south, if we got separated. If anyone was wounded, he was to be put in the middle. We would keep together as long as possible. Roy got us into line. We all unbuttoned the tails of our smocks, usually fastened up the front, between our legs, so the man behind could hold onto it. Stanley Maxted...says we remind him of a procession of elephants, each holding the tail of the one in front of him with his trunk.

And we set off through the trees in the dark. Roy leading with the torn fragment of a map in one hand and my luminous pocket compass in the other.'

Stanley Maxted takes up the story:

'After about 200 yards of silent trekking, we knew we were among the enemy. It was difficult not to throw yourself flat when machine-gun tracers skimmed your head or the scream of a shell or mortar bomb sounded very close – but the orders were to keep going... Major Oliver had reconnoitred the route earlier and had it memorised. The back of my neck was prickling for all that whole interminable march. I couldn't see the man in front of me – all I knew was that I had hold of a coat-tail and for the first time in my life was grateful for the downpour of rain that made the patter on the leaves of the trees and covered up any little noises we were making. At every turn there was a sergeant glider-pilot who stepped out of the shadow and then stepped back into a deeper shadow again.

As we came out of the trees – we had been following carefully thought out footpaths so far – I felt as naked as if I were in Piccadilly Circus in my pyjamas because of the glow of fires across the river. The machine-gun fire and general bombardment had never let up.

We lay down in the mud and rain and stayed that way for two hours till the sentry beyond the hedge on the bank told us to move over the dike and be taken across'.

Guy Byham wrote of the ruthlessness of the SS in their murder of the wounded:

> '*In the morning of the day that we came out I was asked as a non-combatant to go through the lines to contact the enemy, to enable us to evacuate the wounded. As I was making my way back to the area where we dug in, after having seen a German medical officer, I was stopped by an SS lieutenant who said I was his prisoner, this despite the fact that I carried a Red Cross flag. I managed to get away, however, and soon got back to our own lines in a Jeep going to fetch some more wounded. I must admit it was with dread that, in the morning sun, I came back to my lines.*'

Byham reached the banks of the river with Major Oliver's group and lay in the mud waiting for a boat to carry them across:

> '*The mortars were bursting in what seemed like a spray of sparks almost amongst us now, and we lay on the ground pressing our faces into the wet grass. It was then that I decided to have a go at swimming the river....and swept down by the current I at last managed to reach the other bank.*'

Major Oliver managed to get all his party to safety, despite suffering from a wounded arm. The group were fulsome in their praise of him. Wood thought him: '*A genius for organisation and a remarkable flair for leadership. I shall never forget the way he put himself at the head of the nondescript line of censors, wireless operators and unarmed war correspondents and marched us off with as much apparent confidence about getting through as if he were leading a platoon of paratroops.*'

While desperate fighting had been going on, in and around Arnhem, up above the area the Allied aircraft were having a difficult time as they attempted to supply the troops below. The German flak was intense and the supply aircraft stood a good chance of being hit as they flew in low on a predictable course.

Flying in a Stirling bomber of 190 Squadron was *The Daily Telegraph* correspondent, Edmund Townshend. This was his first flight and he had only two minutes of baling out instructions. Sitting in the second-pilot's seat, Townshend watched as they approached the drop-zone through a storm of heavy flak and machine-gunfire. Somehow they were able to drop their cargo of supplies without being hit and began a series of evading manoeuvres to get clear of the flak:

> *'Then with a shock we saw that our port outer motor was on fire, streaming out black smoke… I tried to remember the two-minute instructions given to me a few hours ago. I slipped the pack on to my harness and stumbled with my bulky equipment down to the gaping hatchway already opened by the bomb aimer in the nose.*
>
> *Gripping the parachute release handle to make sure I had it, I leaped into space, too eager to escape from the blazing plane to feel fear at the drop. For minutes like hours, dreading attack by machine-gunners below, I swayed slowly to earth. Breathlessly I watched the Stirling roar away in flames, losing height. With relief I saw other parachutes opening in its wake.'*

When he landed in a ploughed field, he was picked up by a Dutch family and taken to a group of the Dutch Resistance. In the evening he linked up with a party of nine RAF crew, four of whom were from his own aircraft. For four days, the Resistance hid and moved them until they reached the Allied lines.

Although the Arnhem battle had been a defeat, it was an outstanding effort. The 1st Airborne Division lost nearly three-quarters of its strength with 1,984 killed and 6,854 captured. The night-time evacuation, Operation Berlin, successfully saved about 2,400 men with the loss of 95 killed.

Thanks to Major Oliver and the Dutch Resistance, no correspondents were lost.

Chapter 15

The Rhineland Campaign

As the battle front expanded, the numbers of correspondents swelled considerably. The American media in particular sent hundreds of correspondents to supply eyewitness accounts of almost every aspect of the war. Included amongst the American ranks were increasing numbers of female correspondents reflecting the involvement of women in the war effort.[70] With victory in sight, there was a certain amount of relaxation from the censors, although all copy still had to be passed through them. Despite desperate fighting by elements of the German army, everyone knew that the Allies would win.

With the failure to take the bridge at Arnhem and outflank the German defences, the Allies had little alternative than to attempt the breaching of their Westwall or, as the Allies referred to it, the Siegfried Line. The burden of this formidable task fell to the US Army, increasingly manned by new and inexperienced recruits.

The first clash took place in September in the Hürtgen Forest (Hürtgenwald), a densely wooded part of the Eifel mountain range sitting on the border of Belgium and Germany. Lasting from 19 September to 16 December, it turned out to be the longest single battle fought by the Americans. As it was sandwiched between Operation Market Garden and the Battle of the Bulge, the Hürtgen Forest battle is largely overlooked by historians and public alike.

The Hürtgen was a 50 square-mile dense, primordial forest of tall fir trees. The troops who had to fight there found that it an unsettling place, with a twilit, claustrophobic atmosphere something akin to a sinister Grimm's fairy tale. The deep gorges and high ridges made the terrain ideally suited for defence, to which the Germans added extensive minefields and pillboxes. Their artillery was adept at firing tree-high rounds that caused lethal splinters and shrapnel, deadly for anyone caught in the open. With

American armour unable to make much headway except along the muddy forest trails, and the thick tree-cover making air support patchy, the battle was fought almost entirely by the infantry.

The first unit to suffer was the 28th Division, barely recovered from the initial skirmishes in September. The replacements were untrained and under officers and NCOs transferred from other non-infantry units. Ernest Hemingway, back to the action after his exploits in Paris, suggested that it would: *'save everybody a lot of trouble if they just shot them as soon as they got out of the trucks'*. In the four-day long battle for the town of Schmidt, which was won and then lost, barely 300 men of the 28th returned out of 2,000.

Despite the grim conditions, Hemingway was still enjoying the war. Toting a Thompson machine-gun, contrary to the promise he made to the Rambouillet tribunal, he felt at home among the scared, half-frozen soldiers. With Ernie Pyle now in the Far East, Hemingway would slip into a fox-hole and cheerfully introduce himself with: *'Hi, I'm Ernie Hemorrhoid – the poor man's Pyle.'*[71]

He was accompanied by his friend, Bill Walton of *Life*, and they shared a billet together. Hemingway later saved Walton's life during the battle when he recognised the sound of an approaching German plane and threw Walton out of the Jeep just moments before it was strafed.

With the weather growing colder, the rain turned to sleet, then to heavy snow. The tracks were soon churned into a morass of slimy mud. The infantry huddled in their foxholes, suffered frostbite, trench foot and shell shock. The 28th was withdrawn to be replaced by the 8th Division and, Hemingway's adopted unit, the 4th.

Towards the end of the battle, Bill Walton wrote about Colonel Buck Lanham's 22nd Infantry Regiment in its attack on the village of Grosshau:

'In the thunder heaped on Grosshau it seemed impossible for any living thing to survive. Cautiously riflemen and Tommy-gunners hunched down the hill from tree to tree, firing whenever a shadow moved unnaturally in the woods ahead...where every tree was shattered into a naked spear of white ugliness against the dark earth, where weather-soaked corpses had lain so long the stench was unbearable.

As the day advanced, the dirty brown uniforms drove the dirty gray uniforms out of the last woodland west of Grosshau. Emerging onto treeless ground, the Americans felt naked as strip-teasers at a Sunday-school picnic. The forest which had been hateful seemed friendly and protective now that they had only tiny hillocks and shell craters to shield them.

After digging in for the night, the 22nd was ordered to take the village:

'At 0900 under a low gray sky, the first infantrymen raised themselves from their shell-holes into machine-gun fire that spurted from the ruined village... Ducking low, riflemen advanced 200 yards behind the M-10 tank destroyers, using what cover there was, firing toward the village ruins. When the tank destroyers had rumbled beyond four houses and a jagged fragment of a church, the first break came. Fifty Germans, bleary and dust-covered, scrambled from cellars shouting, "Kamarad", above the noise of battle. Then it was a slow, house-to-house fight, warily spraying every doorway and shed with gunfire, hurling grenades into each cellar opening, herding prisoners down one muddy street strewn with dead men and horses, timbers, bricks and dirty straw.

In three hours the worst of the fight was over...Grosshau was ours. Between the edge of the wood and the village, 250 Americans had died.'

Colonel Lanham was distraught at the eighty per cent losses of his 22nd Infantry, confiding in his friend Hemingway that: *'The regiment was a shell of its former self.'*

By 16 December, the Americans had pushed the last German out of the forest. Of the 120,000 Americans involved in this attritional and unnecessary battle, 33,000 were casualties. Many were invalided back to America, suffering battle trauma, trench foot, frostbite and pneumonia. The battle was deemed to have finished on 16 December and Hemingway later described Hürtgen as: *'Passchendaele with tree bursts.'*

On the day that brought the Pyrrhic victory of Hürtgen Forest, the Germans launched their first major assault since the Normandy landings – the Battle of the Bulge. Apart from those who took part, Hürtgen Forest became a forgotten battle.

With the Allies poised to cross the Rhine, Hitler conceived a surprise attack with the 1st and 6th SS Panzer divisions that would divide the Allied forces and, if possible, reoccupy the vital port of Antwerp. If this could be brought about, the German army would be able to devote its forces to repulsing the Russians in the east.

Striking south of the Hürtgen area through the Ardennes, the SS initially made good progress. The Allies had taken a calculated chance and withdrawn many of their units, leaving the area lightly defended. The untried replacements were taken by surprise by the German advance and a considerable number were soon captured. Hitler, in selecting the SS, ordered the battle to be carried out with a brutality more common on the Eastern Front. One of the SS commanders stated that no quarter was to be granted, no prisoners taken and no pity shown towards Belgian civilians. The SS were quick to implement their orders when eighty-four men of an American artillery battalion were captured, taken to a nearby field and mown down by machine-gun fire.[72]

The unprepared Americans pulled back to the west and as they passed through towns they had previously liberated, Jack Belden of *Time* wrote:

> *'Already many vehicles were going toward the rear. Gasoline supply trucks, portable bridges that we might have used to cross rivers, all things that we could use again went back so that the decks could be cleared for action. The inhabitants of the town watched these precautions with frightened faces. Many were refugees from bombed cities and now they had jumped from the frying pan into the fire and didn't know where to go.*
>
> *I noticed in myself a feeling that I had not had for some years. It was the feeling of guilt that seems to come over you whenever you retreat. You don't like to look anyone in the eyes. It seems as if you have done something wrong.'*

One of the deceptions employed by the Germans was to drive captured American and British tanks in a bid to capture the bridges over the Meuse. About forty-four commandos dressed as Americans and speaking perfect English infiltrated behind Allied lines posed as traffic duty soldiers to misdirect Allied traffic, spread rumours of an imminent parachute invasion and generally cause chaos.

The Americans responded with a heavy clampdown, insisting vehicles and personnel show identification and respond to the day's password. A correspondent who came under suspicion was the Hungarian-born Robert Capa, who had hurried to the Ardennes looking for interesting subjects to photograph. Provided with a Jeep, he drove in the general direction of Bastogne, then under siege:

'Every few miles we were stopped by special MPs. They carefully examined our order and identification cards, and asked for the ever-changing password. Then, when we gave them the password, they insisted on asking me a lot of very foolish and very embarrassing questions. "What is the capital of Nebraska?" they wanted to know, and "Who won the last World Series?" They explained that German spies were being dropped by parachute behind our communication lines, and were now promenading around in American uniforms and speaking perfect English. I spoke far from perfect English, and my accent seemed a bit unfashionable. What was worse, I did not know the capital of Nebraska. I was arrested a number of times, each time being delayed for many hours.'

This paranoia extended to the soldiers in the field. About five miles from Bastogne, Capa spotted a good subject to photograph and pulled over. A battalion of infantry was advancing over a snow-covered field with the smoke of exploding shells hanging over their black figures. Climbing up on an embankment he began to click away:

'Suddenly a GI from the battalion about 150 yards away yelled something at me and raised his Tommy-gun at the same time. I yelled back, "Take it easy!" but as he heard my accent he began to shoot. For a fraction of a moment I didn't know what to do. If I threw myself flat on the snow he could still hit me. If I ran down the embankment, he would run after me. I threw my hands high in the air, yelled "Kamerad!" and surrendered. Three of them came at me with raised rifles. When they were close enough to make out the three German cameras around my neck, they became very happy GIs. Two Contax cameras and one Rolleiflex – I was the jackpot! I still kept my hands as high as I could, but when they were rifle's length away from me, I asked one of them to search my breast pocket. He took out my identification and special photographer pass signed by Eisenhower himself. "I should have shot the bastard before!" he groaned.'

UP correspondent, Walter Cronkite, was with Patton's Third Army, which had rushed north to help repel the German attack. Just south of Bastogne, the Jeep he was in hit a bump and Cronkite lost his helmet which bounced off the road and rolled into a field. The driver stopped to retrieve the helmet but signs posted in three languages, warning 'Danger. Mines', changed their minds and they prepared to drive on. One of Patton's inviolable rules was that soldiers must wear helmets at all times and, as luck would have it, the General's three-Jeep entourage appeared with flashing light and siren. A colonel got out of Patton's Jeep and approached Cronkite asking for his name, rank, serial number and where was his helmet? Cronkite replied that he was a war correspondent and that his helmet was now standing in a minefield. The colonel returned to Patton's Jeep, from which a single expletive about war correspondents was heard, and the entourage drove on.

The 101st Airborne Division refused to be shifted from Bastogne, thus robbing the Germans of a vital traffic route. The defence of this town had been somewhat over-praised by the correspondents and when the 101st were relieved, their commander, General McAuliffe, expressed some surprise:

> 'It didn't occur to us, until it was all over, the eyes of the world were on the 101st Airborne Division and the attached armour during the defence of Bastogne. The first thing we heard was that we'd been "rescued" by the 4th Armoured Division. Now I, and everyone else in the 101st, resent the implication that we were rescued or that we needed to be rescued. When General Taylor arrived on the 27th [December] the first thing he asked me was what kind of shape we were in. I told him: "Why, we're in fine shape: we're ready to take the offensive." General Taylor said; "I should have known it, but all that stuff I read in the newspapers was beginning to worry me just a little."
>
> "The fact is we were thinking about what a tough time the Kraut was having."'

Swiftly organised reinforcements from Montgomery in the north and Patton squeezed the German corridor. They managed to get as far as five miles from the Meuse before clear weather allowed the Allied air force to destroy the German armour and fuel trucks for the tanks: many ran out of fuel and had to be abandoned.

On 1 January 1945, in sheer desperation, the Germans launched a major air assault to destroy as many Allied aircraft on the ground as possible. This last throw of the dice proved a disaster for the Germans when they lost 300 aircraft and most of their experienced pilots. This desperate action brought an end to the brief counter-offensive which had cost the Germans an estimated 100,000 killed, wounded or captured.

The Australian correspondent, Osmar White, wrote:

'It was a dreary, sluggish war on the Ardennes Front now that von Rundstedt's sortie to Bastogne was finished: a war of snow-choked mountain forests, fought more to prise loose the clutch of winter than to finish the exhausted enemy. Waiting was hard on the strength and spirit of the men, for the cold bit into their bones and blistered their skin and each one in his heart of hearts said, "What is there to die for now?"'

Another action on the Siegfried Line was the Battle for Aachen fought between 2–21 October 1944. The city had been incorporated into the defensive network and was one of the largest urban battles fought by the Allies in the war. Although Aachen was of little military value, it was deeply symbolic for all Germans. This was the historic capital of Charlemagne and was the first German city to be threatened by the Allies.

George Mucha, a Czech correspondent working for the BBC, reported on 17 October:

'On both sides of the deserted streets stood empty carcasses of burnt-out houses. Glass, wreckage and tree branches were strewn on the pavements and in almost every street a building was burning.

Occasionally we were stopped by the rattle of a sniper's automatic pistol. To get him out, the Americans threw a few incendiaries into the building. The flames did the rest. We came to a huge concrete shelter. These shelters are ugly, gloomy constructions of many floors above and below ground, and in them hundreds of Aachen civilians have been hiding for the last five weeks. In this shelter there were German soldiers also, and they refused to open the doors. For several hours the shelter was besieged by the Americans... who threatened to use flame-throwers. That helped. The doors opened and out came the drabbest filthiest inhabitants of the underworld I have ever seen. They came scrambling into the light, dazed. Then, catching a breath of fresh air, they started to jabber, push, scream and curse. Some rushed up to me brandishing their fists. "Where have you been so long?" they shouted, "Why don't you deliver us sooner from these devils?"

It was a sight to stun you. There were the people of a German town occupied by the Allies... and they were weeping with hysterical joy amid the smouldering ruins of their homes. "We have been praying every day for you to come," said a woman, "You can't imagine what we have had to suffer from them." '[73]

The winter of 1944-45 was one of the coldest on record. After the Allied defeat at Arnhem, the Dutch population in Nazi occupied western Netherlands suffered from lack of food resulting in the deaths of 18,000. Although there was the humanitarian urge to help the Dutch, the Allies could not be deflected from their aim to cross the Rhine and Weser and occupy the Ruhr and north-western Germany.

The Battle of Remagen was fought for the control of the Ludendorff Bridge across the Rhine and was Germany's last natural barrier. On 7 March 1945, in a surprise dash, the US 9th Armoured Division arrived at the village of Remagen and found the railway bridge still standing. The Germans had wired the bridge with more that 600 kilograms of explosives, which could be seen suspended below the roadway. The Germans on the west bank began to fall back over the bridge and the American commander gave the order to closely pursue them in order to establish a position at the east end. As the retreating Germans cleared the bridge, the order to blow the bridge was given, but only a portion of the explosives detonated. Realising they only had a short time before the Germans could repair the fault, a detachment of three men of the Engineer Battalion climbed under the bridge and began to cut the wires. Everett Holles of NBS witnessed the drama:

'At 3:30 o'clock, a platoon... sped down the slope to the bridge entrance. There was a flurry of shooting as the Germans, taken completely by surprise, scurried about trying to organise a defence. A German gun was knocked out, some German soldiers killed. Then the Yanks, crouching low against machine gun fire coming from the bridge towers, ran out onto the bridge. Just as they stepped on the span, an explosion occurred three-quarters of the way down the bridge. The Germans were setting off demolition charges, and the men thought surely their chance had gone. But no, only slight damage was done. They raced on.'

Sergeant Alexander Drabik was the first invader to reach the east bank of the Rhine since the time of Napoleon. Rather than accept the plaudits, his first thoughts were about the engineers who had made it possible. Interviewed by Everett Holles he said:

*'While we were running across the bridge – and, man it may have
been only 250 yards but it seemed like 250 miles to us – I spotted this
lieutenant standing out there completely exposed to machine gun fire
that was pretty heavy by this time.*

*He was cutting wires and kicking the German demolition charges
off the bridge with his feet! He's the one who saved the bridge and
made the whole thing possible.'*

Hitler was furious about losing the bridge, and ordered it be destroyed at all
costs. On 9 March the Germans counter-attacked but were beaten off. One
of the few casualties of this attack was Peter Lawless of *The Daily Telegraph*.
He was about to cross the bridge to Remagen to file his despatch when a shell
exploded nearby mortally wounding him in the stomach. He died fifteen
minutes later: the 16th British war correspondent to die in the war.[74]

The almost accidental capture of the bridge at Remagen opened the
floodgates for the Allies. Regrouping after the Ardennes campaign, which
only delayed the inevitable invasion of Germany, the Allies made great
inroads during March. Industrial centres like München-Gladbach, Krefeld
and Cologne fell as the Allies swept through the industrial heart of Germany.

On 24 March the 6th British and the 17th Airborne divisions took part in
Operation Varsity, the largest airborne operation in history to be conducted
on a single day. The paratroopers were carried five miles inland from the
Rhine by an armada of aircraft and dropped just north-west of Wesel. At the
same time, engineers blanketed 30 miles of the area with smoke to allow the
British Second Army to cross the Rhine and link up with the airborne forces.

Amongst the 16,000 men involved in this mass drop was Stanley Maxted,
fully recovered from his experiences at Arnhem. Landing safely amongst
well defended positions was still a lottery as he found:

*'There was just a minute or two of quiet as the great Hamilcar ran in
with the sound of rushing wind in her wings.[75] Then, when just a few
feet off the ground, pandemonium broke loose – the wicked snap of
Spandau machine-guns, mixed with the slower bong of 20mm
incendiaries for just a fraction of a second before they started
pricking out their trademark in the thin skin of the glider. Things
seemed to happen too quickly for me to take them all in at once. There
was an explosion that appeared to be inside my head, the smell of
burnt cordite. I went down on one knee. Something hot and sticky was
dripping over my right eye and off my chin and all over my clothes.*

There was a doom-like lurch and a great rending as smoke, dust and daylight came from nowhere. I saw the Bren carrier go inexorably out of the nose of the glider, carrying that whole works ahead of it, and wiping two signallers off the top of it like flies. Even then the bullets kept crashing through the wreckage. At the moment of impact, a Jeep trailer that was chained just behind me, came forward about six inches and caught me in the small of my back... I hauled myself out of the mess into a shallow ditch by a hedge. Looking up, and clearing my eyes with the back of my hand, I saw a man pinned across the chest by wreckage. One of the glider pilots was getting him out.'

Following events from the air was CBS's Richard Hottelet, writing for *Collier's*. The mass drop was probably one of the last big stories of the European war and the American Army wanted complete coverage. An unarmed B-17 Flying Fortress had been fitted up to accommodate a group of correspondents, photographers and observers and, what should have been a safe grandstand view of the operation, turned into a terrifying experience:

'We got hit the first time as we swung over the drop zone. Out of the left waist window we were watching parachutes bubble out of a C-47. And then we heard the hammering straight down below us. You could tell by the sound that it was 20 or 37mm, and at 700 feet our B-17 was a fat, lazy bird. We should have known when the first shell knocked against our ship that we ought to get out of the area and stay out.'

Instead the newsmen's airplane followed the waves of C-47s as they dropped their human cargoes. On the third run, however, correspondents had pushed their luck too far:

'It suddenly seemed extremely silly to me that we should be there, because we were a huge bright silver B-17 flying along at almost stalling speed. We were probably the most conspicuous thing in the sky. The Germans must have reached the same conclusion. We had been over the drop zone twenty or twenty-five minutes... and then we really hit trouble.

In the waist we heard the riveter again. A short burst, then a longer one...Then we got hit in a ripple... the ship shuddered. The left wing had been hit and fire was breaking out between the engines. Our pilot [Lieutenant Colonel Benton Balwin] was gaining altitude in a climbing turn. Smoke began to pour down through the plane and in the left waist window. A tongue of flame licked back as far as the window, and the silver inner skin of the ship reflected its orange glow... A crewman reported gasoline was sloshing around in the bomb bay. This Fortress carried 2,000 gallons of aviation fuel, which can almost be ignited in a hot wind. One engine was burning; the one next to it was catching fire.

As we staggered out [of the approach], we watched the C-46s come in and apparently walk into a wall of flak. I could not see the flak, but one plane after another went down. All our attention was concentrated on our own ship. It could blow-up in mid-air any moment.

Up in the cockpit, Colonel Baldwin was keeping the ship under control, watching the fire eat a larger and larger hole in the left wing like a smouldering cigarette in a tablecloth. Suddenly we went into a sharp dip. Back aft all we had was the smoke and the deafening noise, and the tiny fragments of molten metal which the wing was throwing back and which twinkled in the sun as they raced past the waist window.'

Colonel Baldwin was struggling to fly the crippled plane back over the Rhine to friendly territory. As they crossed the grey river, he gave the order to jump. This was Hottelet's first parachute jump which he accomplished without mishap. All the newsmen and crew landed safely except one crewman whose chute failed to open.

Colonel Baldwin intended to bail out as well, but when he reached for his parachute he inadvertently pulled the ripcord and the chute opened in the cockpit. He had no alternative but to attempt a belly-landing in a field. When the burning plane stopped, Baldwin exited by the pilot's window and ran like mad.

Within four days, the engineers had constructed eight bridges across the Rhine. Stewart MacPherson of the BBC described the scene on 29 March:

'Standing on the bank of the Rhine, one can look down on one of the great sights of the war. Stretched across the bridge, and as far as the eye can see, were hundreds of tanks, lorries, carriers, bulldozers, ammo wagons, vehicles of every conceivable type, flooding across the river. Overhead, squadrons of Spitfires, Typhoons, Tempests and Mustangs took their turn in patrolling – giving constant protection to our ground forces, just in case the Luftwaffe should dare to interfere.'

Chapter 16

Final Days

After the brief resistance put up by the Germans, the Allies swiftly moved eastwards into Germany, the pace of which seemed unreal. One of the pleasures of the advance was the freeing of thousands of prisoners of war held in the Stalags and Oflags. One of the first prisoners to be freed was the BBC's Eddy Ward. Captured in North Africa, he and his fellow inmates were liberated when the Americans arrived at Oflag XIIB near Limburg on 31 March 1945. Ward recalled the moment the American soldiers appeared on the west bank of the Lahn River which separated the prisoners from their liberators. Fortunately Ward located a small barge which he was able to manoeuvre across and bring the first soldiers to the camp. Along with Eddy Ward were Pat Crosse of Reuters and Godfrey Anderson of AP who had been captured in North Africa but had managed to keep together despite the constant moving from one PoW camp to another. Within a few days, all three men were filing stories again for their former employers.

Contrasted with the joy of opening the PoW cages were the horrors of entering the nightmare world of the concentration camps. The first report of these terrible camps had been received in July 1944 from BBC's Russian correspondent, Alexander Werth. Along with other journalists, he visited the Majdanek concentration and extermination camp which had been captured intact by the swift advance into Poland of the Russian Army. He filed his report about the terrible atrocities committed and the staggeringly high number of deaths, but the BBC refused to broadcast, believing the story to be incredible and possibly due to Russian propaganda.

In Germany, Ohrdruf was the first camp to be entered on 4 April 1945. Norman Clark of *The Daily Telegraph* was still attached to the American 4th Armoured Division which had crossed the Rhine at Osnabruck on 24 March. They reached Gotha in Thuringia and were searching for a secret Nazi communications centre.[76] Instead, they came upon the abandoned

Ohrdurf-Nord forced labour camp, a satellite of the notorious Buchenwald, some 20 miles east of Gotha. Clark recalled the terrible scenes:

> 'When we arrived, the camp gates were open and the Nazis already gone. Most of the prisoners had been force marched to Buchenwald leaving a few living amongst the hundreds of dead. There was even an American flyer who had been killed and suspended in a gibbet. Patton ordered the townspeople of Ohrdurf to see for themselves what crimes had been committed on the outskirts of their community. That evening, the mayor and his family committed suicide.' [77]

Clark mentioned that the reports were again not entirely believed, and the government sent over a commission to verify the facts. When they had finished their investigation and returned to London one of their members, Mavis Tate, was so distressed she took her own life.

As the American forces closed in on Buchenwald, the Gestapo telephoned the camp administration that it was sending explosives to blow up any evidence of the camp, including its inmates. The Gestapo did not know the camp commandant and his staff had already fled in fear of the Allies. A prisoner answered the phone and told the Gestapo that the explosives would not be needed as the camp had already been blown up. When the American arrived on 11 April, they found the camp intact, no guards and 21,000 starving emaciated prisoners.

Eddy Ward, now back in harness with the BBC, met up with Harold Denny of the *New York Times*, who had been captured at the same time as Ward. As an American correspondent, Denny had been separated from his British colleagues when they reached Italy. He appears to have displeased the Germans for he was singled out by the Gestapo, taken to Germany and placed in isolated custody in a prison camp. Here his health deteriorated and he was freed seven months later in a prisoner exchange.

The pair decided to drive from their Press Camp in Wiesbaden to Leipzig. On the way, they diverted to Buchenwald, which had been liberated a few days before. Ward described their visit:

> 'I stopped and asked several Germans where Buchenwald was and they professed not to know. Then I saw an emaciated looking Russian and asked him. He knew only too well...
>
> We stopped at the gates of this terrible monument to Nazism. Just inside was a large open space where the prisoners had mustered on

roll-call. It was crowded with men and boys of practically every European nation, though the bulk was made up of Russians, Poles, Germans and Frenchmen. And, of course, Jews from all these countries and many others. Most of them were dressed in the hideous blue and white striped pyjamas which were the official prison garb. Most of them were so dreadfully emaciated that they looked like ghastly scarecrows. A few American soldiers were walking around, but as yet, nothing much had been done officially to relieve the awful lot of the wretched inhabitants of Buchenwald.

Behind the parade ground row upon row of wooden huts disappeared down a hill. I walked down through indescribable filth. All attempts at hygiene had been abandoned and the stench was overpowering. My guide took me into a hut whose occupants were so weak from lack of food that they were unable to move outside. A four-tiered row of shelves ran along its hundred-foot length. Lying on them were several hundred poor caricatures of humanity, who needed the hand of some twentieth-century Goya to portray them in their awful, terrifying misery.'

Osmar White, who had reported the events on the Kokoda Track during the New Guinea campaign with Chester Wilmot, had just returned to work with Sir Keith Murdoch's *Herald and Weekly Times*. He had recovered from serious injuries sustained when the LST tank landing ship he was on was struck by a Japanese 500lb bomb. The four men who were standing beside him in the wheel-house were killed but White survived, albeit with severely wounded legs. Recovery was slow but Murdoch was keen that White should report the advance into Germany and in February 1945, he joined Patton's Third Army as it pushed further into the enemy's own country. [78] White expressed what all correspondents experienced as horrors of the Nazi's concentration camps came to light:

'We are in the heart of Germany, in a diseased nation. We are in concentration camp country. Today I've seen the Buchenwald, and moved among the living dead. I cannot now nor ever will be able to write objectively of what I have seen. One cannot observe war for three-and-a-half years as a newspaperman and remain either sentimentalist or supersensitive about spectacles of human suffering. Yet what I saw today moved me to physical illness... This, they told me, was the Buchenwald – the deepest pit of the hell Hitler has dug.'

FINAL DAYS

Ed Murrow visited Buchenwald and delivered his usual measured version of what he had witnessed. Stunned by what he had seen, he concluded his broadcast:

> *'I pray you to believe what I have said about Buchenwald. I have reported what I saw and heard, but only part of it. For most of it I have no words.'*

Margaret Bourke-White, the *Life* photographer, travelled with Patton's force and wrote about her Buchenwald experience:

> *'Using a camera was almost a relief. It interposed a slight barrier between myself and the horror in front of me.'*

The correspondents who entered these hellish camps carried the sights they saw for the rest of their lives. Osmar White wrote:

> *'Buchenwald, Belsen, Dachau, Auschwitz – names that enraged the world too late. I spent, in all, fourteen or fifteen days in concentration camps – not one hundredth part of the time needed to learn the whole truth.'*

Martha Gellhorn expressed this change after visiting Dachau and its indescribable medical experiments:

> *'A darkness entered my spirit and it was there that I stopped being young.'*

In the north, Richard Dimbleby found similar scenes when he entered Belsen concentration camp in Lower Saxony:

> *'In the shade of some trees lay a great collection of bodies. I walked about them trying to count, there was perhaps 150 of them flung down on each other, all naked, all so thin that their yellow skin glistened like stretched rubber on their bones. Some of the poor starved creatures whose bodies were there looked so utterly unreal and inhuman that I could have imagined that they had never lived at all...'*

When the camp was liberated by the British 11th Armoured Division, the soldiers found approximately 60,000 prisoners, most of who were beyond saving. The horrors of the camp were documented on film which shocked the world and the name of Belsen became emblematic with the depth of Nazi atrocities.

The Allied advance continued and any resistance was dealt with by aerial bombing or artillery shelling. As Omar White described it: '*The whole of Germany, with the exception of south-eastern Bavaria, was mauled beyond belief.*'

White was in that region of Bavaria during the last weeks of the war when the Americans learned of Nazi treasure buried deep underground. In all, the Americans unearthed fifty-three sites containing gold, banknotes and art treasures. The most valuable discovery was the Reichsbank's entire bullion reserves worth several thousand million dollars. On 8 April, White was one of the correspondents who accompanied General Earnest and men of an engineering battalion as they descended the Kaiseroda salt mine to a depth of 2,100 feet. Here the engineers blasted an entrance through a masonry wall and entered a large vault.

> '*The floor was covered with little, red-sealed canvas bags. "Open them up," said the general. A staff officer jerked the seals off a bag, fumbled, and pulled out a gold brick. The general hefted it. We all hefted it – and handed it back to the general. Yes…50 pounds, near enough. The 100 ton estimate was not so far wrong.*'

Back on the surface, the correspondents were shown some of the art treasures that had been recovered elsewhere in the mine:

> '*Crate upon crate of Greek, Chinese and Egyptian ceramics, packing cases full of canvases by Menzel, Dürer, Manet, Constable, Raphael, Titian, Van Dyke, da Vinci – coffers in which were packed the manuscripts and relics of Goethe, loose albums with engravings, etchings and drawings by the masters of all nations. They were stacked on the naked floor with salt softly falling on them.*'

With little to stop them, the Allies and Soviet forces were advancing towards each other. Finally, on 25 April, the US First Army linked up with the Russians at Torgau on the River Elbe. Eddy Ward, a Russian speaker, was probably the first correspondent to meet up with the Russians. He and his recording engineer had joined a three-Jeep reconnaissance party sent to check if the road to Torgau was safe. On the way they accepted the surrender of several groups of German soldiers but also found entry into the town blocked by barricades and rubble. Ward came upon a young Russian worker who offered to guide them:

> *'We turned a sharp corner, and there on the pavement, coming towards us, I saw three Red Army soldiers, with their machine-pistols at the ready... The convoy stopped instantly. The Russians looked at us for a few minutes, not quite sure who or what we were. Then, realising that we were an American force, they rushed forward to greet us. It was a moment of great excitement, for these were the first Russian troops any of us had seen in the field.*
>
> *"Zdrastiya tovarishchye!" they shouted. I shouted the same back. "Greetings, comrades!" There was great hand-clapping and back-slapping... Burly Russians threw their arms round the dusty GIs. A gigantic fellow, who told me later that he came from Kharkov, flung his arms round my neck and insisted on kissing me on both cheeks. This kind of thing seemed likely to continue indefinitely.'*

Two of the many correspondents to witness the formal meeting of the two armies were the determined *St Louis Post-Dispatch* correspondent, Virginia Irwin and Andrew Tully of the *Boston Traveller*. After a morning of vodka-fuelled celebration, the pair unofficially decided to travel the 80-miles to Berlin, where the Russians were on the point of victory. Along with their GI driver, Sergeant John Wilson, Irwin and Tully drove to the capital with sketchiest details of the route, which was not helped as the Russians had replaced all German road signs with Russian. After driving north from Torgau which took them through dark forests and deserted roads, they came upon a highway, along which travelled the Russian army:

> *'The Red Army in action is terrific. On the move it looks like...a scene from a De Mille movie of the Crusades... American Studebaker 2½-ton trucks rub axles with antiquated farm carts loaded down with Russian infantry. Great herds of sheep and cows are mixed in with armoured cars and half-tracks with household belongings lashed to their sides. Super tanks tangle with a fantastic mess of horse-drawn buggies, phaetons, surreys, old-fashioned pony carts and farm wagons, all loaded down with ammunition, food, women, wounded and animals.*
>
> *Before 8pm, we were well into Berlin with the forward elements*

of the Russian troops... German dead lay on the sidewalks, in the front yards of bomb-shattered homes in the Berlin suburbs. All streets were clogged with Russian tanks, guns, infantry in their shaggy fur hats, and everywhere the horses of the Russian Army ran loose about the streets.

As I write, the Russian artillery is pounding the heart of the city with a barrage I have never heard equalled in an American battle. The earth shakes. The air stinks of cordite and the dead. All Berlin seems confusion.

In the territory over which I travelled to reach Berlin, I saw very few Germans. They fear the Russians as no nation has ever feared a conquering army... We found a German woman who spoke English, but she was too frightened to be coherent... One look at this woman told more than she could have said in words. There were circles under her eyes so deep and dark that they might have been etched there with lamp black. She shivered like someone with the ague.

The Russians have shown no mercy. They have played the perfect game of tit-for-tat. They have done to Berlin what the German Army did to Leningrad and Stalingrad.'

Irwin, Tully and Sergeant Wilson were overwhelmed by the Russians' hospitality, which used their presence as an excuse for a prolonged party involving strange food, much dancing and plenty of vodka. For Irwin, it had been worth it: *'It had been a mad day, but a wonderful one.'*

The following day the very hung-over trio continued towards the centre of Berlin. On 28 April, Andrew Tully sent this report back to the *Boston Traveller*:

'Running a gauntlet of bursting shells, seemingly falling in aimless fashion throughout the city, I got to within sixteen blocks of the famous Unter den Linden today. I was within ten blocks of the historic Wilhelmstrasse, where a little man named Hitler once ruled the Third Reich. Unless I wanted to form a one-man task force, I could go no further, for the entire centre of the city is no-man's-land, with shrapnel spraying the air and whole buildings collapsing under the weight of a thunderous artillery attack. The air was a permanent blueish gray from the numerous pitched battles which went on all around us and the reek of gun powder was almost stifling. It was the most desperate fighting I have ever seen, surpassing for pure violence and

desperation the battles of Metz, Frankfurt and Nürnberg. At long last it seemed that the German military automaton was heeding his mad dictator's orders to fight to the death.

Almost every square inch of the city seemed to be the scene of fighting. On rooftops all around us snipers peppered the streets with automatic rifle and machine-gun fire. Russian soldiers with a cold, magnificent courage were mopping up road blocks and street barricades of huge fir logs. Houses and apartment buildings were being ransacked one by one.

As our Jeep drove up the Eberstasse and stopped, two Russian soldiers were herding half a dozen members of the Wermacht from a department store building. These Nazis were lucky, for their comrades lay dead on the sidewalk. German dead, for that matter, are everywhere. I counted at least fifty bodies sprawled in assorted positions along our route.'

As it was becoming evident that the Soviet authorities were tightening restrictions on travel by non-accredited personnel, the Americans left Berlin. Finally, the enterprising correspondents made their way back to the American lines, filed their stories and were then told that they had had their accreditation revoked. [79]

With Adolf Hitler's suicide in his Berlin bunker on 30 April, the apparently simple act of surrender had become complicated. On 2 May, Field Marshal Montgomery's troops had reached the Baltic Sea, made contact with the Russians and isolated the Germans in Denmark and Norway. Admiral Karl Dönitz, nominated President and Supreme Commander of the German forces in Hitler's last will and testament, made the approach. He hoped that a protracted partial and local surrender might buy time for his troops fleeing from the Russians. Instead, Montgomery insisted on an unconditional surrender of German forces in the Netherlands, north-west Germany and Denmark.

The BBC's Chester Wilmot and Bill Downs of CBS were the only correspondents present at the surrender, which was also filmed. On 4 May, Wilmot broadcast from Montgomery's headquarters on Lüneburg Heath. For the surrender ceremony Montgomery sat at the head of the table covered with an army blanket and two BBC microphones in front of him:

'It is ten past six on Friday 4 May: the hour and the day for which British fighting men and women and British people throughout the

world have been fighting and working and waiting for five years and eight months.'

The following day, the Germans handed a hastily written message for transmission by radio to German headquarters:

'The paper was spotted with raindrops and the ink had begun to run; so much so, that some of the letters were indistinct. It didn't look like an historic document, but it was...It was a message telling the German Command that the armistice was signed.'

Another correspondent present was Leonard Mosley of the *Daily Express*, who wrote:

'Montgomery kept the German delegation waiting, standing miserably about in the rain, first while he told us of the events which led up to the Armistice, and later while he confirmed with his aides inside the caravan... Montgomery kept them standing there letting them watch and think, letting the rain splash over them until he judged the moment right.'

Bill Downs summed up the surrender:

'This is it! It was a great moment, a historic moment, there in the cold rain, the blustering winds on the Lüneburg Heath, in the heart of northern Germany: a great moment not only for Britain and Canada but for the 82nd Airborne Division, the American Eighth Infantry Division, and the American Seventh Armoured Division, who fought under the Second Army in its hour of victory.'

The next episode of the piecemeal surrender took place at SHAEF headquarters at Reims on 7 May. This went ahead despite the Soviet objection that the terms were not what was discussed at the European Advisory Commission (EAC) in 1944, which proposed that: 'the capitulation of Germany should be recorded in a single document of unconditional surrender'. Already the shoots of distrust were appearing between East and West. Furthermore, they insisted that the ratified surrender should be held in Berlin and not on liberated territory. This was hastily implemented and the final surrender was signed on the evening of

8 May at the Soviet Military Administration Headquarters in Berlin-Karlshorst.

These events were overshadowed by the action of the American AP correspondent, Edward Kennedy. He was one of sixteen mixed-nationality correspondents who witnessed the surrender at Reims. Significantly, there were no correspondents from any US newspapers, only three representatives from news agencies: Associated Press, United Press and International News Service. Having witnessed the surrender ceremony, all the newsmen were ordered to keep the story under wraps for thirty-six hours for fear of offending the Russians. Risking the wrath of the censors, Kennedy telephoned his report to his Paris office which was relayed to New York via the London office. Within hours, the news was headlined in the *New York Times*. At this point, the censors pursued the policy of shutting the stable door after the horse had bolted. The SHAEF administration added to the problem by bullying the other correspondents into denying the story. The result was total confusion. Despite the denials published by the American papers, street celebrations still went ahead in America and Britain.

Edward Kennedy was about to see his career take a nose dive.

The Allied commanders and politicians, in order not to upset the Russians, wanted news of the Reims ceremony held back until the Berlin surrender had been signed. Kennedy protested that a German radio station had already broadcast the news, as had the American Broadcasting Station in Europe, and he believed the military censors must have allowed it. Also, he believed that previous embargoes had dealt with military security, which this was not, and that it was purely a political decision and, therefore, fair game for a journalist.

Kennedy was robustly defended by A.J. Liebling in *The New Yorker*. Taking the opportunity to expand the subject, Liebling voiced what most newspaper correspondents felt about the army of censors with whom they were forced to deal and also the role of the news-agencies:

> *'The Public Relations officers, mostly colonels and lieutenant-colonels, had for the most part been Hollywood press agents or Chicago rewrite men in civilian life. They looked as authentic in their uniforms as dress extras in a B picture...The news-agency men adapted themselves to this squalid milieu and flourished in it. They agreed with everything the dress extras said, especially with the thesis that on 50 miles of Normandy coast there would be room for*

only about 20 correspondents, who would, of course, represent the larger news organisations. The habit of saying yes to people you don't respect is hard to break, which is one reason I think well of Edward Kennedy for breaking it.'

In the event, Edward Kennedy was vilified by the newspapers and many of his colleagues. The *New York Times* went so far as to publish an editorial saying Kennedy had committed a 'grave disservice to the newspaper profession'. He continued in newspapers, albeit in the back-waters of California. A wartime drinking companion of Ernest Hemingway, he continued his heavy drinking and was killed as he left a bar and walked in front of a car.[80]

Dealing with the military's public relations was a Kafkaesque experience and neatly illustrated by General Eisenhower at his farewell press conference for war correspondents. He repeated his view that journalists accredited to his command were 'auxiliary staff officers', whose job had been to support the war effort through objective reporting. He must have raised a few eyebrows when he declared that there had been no serious censorship of their stories. He finished by reminding the assembled correspondents to clear any statement they wanted to quote with a PR officer!

Eddy Ward voiced what many correspondents felt: '*I had grown tired, and I felt I wanted to get out of Germany and stay out for a long time.*'

Now the war was finished the Occupying Powers, as the Allies were renamed, had the task of governing a population reduced to destitution. An immediate priority was to bring the more prominent Nazi members of leadership to trial and many wartime correspondents stayed to cover the Nuremberg trials held between November 1945 and 1 October 1946.

Both the West and the East cherry-picked German experts in the sciences and aeronautics, having glimpsed at the end of the war just how advanced the Germans were in technology. Osmar White wrote:

'I visited the Zeiss optical laboratories and factories in Jena before the town was officially occupied. Senior members of the research staff calmly, smugly, informed me that they had already been promised well-paid jobs in the United States and were awaiting evacuation. Their only anxiety was that the Russian tanks would get to town first and they would be forced to accept less well-paid employment behind the Urals.'

FINAL DAYS

The drive for de-Nazification meant, as Osmar White wrote: *'Skimming the most offensive scum off the melting pot into which the parts of the dismembered nation had been thrown, destroying it with judicial pomp and ceremony, and reducing what was left to a broth from which reparations could be distilled... Adult Germans had been de-Nazified by the abject defeat of Hitler's regime. Chastising them with payback could teach them nothing they did not already know.'*

Many war correspondents returned home to write their memoirs, freed from the restraints of the censors. Although some correspondents regarded their reporting of the war as inadequate, there were many who could look back with some pride despite the censorship strictures. Some were pleased to get back to their papers and again take up non-war reporting.

One who fell foul of his publisher for telling the truth as he viewed it was Osmar White. He followed his best-selling book, *Green Armour* about the New Guinea Campaign, with his experiences in Germany in 1945. After initial enthusiasm for *Conqueror's Road*, the publishers rejected it as it did not conform to the 'political correctness' of the time with his criticism of the occupation, both East and West. It would take another forty years before it was published.

There were correspondents who had become hooked on the adrenaline rush of front-line war reporting and actively went in search of new conflicts. They did not have to go looking far for action for the post-war years were littered with plenty of left-over disputes and colonial wars. Almost inevitably, some of those correspondents who had survived the Second World War would soon lose their lives in these lesser conflicts.

The Times special correspondent Ian Morrison, who had escaped from Singapore, was one such restless soul. During the war, he spent very little time with his wife and two children and the defeat of the Japan did little to still this restlessness. The post-war years were spent travelling South East Asia, visiting Burma and Indo-China and reporting the civil war in China. In 1950 he visited Hong Kong, met and fell in love with Han Suyin, a local doctor. His paper sent him to cover the Korean War and within a few weeks Morrison was killed on 12 August 1950 when his Jeep carrying him and Christopher Buckley of *The Daily Telegraph* struck a landmine. Both were buried in the UN Memorial Cemetery in Pusan. Han Suyin wrote a book about their doomed love-affair which was made into the successful film, *Love Is a Many-Splendored Thing*.

The outstanding photo-journalist, Robert Capa, co-founded Magnum Photos with the French photographer, Henri Cartier-Bresson. Capa swore that he was finished covering wars but, while attending a photographic exhibition in Japan, he was asked by *Life* magazine to cover the war in Indo-China. On 25 May 1954, he stopped to photograph a French regiment as it advanced up a road. Going ahead, he stepped on a landmine and was mortally wounded.

Chester Wilmot returned to England to live and continue working for the BBC. In 1952, he wrote a well-received book entitled, *The Struggle for Europe*. He returned to Australia to take part in the BBC's 1953 round-the-world Christmas Day broadcast. On the return flight, he was killed when the Comet airliner in which he was flying crashed into the Mediterranean on 10 January 1954. This was the first of a series of Comet crashes that effectively ended Britain's lead in jet airliners.

Fellow BBC correspondent, Eddy Ward took part in a round-the-world link-up in 1946. Sent with an engineer to the remote Bishop Rock lighthouse, standing seven miles west of the Isles of Scilly, Ward's contribution to the broadcast was that a gale was blowing and heavy seas were crashing against the lighthouse. Ward expected to be spending a maximum of four days on Bishop Rock. The stormy weather continued and it was a month before the marooned correspondent could be rescued by breeches-buoy. In 1950 Ward succeeded his father as the 7th Viscount Bangor, but still worked as a freelance for the BBC.

While Ernest Hemingway was on his way to cover the Battle of the Bulge, he came down with a high fever. His friend, Colonel Buck Lanham, recognised it as pneumonia and Hemingway was immediately hospitalised for the rest of the war. After the war, to his delight he was awarded the Bronze Star as recognition '*for his valour having been under fire in combat areas in order to obtain an accurate picture of conditions. Through his talent of expression, Mr Hemingway enabled readers to obtain a vivid picture of the difficulties and triumphs of the front-line soldier and his organisation in combat.*'

In 1946, he married Mary Welsh and in 1954 received the Nobel Prize for Literature. A series of accidents, depression and increased drinking took their toll and on 2 July 1961, Hemingway committed suicide with his favourite shotgun.

Bill Walton, Hemingway's friend and companion, left journalism in 1949 to concentrate on painting. He worked primarily in abstract expressionism and became highly regarded in his home country. He also became a close confident of John Kennedy and was considered the most popular of the president's friends.

FINAL DAYS

Until she was struck down with Parkinson's disease, Margaret Bourke-White continued to take beautifully composed photographs even in the most horrific of circumstances. Like many top war photographers, she came in for criticism from other correspondents. Edward Behr wrote scathingly about the dedication of star *Life* photographers to their craft:

> *'Their finicky passion for perfection, drove otherwise sane reporters into a shaky determination to seek out some other way of making a living. And since most of them were thick-skinned and egotistical beyond belief, they never realised how impossible they were.'*

As if to illustrate this obsession for perfection, during the time of the 1947 partition, which bloodily produced the independent countries of India and Pakistan, Bourke-White made an Indian refugee family bury and rebury its dead several times before extracting sufficient pathos from the scene.

Virginia Cowles and Martha Gellhorn collaborated on a play entitled *Love Goes to Press*, a romantic farce set in a press camp on the Italian front. Complications ensue when one of the heroines encounters her ex-husband, a famous writer whom she divorced on the grounds of plagiarism. It is fairly obvious that this male protagonist is based on Gellhorn's ex-husband, Ernest Hemingway. The play had a successful opening in London in 1946 and but had a disappointing reception on Broadway the following year.

Virginia Cowles married the writer and politician, Aidan Crawley, in 1945. She wrote several biographies and in 1974, left England for southern Europe. Diagnosed with terminal emphysema, she died in Spain when the car her husband was driving overturned, killing her instantly.

Both Martha Gellhorn and Clare Hollingworth continued to go to the wars, write books and outlive most of their male counterparts. Gellhorn chose to live in London after the war but near blindness and cancer caused her to commit suicide in 1998 at the age of 89.

Clare Hollingworth went on to have a long and distinguished career, reporting on conflicts in Palestine, Algeria, China, Aden and Vietnam. She was among the survivors of the King David Hotel bombing in Jerusalem in 1946 which took the lives of ninety-one people. At the time of writing, she is 104 years old and lives in Hong Kong.

After the war, Alan Moorehead concentrated writing such critically acclaimed books as *Gallipoli, The White Nile, The Blue Nile* and *Darwin and the Beagle*. Tragically, at the height of his popularity, Moorehead suffered a major stroke at the age of 56 which left him unable to speak, read or write.

Ed Murrow, Walter Cronkite and Richard Dimbleby made successful transitions from radio to television, becoming household names and models of the now-familiar anchor man.

The Second World War was the most reported war to date and re-established the public's love of war correspondents and their willingness to accompany their servicemen into dangerous situations. Indeed, many had lost their lives including fifty-four Americans, about twenty British and six Australian. They tried to convey a taste of what the war meant and felt to the enlisted men. Most war correspondents are like spectators in the front row at a prize fight – closest to the ring but never in it. This was put eloquently in a sort of confessional by CBS's Eric Sevareid in a broadcast at the end of the war:

'Only the soldier really lives the war: the journalist does not. He may share the soldier's outward life and dangers, but he cannot share his inner life, because the same moral compulsion does not bear on him. The observer knows he has alternatives of action: the soldier knows he has none. Their worlds are very far apart, for one is free – the other, a slave. This war must be seen to be believed: but it must be lived to be understood. We journalists can tell you only of events, of what men do. We cannot really tell you how, or why they do it. We can see and tell you that this war is brutalising some among your sons, and yet ennobling others. We can tell you little more. War happens inside a man. It happens to one man alone. It can never be communicated. That is a tragedy – and perhaps, a blessing. A thousand ghastly wounds are really only one. A million martyred lives leave an empty space at only one family table. That is why, at bottom, people can let wars happen, and that is why nations survive them and carry on. And, I am sorry to say, that is also why, in a certain sense, you and your sons from the war will be forever strangers.'

Bibliography

Churchill and the Norway Campaign by Graham Rhys-Jones. Pen & Sword 2008

The First Casualty by Phillip Knightley. Harcourt Brace Jovanovitch. 1975

The Accidental Journalist: The Adventures of Edmund Stevens 1934-1945 by Cheryl Heckler. University of Missouri Press 2007

The Nine Days of Dunkirk by David Divine. Faber & Faber 1959

The Desert War – The Classic Trilogy on the North African Campaign 1940-43 by Alan Moorehead. Hamish Hamilton & Harper 1945

Looking for Trouble by Virginia Cowles. Faber & Faber 1941

Reporting World War II Vols. 1 & 2. Library of Congress 1995

The Murrow Boys – Pioneers on the Front Lines of Broadcast Journalism by Stanley Cloud & Lynne Olsen. Houghton Mifflin NY 1996

'I Was There' US War Correspondents reporting World War Two 1938-1945 by Martin Chekel 2006

Slightly Out of Focus by Robert Capa. Henry Holt and Co. 1947

Give Me Air by Edward Ward. John Lane The Bodley Head 1946

The Privileged Nightmare by Giles Romilly and Michael Alexander. Weidenfeld and Nicolson 1954

Churchill, Roosevelt and India: Propaganda during World War II by Auriol Weigold. Routledge 2008

Selling War: The British Propaganda Campaign against American 'Neutrality' by Nicholas John Cull. Oxford University Press 1995

Rehearsal for Invasion by Wallace Reyburn. G. George 1943

Dress Rehearsal – The Story of Dieppe by Quentin Reynolds. Random House 1943

Inappropriate Conduct by Don North. iUniverse.com 2013

Ortona, Canada's Epic WW2 Battle by Mark Zuehike

Whicker's War by Alan Whicker

The Capture of Attu Edited by Robert J. Mitchell. University of Nebraska Press 2000

On the Air: The Encyclopaedia of Old-Time Radio by John Dunning.

Foreign Correspondence: The Great Reporters and Their Times by John Hohenberg

The Race for the Rhine Bridges 1940, 1944 by Alexander McKee. Souvenir Press 1971

Hemingway Lives! by Clancy Sigal. OR Books 2013

The Women Who Wrote the War: The Compelling Story of Path-breaking Women by Nancy Caldwell Sorel. Arcade Publishing 1999

Countdown to Victory by Barry Turner. Hodder & Stoughton 2004

The Battle of Hurtgen Forest by Charles Whiting. Leo Cooper 1989

Richard Dimbleby by Jonathan Dimbleby. Hodder & Stoughton 1975

War Report – D-Day to VE-Day Ed. Desmond Hawkins. Ariel Books 1985

A Traveller's War by Alaric Jacob. Collins 1944

Martha Gellhorn – A Life by Caroline Moorehead. Chatto and Windus 2002

Conqueror's Road by Osmar White. Cambridge University 1996

The Race for the Rhine Bridges by Alexander McKee. Souvenir Press 2001

Reporting the Wars by Joseph James Matthews. University of Minnesota Press 1957

Berlin: Story of a Battle by Andrew Tully. Simon and Schuster 1963

Notes

1 Narvik was strategically valuable and became the focal point of the ill-fated Norwegian Campaign. The port acts as a gateway to the Swedish iron ore mines in winter when the Swedish ports in the Gulf of Bothnia are frozen.

2 There is another more heroic version of Webb Miller's death. He was reporting the fighting on the Karelian Isthmus when he stepped out of the bunker to observe the artillery fire. When he did not reappear, his accompanying Information Officer went in search of him. His body was found some way off, where it appeared that he had fallen over a bank and struck his head on a rock and died.

3 The Battle of Suomussalmi, fought from 7 December 1939 to 8 January 1940 was a major Finnish victory against vastly superior Russian forces. It resulted in the Russians losing about 27,000 dead, 2,100 captured and 43 tanks taken. The Finnish casualties were 1,000 dead and 1,000 wounded.

4 The beached motor-boat was the *Singapore*, which managed to refloat with the rising tide and brought away three French officers.

5 As British gallantry medals were not awarded to civilians, it seems likely that David Divine was serving in the RNVR.

6 The British launched Operation Dynamo with the hope of rescuing between 20,000 – 30,000 men before the Germans advanced. In fact, circumstances led to the evacuation of 338,226 men safely across the Channel to British shores. The BBC reports that men were also rescued from other coastal towns, for a total of 558,000.

7 Of the 100,000 French troops evacuated at Dunkirk, fewer than 10,000 joined de Gaulle's Free French, while the others returned home. France's colonies remained under Vichy control. Although France had made solemn promises to keep its fleet beyond German or Italian control, Churchill was not convinced and ordered the choice of surrender or destruction.

8 By 11 August, 22 colliers and four destroyers had been sunk. The Navy cancelled all further convoys and coal was transported by rail.

9 Joseph Kennedy argued strongly against giving military and economic aid to Britain and declared that; 'Democracy is dead in England'. He was forced to resign in November 1940.

10 Murrow had become so closely associated with the British that Churchill

offered to make him joint director general of the BBC in charge of programming. He fell in love with Churchill's daughter-in-law, Pamela, but would not leave his wife. Pamela later married Averell Harriman.

11 William Shirer had requested that CBS transfer him away from Germany, but they tried to get him to stay. The Gestapo plot may have been a ruse to persuade CBS that his life was in some danger and that he should leave. He fell out with Murrow and CBS in 1947 and went on to write a series of successful books about the war.

12 Alexander Clifford was married to the actress and journalist, Jennie Prydie Nicholson, the eldest daughter of the poet Robert Graves and Nancy Nicholson, the daughter of the painter, William Nicholson.

13 One of the first civil servants at the MOI was one Eric Blair, better know as George Orwell. Brendan Bracken was referred by his employees as 'BB'. He was also not very popular with his civil servants, in particular Orwell, who resented the war time censorship and manipulation of information, which he felt came from Bracken's office in particular. He later used Bracken's initials, 'BB' as his monstrous 'Big Brother' in *1984*. Incidentally, the Senate Building has all the exterior features of the 'Ministry of Truth'.

14 Bracken was elevated in 1952 to Viscount Bracken of Christchurch. He was a newspaperman and published the *Financial Times* and *The Economist*.

15 Scrap iron was useful for melting down for use in industry. An aluminium-scrap drive, however, saw all those pots and pans needlessly donated as only virgin aluminium could be used to manufacture aircraft. There's no denying scrap drives and other Second World War home-defence efforts were meant in part as morale builders.

16 Released in March 1943, *Desert Victory* became the biggest box-office success of all British war documentaries, grossing an impressive £77,250 in first 12 months (production cost £5,793).

17 The Australians casualties were 1,552 with a further 3,150 who fell sick during the campaign. The Free French had 1,300 casualties and the British and Indian casualties amounted to 1,200.

18 In fact Wavell swopped jobs with Auckinleck and was appointed Commander in Chief of India.

19 The relative strength of either side was reflected in the increased numbers compared with previous battles. The British fielded 118,000 men against the Axis force of 119,000. The British outnumbered the enemy in tanks and aircraft.

20 Operation Crusader was fought from 18 November to 30 December 1941.

21 Edward Henry Harold Ward succeeded as seventh Viscount Bangor in 1950. He was married and divorced three times. His fourth wife and writing collaborator, Marjorie Banks, committed suicide in 1991.

22 Under cover of darkness, HMS *Illustrious* reached the Grand Harbour in Malta. Even here she was not safe and the daily bombing went until 19 January, but only one bomb hit the carrier. She managed to leave Malta and reached the comparative safety of Alexandria. Later she travelled to America for repairs but returned in time for the invasion of Sicily.

23 By a strange ironic twist, *U-557* set course for Greece and was sunk by an Italian motor gun boat, who mistook her for a British submarine.

24 Churchill remarked that it; 'may almost be said, before Alamein we never had a victory. After Alamein we never had a defeat.' It was the only great land battle won by the British and Commonwealth forces without direct American participation. Victory was greatly helped by a string of setbacks suffered by the Germans. Rommel was ill when the battle started and had to return to Germany for treatment. His deputy suffered a heart attack and died leaving a third general in charge. Rommel did return in time to command the defence of Tunisia.

25 There has always been some mystery as to why this Dutch KLM civilian plane was shot down. One explanation was that Leslie Howard, a Jew by birth, had bought himself out of his studio contract in order to appear in propaganda films for the Ministry of Information. He particularly irritated Goebbels by appearing in *Pimpernel Smith*, about freeing Jewish refugees from the Nazis, and *The First of the Few*, about the designer of the Spitfire, R.J. Mitchell. A more plausible explanation was that the Luftwaffe had been misinformed by agents in Lisbon that Winston Churchill was on board.

26 Both the accused, West and Compton, were court martialled. West received a life sentence but was reprieved the following year. He ended the war with an honourable discharge. Compton pleaded not guilty of murder and all charges were dropped. He was killed in 1945. Both claimed to be following General Patton's instructions in killing prisoners.

27 The St Nazaire raid was a bold Combined Services attack on the dry dock which had been built for the French liner, *Normandie*. An old destroyer, the *Campbeltown*, was packed with twenty-four depth charges primed to explode six hours after it had rammed the gates of the dry-dock. Eighteen motor launches carrying Commandos would attack and destroy other dock installations. The raid was deemed a success despite the loss of 400 dead or captured.

28 Of the 523 South Saskatchewans who landed, only 184 returned to England. Their commanding officer, Lieutenant Colonel Charles Merritt, was awarded the Victoria Cross.

29 None of the tanks that made it ashore were able to get off the beaches and were abandoned.

30 Alaric Jacob was a descendant of Brigadier General John Jacob, commander of the famous irregular cavalry regiment, Jacob's Horse.

31 During the war, modern Iran was divided between the British and the Russians in South Persia and North Persia respectively. Most Russian-bound journalists entered the country by this route.

32 Another couple were not so fortunate. Carl and Shelley Mydans reporting for *Life* magazine were captured and interned in a Japanese concentration camp.

33 The Japanese bombed and destroyed many of the RAF aircraft on the ground and rendered the airfield inoperable. Practically all the fighters were obsolete and no match for the Japanese Zeroes.

34 Salerno was chosen as it was the furthest point from which air support could be provided from Sicily.

35 General Mark Clark was a vain and publicity seeking general and not the only one of that rank. British officers were reluctant to move against him without US backing and the Americans were wary because of Clark's close relationship with Eisenhower.

36 Invented in 1912 by the Madras Sappers and Miners, the Bangalore torpedo is an explosive charge packed in one or several connected tubes that could be pushed towards an enemy strongpoint or minefield from a concealed position and then detonated.

37 General Lucas was definitely not a fighting general. Major General Gerald Templer summed him up; 'He had no qualities of any sort as a Commander – the antithesis of everything a fighting soldier and General should be.' He was dismissed and died soon after the war while ballroom dancing.

38 The phrase was popularised in connection with the Marines fighting in the Pacific. In particular the artist and correspondent for *Life* magazine, Tom Lea, published his painting 'The 2,000 Yard Stare'.

39 Paul Morton was very badly treated and turned to alcohol. Many years later, he was defended by the Italian Partisans, who asked him to write a book about them. The British Ministry of War also vouched that Morton had been assigned to the mission as a war reporter and had completed his task.

The only body that refused to apologise or recognise his service was his paper, the *Toronto Star*.

40 For details, see *Reporting from the Front* by Brian Best. Published by Pen & Sword 2014.

41 Major-General Orde Charles Wingate aged 41, is regarded as one of the founders of modern guerrilla warfare. He came from a deeply religious family who were Plymouth Brethren. As a leader he was regarded by his fellow officers as argumentative and aggressive and was known for his eccentricities. He often wore an alarm clock around his wrist and sported raw onions and garlic on a string around his neck to repel mosquitoes. Lord Moran, Churchill's personal physician wrote, 'he seemed to me hardly sane – in medical terms a borderline case'.

42 The American government sent $100 million to spend on constructing airfields in order to start bombing operations against Japan, but about half this sum was embezzled by Chiang and his Nationalist party officials.

43 Stuart Gelder was an experienced China-hand and very much supported the Chinese communists in their struggle against the Japanese.

44 The Territory of Alaska became an American State in 1959.

45 The Higgins boat originally designed to rescue Mississippi River flood victims and was later accepted by the military as a landing craft (Landing Craft, Vehicle, Personnel – LCVP). Typically constructed of plywood, it could carry 36 men with two machine guns in the bow.

46 The Amphtrack was a Landing Vehicle Tracked (LVT), rather like a small turretless tank. Originally intended as a cargo carrier, it was the only way to convey the Marines over the coral reef to reach the beach.

47 USS *New Mexico* was attacked again by two kamikazes on 12 May 1945 with the loss of 54 killed and 119 wounded.

48 Lieutenant Colonel James Doolittle gained fame a few months later when he led the famous carrier-born 'Doolittle Raid' on Tokyo.

49 This was five months before Guy Gibson was given command of the specially formed 617 Squadron of Dam Buster fame.

50 The demise of 'The Writing 69th' did not mean an end to the correspondents taking part in future bombing missions.

51 Flying in the other unarmed aircraft were the British observers, Group Captain Leonard Cheshire and Dr William Penney, who was one of the group of British scientists that had been working on the Manhattan Project.

52 St Elmo's Fire is a weather phenomenon caused by a strong electrical field in the atmosphere generated by thunderstorms.

53 William Lawrence is confused over the naming of the aircraft. He was in *The Great Artiste* flown by Captain Fred Bock, whose aircraft, nicknamed *Bock's Car*, was carrying the bomb.

54 Lawrence was known at the *New York Times* office as 'Atomic Bill'.

55 The 530 accredited correspondents were distributed as follows:

Press associations, Radio, Newspapers, Magazines, Photographers & Newsreel

      US. 72 25 79 35 25

      British. 30 48 118 7 12

      Canadian. 7 5 13 1

      Australian. 10 15

      Allied French, Dutch, Norwegian 9

56 On 6 June, General Patton had been in England at the head of a fake army. He was part of the largest and most successful deception of the Second World War. This concealed the true destination of the invasion. Patton was well known to the Germans, who expected him to be prominent in any invasion attempt. As he was spotted in the south-east of England, it was thought by the enemy that the Pas de Calais was probably the invasion target.

57 In 2014 a new pedestrian bridge was opened and the old causeway removed.

58 This wounded correspondent was certainly the one described in Anthony Beevor's *D-Day: The Battle for Normandy*, page 443. He describes the correspondent as American, who hoped to be the first into Chartres and beat his rival reporters. Unfortunately, he arrived two days early.

59 William James Makin was born in 1896 in Manchester. He was invalided in the early years of the First World War and joined the *Manchester Guardian* in 1916. He travelled extensively in his journalist career writing for newspapers in India, Australia, Jamaica and South Africa. He was also attached to the Colonial Office as an Intelligence Officer just prior to the Second World War.

60 Alexander Gault MacGowan was born in Manchester in 1894 and was described by Ernie Pyle as 'the oldest war correspondent'. He reported the Dieppe disaster, North Africa and Italy as well as the liberation of the death camps in 1945.

61 As well as being a soldier, Colonel Charles Lanham was a poet and author who greatly admired Ernest Hemingway and was probably flattered by the writer's friendship.

62 The group of resistance fighters thought Hemingway was an American

senior officer for he discarded his correspondent's tunic and went about in shirt sleeves due to the summer heat.

63 A total of 9,251 V-1s were fired at targets in Britain, the vast majority aimed at London: 6,184 civilians were killed and 17,981 injured.

64 The Allies finally cleared the port areas on 8 November at a cost of 12,873 casualties (killed, wounded or missing). The Allies were now able to use Antwerp to bring in supplies.

65 General James 'Jumpin' Jim' Gavin was a handsome 36-year old and the youngest American major general in the Second World War. Women found him irresistible and he could count Martha Gellhorn amongst his wartime lovers.

66 Major Roy Oliver was awarded the American Silver Star. Part of the citation mentions: 'In the withdrawal to, and crossing of, the Rhine, he was again wounded and lost his boat, necessitating his swimming the remaining distance, carrying film negatives, still photographs, and radio discs of the operation. His coolness under fire and marked devotion to duty are highly exemplary.'

67 Wood refers to the 1st (Polish) Parachute Brigade, who landed on the south bank of the Rhine and was able to help cover the withdrawal from Arnhem.

68 After he was liberated, Jack Smyth was sent to the Far East and was onboard the last British cruiser to bombard Japan. He was one of the first correspondents to enter Tokyo and visit the site of the atomic explosion at Hiroshima. He had a book published in 1956 about his war experiences (*Five Days in Hell*). His life ended tragically shortly after, when the car he was driving accidentally drove into the River Liffey in Dublin, killing Smyth and his wife.

69 *Völkischer Beobachter* was the newspaper of the National Socialist German Workers' Party and was the official public face of the Nazi party.

70 After the war, the ranks of newswomen thinned out mainly through demotion. By 1968, there were actually fewer female foreign correspondents that in the pre-war years.

71 Hemingway did not like Ernie Pyle's folksy style of reporting, or his bouts of introspection.

72 This atrocity became known as the Malmedy Massacre and the Americans soon responded in kind with the killing of 60 German PoWs at the village of Chenogne in Belgium.

73 Jiri Mucha, also known as George, had served with the Free Czech Army

in France during 1939-40 before reaching England. He then served as a Flying Officer in the Royal Air Force before joining the BBC and became a regular contributor. In May 1945, with the battlefront disintegrating, Mucha drove his Jeep into Prague ahead of the advancing American armies. His Scottish composer wife joined him and they lived in Prague. In 1951, he was imprisoned because of his wartime links with the West. Sentenced to death, he was ultimately given a sentence of hard labour in the uranium mines, which were known as the Czech Gulag. Released in 1954, he continued to fight for change but died in 1991, soon after Czechoslovakia regained its freedom.

74 Peter Lawless was born in 1891, served in the First World War and was awarded the Military Cross. His grandson, Sebastian Faulkes, drew upon Lawless's experiences during the writing of his best-selling novel, *Birdsong*. After the Great War, Lawless played rugby against New Zealand, South Africa and Canada. A keen golfer, he was golfing correspondent for the *Morning Post*, which was acquired by *The Daily Telegraph* in 1937. Most of the Second World War was spent with the Army Intelligence Corps but he was released in 1944 in order to return to *The Daily Telegraph* as war correspondent with the American First Army.

75 The General Aircraft Ltd Hamilcar was a large British glider designed to carry heavy cargo in support of airborne troops.

76 Situated close by Ohrdurf was the Kaiseroda salt mine, used by the Nazis to hide priceless art treasures and virtually the entire gold and currency reserves of the German Reichsbank.

77 Beside General Patton, Generals Bradley and Eisenhower visited Ohrdurf, the only camp to be visited by high ranking officers.

78 Osmar White did not like General Patton: 'His childish love of notoriety, his foul mouth, his preoccupation at his periodical press briefings with corpses – it was distasteful to admit that the man's genius as a commander in the field overshadowed that of his fellow generals.'

79 The American censors were furious that Irwin and Tully had travelled to Berlin without permission and refused to send their stories for a week. Also, the War Department did not invite her to the big dinner in Washington on 23 November 1946, honouring overseas war correspondents. Later, they did send her a citation thanking her for her outstanding and conspicuous service.

80 Thanks to Edward Kennedy, VE day is celebrated on 8 May in the West and on 9 May in the former Soviet block.

Index of Names

Allen, Laurence, 66
Anderson, Alexander Massy, 64–6
Anderson, Godfrey, 62, 64, 196
Annabel, Russell, 125
Austin, Alexander, 83, 100

Baldwin, Harold, 125
Beauchamp, Tony, 114
Behr, Edward, 209
Belden, Jack, 188
Bennett, Lowell, 141
Bewley, Cyril, 109
Bewsher, Paul, 166
Bigart, Homer, 109–10, 139–40
Bourke-White, Margaret, viii, 86, 136, 199, 209
Bowen, James, 18
Brewer, Sam, 63
Brown, Cecil, 92, 94–5
Buckley, Christopher, 104–106, 171
Buckley, Henry, 4
Burdett, Winston, 87, 134
Busvine, Richard, 61
Byam, Guy, 147, 178–80, 183

Calder, Peter Ritchie, 44–5
Capa, Robert, 4, 106–107, 110, 152–4, 163, 167, 188–9, 207
Cardozo, Harold, 2
Cassidy, Henry, 32
Chickering, William, 131
Chinigo, Michael, 75–6

Clapper, Raymond, 90, 141–2
Clark, Norman Maynard, 106–108, 162, 166–7, 173, 196–7
Clifford, Alexander, 17, 43, 55, 57, 61, 68, 76–7
Collingwood, Charles, 163, 168–9
Corman, Mathieu, 9
Cowles, Virginia, 19–21, 32–3, 35, 209
Crockett, Edward, 66
Cronkite, Walter, viii, 139–40, 189–90, 210
Crosse, Pat, 196
Cuhel, Frank, 76

Davis, Eric, 98
Delaprée, Louis, 7–9
Delmer, Tom Sefton, 45, 47
Denny, Harold, 62, 64, 197
Dimbleby, Richard, vii–viii, 29, 47–8, 55, 66, 70–1, 132, 137–9, 147, 158, 199, 210

Emeny, Stuart, 114, 116–17

Fisher, John, 31
Fyfe, Ian, 149

Gallagher, O'Dowd, 5, 92, 94
Gardener, Charles, 34–5
Gellhorn, Martha, viii, 4, 13, 108, 137, 154, 155, 199, 209
Gibb, Philip, vi

Gillard, Frank, 83, 101, 170, 178
Gingell, Basil, 101, 106
Gorrell, Henry, 135
Gray, Bernard, 67

Halton, Matthew, 63, 105, 172
Harriot, Guy, 52, 60
Hartrich, Edwin, 21
Haugland, Vern, 117
Healy, Tom, 32
Heinzerling, Lynn, 17
Hemingway, Ernest, 4, 12, 154,
    156–7, 163, 166–9, 187, 208–209
Hill, Gladwin, 139
Hippie, Bill, 127
Holles, Everett, 192
Hollingworth, Clare, viii, 16–17,
    209
Holmes, Christopher, 9
Hottelet, Richard, 85, 141, 194–5
Hughes, Robert, 69

Irwin, Virginia, 201–202

Jacob, Alaric, 63, 86, 114, 117
Jacoby, Mel, 90–1
Jameson, Henry, 154
Johnson, Brandish, 7

Kennedy, Edward, 78, 134, 205–
    206
Kerr, Walter, 32
Kirkpatrick, Helen, 37, 169

Lait, George, 134
Lawless, Peter, 193
Lawrence, William, 142, 144
Lee, Clark, 91

Lennard, Hayden, 122
LeSueur, Larry, 87
Liebling, A.J., 163, 205

MacDonald, Roderick, 109
MacGowan, Alexander 165
MacPherson, Stewart, 195
Makin, Bill, 165
Manning, Paul, 139
Marshall, Howard, 151–2
Matthews, Ronald, 132
Maxted, Stanley, 178–80, 182, 193
McCullagh, Francis, 2
Metcalf, Hedley, 98
Miller, Webb, 2, 21
Minifie, James, 2
Monks, Noel, 2, 9, 11, 12, 54, 79
Monson, Ronald, 54, 59
Moore, Martin, 114
Moorehead, Alan, viii, 51, 54–7,
    60–1, 67–9, 73, 77, 132, 209
Morrison, Ian, 94–6, 121–3, 207
Mosley, Leonard, 204
Mucha, George, 191
Munday, William, 101, 109
Munro, Ross, 82, 105
Murrow, Edward, vii–viii, 37–9,
    88, 140–1, 199, 210

Neil, Edward, 7

Parer, Damien, 120–1
Parker, Ralph, 86
Parr, Grant, 134
Pearson, Drew, 78
Philby, Harold 'Kim', 7, 32, 86
Phillips, Percival, 2, 3
Post, Robert, 41–2, 139–40

INDEX

Pyle, Ernie, vii, 41, 72, 80, 107–108, 130–1, 135, 186

Ray, Cecil, 105, 175–6
Raynor, Pendril, 122
Reid, Bill, 169
Reyburn, Wallace, 82, 84
Reynolds, Quentin, 83–4, 86
Robertson, Ben, 76
Romilly, Giles, 22, 28
Rooney, Andy, 139
Ryan, A.P. 47–8
Ryan, Cornelius, viii, 161–2

Sale, Stewart, 100–101
Schultz, Sigrid, 40–1
Selby-Walker, Kenneth, 98
Sevareid, Eric, 88, 107, 110, 117–18, 132, 210
Sheepshanks, Ernest, 7
Sherrod, Robert, 125–30
Shirer, William, 39–40, 95
Slessor, Kenneth, 59
Smith, Howard, 85
Smyth, Jack, 178, 180–1
Steer, George, 9, 11
Stevens, Edmund, 22, 25, 27
Stevenson, Kent, 139
Stockton, Norman, 141
Stonehouse, Kenneth, 76
Stowe, Leland, 24–7
Stubbs, Bernard, 29

Talbot, Godfrey, 70–1
Taro, Gerda, 4–5

Taves, Brydon, 122
Thompson, John, 75
Thorpe, Arthur, 160
Tighe, Desmond, 159
Townsend, Edmund, 183
Treanor, Thomas, 164–5
Tregaskis, Richard, 102–104
Tully, Andrew, 201–202

Vaughan-Thomas, Wynford, 106, 108, 141

Wade, William, 139
Waite, David, 97–8
Walton, William, 149, 163, 186, 208
Ward, Eddy, 33, 61–4, 196–7, 200–201, 206, 208
Weaver, Denis, 2
Welsh, Mary, 12, 167, 208
Werth, Alexander, 86, 196
Whicker, Alan, 107
White, Osmar, 120–1, 191, 198–200, 207
Williams, Desmond, 44, 170
Wills, Eric Lloyd, 99–100
Wills, Stanley, 117
Wilmot, Chester, 51, 59, 119–21, 148, 171–2, 174, 203, 208
Wood, Alan, 54, 178–81
Woodward, David, 146

Yarrow, Marshall, 157–8